Introducing Organizational Behaviour

Other books by the authors

J. Beck and C. Cox (eds), *Advance in Management Education*

C. L. Cooper, *The Stress Check*

C. L. Cooper (ed.), *Developing Managers for the 1980s*

C. L. Cooper (with Peter Makin), *Psychology for Managers*

R. N. Ottaway, *Humanizing the Workplace*

Introducing Organizational Behaviour

Mike Smith, John Beck, Cary L. Cooper, Charles Cox,
Dick Ottaway and Reg Talbot

MACMILLAN

First published 1982
Reprinted 1984, 1986

Published by
MACMILLAN EDUCATION LTD
Houndmills, Basingstoke, Hampshire RG21 2XS
and London
Companies and representatives
throughout the world

Printed in Hong Kong

ISBN 0-333-30513-2 (hardcover)
ISBN 0-333-30514-0 (paperback)

Contents

SECTION 4: OTHER MATTERS

The authors and publishers wish to thank the following who have kindly given permission for the use of copyright material. American Management Associations for a chart from 'Organizational Stress and Individual Strain' in *The Failure of Success* edited by A. J. Marrow © 1972 by AMACOM, a division of American Management Associations. All rights reserved. British Institute of Management for tables from reports 'Profile of the British Manager', *Management Survey Report*, No. 38 by Melrose-Woodman, (1978), and 'The British Manager: Careers and Mobility', *Management Survey Report*, No. 39, by Guerrier and Philpot (1978). The Controller of Her Majesty's Stationery Office for two tables from *Occupational Segregation*, Department of Employment, London (1979). E. P. Dutton & Co. Inc. for a figure from *Man and Society in Calamity* by Pitirim A. Sorokin. Copyright 1942 by E. P. Dutton & Co. Inc. Renewed 1970 by Helen P. Sorokin. Gower Publishing Company Ltd for an extract from *Problem Solving Through Creative Analysis* by T. Rickards (1974). Harvard Business Review for a table adapted from *How to Choose a Leadership Pattern* by Robert Tannenbaum and Warren H. Schmidt (HBR May–June, 1973). Copyright © 1974 by the President and Fellows of Harvard College. All rights reserved. International Publications Ltd for the diagram 'The 3-D grid'. Irvington Publishers Inc. for figures 3.3 and 3.4 from *The Achieving Society* (1976) by D. C. McClelland. McGraw-Hill Book Company for a figure from *A Theory of Leadership Effectiveness* by Fiedler and a table from *Psychology of Industrial Behaviour* by C. H. Smith and J. H. Wakeley (1972). Penguin Books Ltd for a figure from *Creativity in Industry* by P. R. Whitfield (Pelican Books, 1975). Copyright © 1975 by P. R. Whitfield. Professors M. M. Webber and H. W. J. Rittel for an extract from their essay 'Dilemmas in a General Theory of Planning' reprinted by the Design Methods Group, California, from the original publication in *Policy Sciences*, No. 4 (1973).

Every effort has been made to trace all the copyright holders but if any have been inadvertently overlooked the publishers will be pleased to make the necessary arrangements at the first opportunity.

List of Figures

List of Tables

1
Introduction: The Relevance and Scope of Organizational Psychology to Management

Many managers will regard this book as a threat. These managers will have been formed in the same mould as the overseers of the dark satanic mills of the early part of the first industrial revolution. Their simple belief in the use of economic power and authority will be typified by the earthy comment, 'When you've got them by the balls, their hearts and minds will follow later.' To these managers all the organizational psychology you need to know is how to apply the right pressure, in the right place, at the right time.

This book takes a different view. The difference is derived from a mixture of ethics, fear and reason. The ethical considerations are, to a large extent, a matter of individual conscience. The fear arises from the realization that when people are squeezed it is highly likely that they start to squeeze back. For at least some of the time they will be able to squeeze hardest and inflict more pain than they receive. In between the waves of mutual pain, even the most neanderthalic manager must begin to wonder if there is a better way of doing things. Perhaps observation and reason provide a better way.

The essential rationale behind any book on organizational behaviour can be quickly explained. An organization exists to achieve certain objectives; it extracts from its environment certain resources; by working on these resources the organization produces something of greater value, and which furthers the organization's progress towards its objectives. The people in an organization can process resources in many ways. Some of these ways are efficient and others are inefficient. By taking careful observations and recording them accurately, one should begin to differentiate between the effective and the ineffective organizations. Of course, there are many complexities, the objectives may not be clear and observations may be difficult or impossible. Nevertheless, the basic rationale remains valid.

Most organizations are incredibly complex and there is always the problem of where to start observing them. Probably the best starting-point is to begin with the *individuals* who make up the organization. Who are they? What are they like? In the present context the emphasis is upon management, the questions become: Who are our managers? What are their characteristics? The next set of questions concern the positions that these individuals occupy within the organization. In the context of management, the question becomes 'What does a manager do?' These and similar issues are dealt with in Chapter 2.

Once the individuals and their roles have been identified, we need to know what makes them tick? What are the processes within an individual which allow him or her to operate. Psychologists have typically identified three processes: motivation, learning and perception. In the chapters that deal with these topics we have tried to give greatest attention to those aspects of motivation and learning which seem to have important implications for managers rather than delivering detailed expositions of each area. The final chapter in the section dealing with the individual reminds us that life is a two-way street. The individual influences his organization and the organization influences the individual. The organization can provide sources of both satisfaction and stress.

In observing individuals within an organization, it soon becomes obvious that they perceive each other, make judgements about each other and act upon the basis of these judgements. This process of social perception is discussed in the second section of the book, which focuses on the way that *groups* of individuals operate. Another characteristic of groups is that their members communicate with each other and influence each other's attitudes. When groups exist they are faced with the problem of getting the job done and in keeping together. Further, certain patterns of acceptable behaviour emerge. Observations of a group quickly reveals that some individuals have more influence than others — they become either official or unofficial leaders and consequently a group must face up to the problems of leadership and supervision.

Even groups of individuals rarely exist in isolation. Usually they exist side by side with other groups, and in order to avoid chaos the groups within an organization need to be structured in some way and their activities co-ordinated.

The final section of the book concerns change. Even a well-structured organization, that has well formed groups consisting of well-adjusted individuals, will sooner or later become extinct unless it is prepared to change. The impetus for change can arise from many directions. Perhaps the impetus for change may arise from the creativity of the people within the organization. One of the most ubiquitous changes in modern organizations is the greater participation of all levels of workers in making decisions — especially where traditional methods of work are being overtaken by technological advances. Creativity and participation are only two of the many examples of changes which we have to face, and both examples have to be set against the wider context of organizational change.

The objectives of this book are very well defined. We have attempted to produce an introduction to a very important and fascinating aspect of management. In our correspondence, in our informal contacts with managers, in our teaching on management courses and in our teaching of new undergraduates we are constantly asked to recommend a book which will serve as a first introduction to organizational behaviour. Of course, in a book of this kind we have had to be selective, yet clearly we have had to reflect the main developments in our subject, so that when the reader has finished with our book he will be eager and able to tackle other texts and specialist volumes.

Note to the reader. In the interests of clarity the masculine form has been used throughout this book.

Section 1: The Individual Within the Organization

2
The Manager and His Job

In essence, management is concerned with the efficient use of the three Ms – Men, Money and Materials. Each of these three ingredients is an essential part of the work activity of a manager, whether he is producing silicon chips, optical fibres or cotton T-shirts. The same three Ms – Men, Money and Materials – are also involved in the work of managers in service industries as widely different as merchant banking, hospital management or publishing. In all these settings, managers are concerned with the efficient use of resources so that the services and goods leaving their organizations are worth more than the resources which their organization consumes.

This book is largely about the first of the three resources – the men and women who staff the agricultural, industrial and service organizations in the world of work.

A book produced for practising managers and the students of management needs to start with a clear idea about who is and who is not a manager. It has been said that, by definition, all definitions are unsatisfactory. It might also be said that definitions of managers are among the most unsatisfactory of all. Melrose-Woodman (1978) observed that 'The term "manager" has defied definition ever since people first began to analyse its meaning. It is possible to draw up a definition based on more or less arbitrary parameters for a particular purpose but it is hard to arrive at a generally acceptable definition.' For many practical purposes the most acceptable definition of a manager is 'someone who is directly responsible for getting work done by other people'. This approach has the advantage of emphasizing the 'men' aspect of the 'men–money–materials' triangle, and it also neatly differentiates between the manager and the specialist. The specialist may have a high status and a high income but he is not a manager until he is responsible for the work of others. For example, an investment analyst has a prestigious occupation with high earnings, yet investment analysts are not managers until they are put in charge of junior analysts, researchers or office staff. Similarly, a paediatrician becomes a manager only when he is responsible for the work of, say, other paediatricians or perhaps the ancillary staff at a health centre. Of course, neither of these examples is typical of managers in agriculture, industry or commerce. In all probability a completely typical manager does not exist. Yet a profile of a modern-day manager is a key element in establishing a manager's role in an organization and the relevance of organizational psychology to the role he has to perform.

Profile of a manager

The British Institute of Management's survey of almost 4,500 members probably produced the best available data base for drawing up a profile of a British manager (Melrose-Woodman, 1978). In spite of the fact that the Institute's membership is not totally representative of all British managers — for example, managers in small firms are underrepresented — and despite the fact that only 4,479 of the 10,000 managers in the sample responded to the questionnaire, the BIM survey is more up to date and based on a larger sample than previous surveys by Copeman (1955), the Acton Society Trust (1956) and Clark (1966).

The BIM survey highlights the obvious — but nevertheless startling and important fact — the typical manager is not a woman. Although 42 per cent of the British work-force is female, less than 1 per cent of managers in the BIM survey were women. Similar structures exist in both Western Europe and North America. In many developing countries the discrepancy between the proportion of women in the work-force and the proportion of women in management positions is even larger. The underrepresentation of women in management positions is one of the most serious management issues of today, and will be considered in greater depth later in this chapter.

The 'average' manager in the BIM survey could be classified as a Senior Manager reporting directly to a Board member. He is about 50 years old and works in an organization employing less than 2,000 workers. The 'average' manager attended grammar school and left school at 17. However, a substantial number of managers will have attended technical college on a part-time basis. As Table 2.1 shows, about a quarter of managers replying to the BIM survey held university degrees.

International comparisons are notoriously difficult, because differing standards and differing traditions may lie behind apparently comparable statistics. However, Table 2.2, showing data from ten different countries, suggests that the educational

Table 2.1 *Qualifications of managers*

Qualification	Percentage ($N = 4,196$)
Two or more O-levels	58
Two or more A-levels	45
Diploma in management studies	28
First degree	27

Source: J. Melrose-Woodman (1978) 'Profile of the British Manager', BIM *Management Survey Report*, No. 38, London.

Table 2.2 *Comparison of educational level of managers in ten countries*

Country	% of executives with higher education
France	91
Belgium	85
USA	83
Germany	81
Ireland	78
Norway	63
Netherlands	60
Denmark	51
Great Britain	50

Source: H. C. De Bettignies and P. Ebans (1971) in *European Business*, no. 31.

background of British managers is not typical of managers in all industrialized countries.

While the BIM indicates that younger managers tend to have better educational qualifications than previous generations, it is still possible to agree with Glover's (1974) conclusions that managers are not becoming better educated at a faster rate than that of the general population, that management education is a new, relatively small-scale, phenomenon, that British graduates tend to prefer small firms to large ones, and that British managers are still not as well educated as their Continental and North American counterparts.

The employment profile of managers may also be strongly influenced by cultural factors, especially since educational background is known to influence career pattern. Until recently it appears that the majority of managers started in technical or clerical jobs and entered a managerial position in their mid-twenties. Among the younger managers, however, this traditional pattern seems to be breaking down, and almost a third of entrants are joining management as their first full-time employment. This direct entry at management level is particularly typical of managers who had previously attended public school.

Several studies have commented on the low level of mobility among British managers. For example, the Acton sample indicated that 44 per cent of managers spent their entire career in one company. To an extent, low mobility may be a result of the pattern of educational qualifications. It is often said that one's present employer is most influenced by the results achieved at the job.

Length of experience with the specific procedures and processes which the particular company uses is the most important factor in achieving these results, as long as there are no major changes. On the other hand, a future employer is concerned with managerial potential, which is reflected by educational qualifications. If these beliefs are true, managers without qualifications are of greatest economic value to their present employer, and may be less prepared to accept changes which may undermine their value.

In the BIM survey over half of the managers had been working for their present organization for more than ten years. This over-all result is modified by many other factors such as the age of the manager, his educational qualifications and the industry he is in.

The influence of age is very much according to expectation: the young manager (aged 25—35) will have been working in his organization for about five years, while a manager aged 36—45 will have been working in his organization for about seven years. Length of service shows a disproportionate increase for managers over the age of 45. Type of education also influences employer mobility. Melrose-Woodman (1978) writes that 'A high proportion of elementary school pupils, 39%, have been with their firms for over 20 years. Presumably, this figure includes those manual workers who slowly worked their way up through the organization.' Respondents with postgraduate qualifications seem to have been with their employers for a shorter period than the rest. Since the 'educated' managers tend to be the younger managers, it is unfortunate that the available data do not allow the influences of the two factors to be disentangled.

The mobility data from the BIM seem to provide a close fit to Super and Hall's (1978) model of career development. During their late teens and early twenties, potential managers are exploring a number of careers while they are either at university or performing a technical or clerical job. In their mid-twenties the opportunity arises to try out a management post, and if this trial is successful, establishment and advancement ensue up to the mid-forties. Super and Hall's model (Figure 2.1) predicts further growth, or a plateau of maintained performance, or decline, depending upon personal and organizational factors.

Guerrier and Philpot (1978) took a closer look at managerial mobility. As Table 2.3 shows, the most frequent reasons managers give for staying with their present employer are a realisation of career progression within the organization, enjoyment of the job and the variety of experience with the organization. On the other hand, the major reason for changing to their present employer was to improve long-term career prospects. Guerrier and Philpot also note that managers are becoming more willing to change employer. Of course, these generalizations conceal considerable differences between industries:

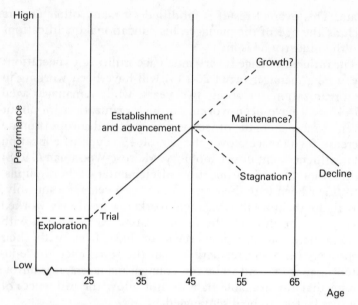

Figure 2.1   *Super and Hall's model of career paths*

long service of over twenty years in an organization is the typical position of managers within manufacturing industry, distributive industries and national industries. On the other hand, shorter service seems more widespread in the local government, education and financial sectors.

So far we have looked at managerial mobility in terms of *external* mobility, which involves a complete change of employer. In many organizations, however, there is considerable scope for internal mobility, where managers change their *function* but not their employer. The inclusion of *internal* mobility considerably alters the previous picture of relatively immobile managers. The Melrose-Woodman survey suggests that half the managers have been in their present jobs for less than five years. Indeed, analysis by age reveals that 80 per cent of managers aged 25–35 and 74 per cent of managers aged 36–45 have been in their present jobs for less than five years. Furthermore, this pattern of frequent internal job

Table 2.3 *Attitudes concerning job mobility*

Reasons for changing to present employer given by at least 25 per cent of sample	*Percentage (N = 800)*
To improve long-term career prospects	57
Dissatisfaction with career opportunities	36
Offered job thought to be enjoyable	32
Wanted opportunity to influence the way things are run	29

Reasons for staying with present employer given by at least 25 per cent of sample	*Percentage (N = 462)*
My career has progressed well in present organization	65
I get a lot of enjoyment from my job	55
I can get a variety of experience within my organization	50
It would be difficult to find a better job	30

Source: Y. Guerrier and N. Philpot (1978) 'The British Manager: Careers and Mobility', BIM *Management Survey Report*, No. 39.

change can be seen across all sectors of management. A clear picture emerges where the norm is frequent internal job changes.

Thus our typical manager is a 50-year-old man reporting to a Board member. He has received an education which is a little better than the legal minimum and has changed his employer two or three times in his career, but frequent changes of function within the organization have given him a wider range of experience.

Alistair Mant (1969) drew up seven characterizations of experienced managers.

(1) There is the *mobile manager I (internal)*, who is on a reasonably fast track inside a dynamic company which is growing and changing. He is attuned to the climate of his company and he has developed the knack of quickly picking up the small number of factors in successive jobs which account for most of the results. He is politically sensitive and trusted in high places.

(2) The *mobile manager II (external)* — sometimes known

as the 'hopper' or 'wheeler-dealer' — is similar to the mobile manager I but his loyalty is primarily to himself and he needs a great deal of freedom to operate in his own way.

(3) The *thwarted manager* is immobile and frustrated. Mant considers that he is most likely to be seen in a conservative, declining industry. He is loyal and once had ambition. In a sense he is now getting too good at his job. Although he may be expecting better things around the corner, he is aware that he is becoming less salable on the grounds of age and narrowness of experience.

(4) The *technocratic manager* is seen most clearly in science-based industries. He is often faced with a mid-career crisis, when he rises in the managerial hierarchy and has to leave his specialism to focus on pure management or administration.

(5) The *recessional manager* is sometimes called the 'hidden redundant', and he does just enough to get by. He lacks confidence and flexibility. He is politically sensitive but he is also cynical about promotion.

(6) Mant's characterization of the *old boy manager* has great appeal. Mant writes: 'The experienced manager, frequently seen on short seminars, conferences and the more senior courses for experienced managers, tends to come from rather slow, friendly companies of a fair size operating in the gentler markets. The firm is characterized by woolly objectives and a "system" of informal criteria for promotion — the road to the top is paved with mimicry'.

(7) *The backbone manager* comes closest to our profile of the typical manager. He can be seen in all functions in most types of company. He is no longer young but has a substantial part of his managerial life in front of him.

Although Mant's characterizations are not empirically based, they strike a chord of recognition and most managers can think of colleagues who fit neatly into his categories.

The owner-manager of a small firm

A large part of the literature about managers has concentrated upon managers in organizations of considerable size – the companies whose products are household names. Yet in most industrial countries about a third of all production comes from organizations with less than 500 employees. Small firms also have a strategic importance since some of them will, one day, become large multinational corporations. The managers of small firms are a significant sub-group of managers who, in many ways, have a greater personal impact on their organization. Often, small firms with less than 100 employees are the inspiration of one man, the owner-manager. Often, it is the ingenuity, perseverance and 'personability' of this one man who holds together the whole fabric of his organization from supplier to manufacturing process, and ultimately to customer. In many small firms there is no division of managerial labour, no organizational systems and procedures, only the abilities of the owner-manager. In spite of the crucial role of the owner-manager very little is known about his background. Fortunately, there is a small survey by Deeks (1970) about managers of small firms. The survey included fifty firms in the furniture and timber industry and included a total of ninetyfour owner-managers. The typical owner-manager is in his fifties, with a number of relations working in his company. Almost 30 per cent of the owner-managers had received fulltime further education. However, just over half of the managers in the sample had received part-time further education, usually craft and technician courses relating to the furniture industry. Only 8 per cent of the managers in the sample had attended *any* management courses. Most owner-managers had limited outside experience – typically they had worked for about three firms, including their present one. However, even this outside experience was out of date: almost half (46 per cent) had worked in their present company for more than twenty years; 43 per cent of owner-managers had not changed their function since they had joined the firm.

Thus the profile of the manager in a smaller firm indicates that while he is roughly the same age as his counterpart in larger firms, he has less formal education and he has been with his present company for a longer time and has had fewer, if any, changes in the function of his job.

The woman manager

It is paradoxical that at a time of great discussion about the advent of the leisure society, more people are at work than at any other period in history. A part of the increase in the number of workers is due to the growth of the population, but in industrialized countries at least the major influence in the expansion of the work-force has been a greater rate of economic participation by women. Women's economic participation is particularly high in Great Britain, but as Table 2.4 shows the trend is clearly discernible in other industrialized nations.

Table 2.4   *Participation rates for women, 1901–71*

Year	USA	Canada	Great Britain
1901	20.4	14.1	34.5
1911	25.2	–	35.5
1921	23.3	19.9	33.7
1931	24.3	21.8	34.2
1941	25.4	22.9	–
1951	29.0	24.4	34.9
1961	34.5	29.3	37.7
1971	39.6	39.2	42.6

Source: C. Hakim (1979) *Occupational Segregation*, HMSO, London.

Although women play a significant role in a nation's economic life, they are markedly underrepresented among managers. Table 2.5 shows that in thirty-seven countries out of thirty-nine, women managers and administrators are underrepresented. The exceptions are Bahrain and Algeria.

There seems to be little or no evidence to suggest that women are inherently less suitable than men for management positions, so the question arises: why does such widespread underrepresentation occur? Undoubtedly, a part of the answer is that women have available alternative family roles and that a substantial proportion of women prefer to give these roles priority. However, this cannot be a complete answer because a substantial and possibly growing proportion of women would make an alternative choice. Preliminary results from an investigation by the Ashridge Management Research Unit (1980) suggests that the factors which retard women's progression into management can be categorized under three headings. First, *career paths* may require up to twenty years' continuous service, recurrent mobility and a commitment to a long period of part-time study. The Ashridge Management Research Unit contends that hurdles along these career paths are often more difficult for women to overcome. The second group of factors concerns the *attitudes of senior executives*. Rightly or wrongly, managers have stereotype ideas of different categories of workers and these stereotypes influence promotion and placement decisions. Consequently, and often with the very best of intentions, women are channelled into 'suitable' positions – and away from management! The third area concerns the *attitudes of women themselves*. Some women may lack confidence in their abilities, and concentrate upon being conscientious and meticulous with detailed work on the assumption that these abilities will be rewarded by their superiors. Other writers such as Larwood and Wood (1977) explore the possibilities that women's motivation, assertiveness, self-reliance and risk-taking are related to the underrepresentation of women in management.

Melrose-Woodman's (1978) survey can only give a tentative profile of the typical woman manager because the sample of nearly 4,500 managers contained only twenty-nine women. However, the data suggest that in spite of the fact that women had slightly better educational qualifications than the men, they waited longer for their promotion to management and very few women indeed progressed beyond middle-management level. In the USA, however, much more information is available about the successful woman manager. Larwood and Wood (1977) attempt to bring together a number of wide-ranging surveys to produce a profile of the successful woman manager. They note that 'studies have revealed that almost all women managers are pleased with their jobs and hold the same expectations as males . . . in short, the woman executive thoroughly enjoys her success, believes she has made the right decisions and looks forward to future advancement'. The

Eastern Europe				
1970	Poland	50	27	46
1970	Hungary	47	15	41
1971	Yugoslavia	46	9	36
1970	Czechoslovakia	42	14	45
North America				
1976	Canada	48	20	37
1975	USA	42	20	39
Latin America				
1970	Brazil	59	11	21
1972	Paraguay	55	15	21
Middle East and Africa				
1970	Lebanon	38	2	17
1971	Bahrain	35	7	5
1975	Kuwait	34	2	12
1966	Iran	26	3	13
1966	Egypt	24	4	7
1970	Syria	23	2	11
1966	Algeria	21	6	4
Asia				
1970	Philippines	57	29	32
1973	Thailand	49	9	45
1971	Hong Kong	44	8	34
1971	Sri Lanka	41	6	26
1975	Japan	38	5	37
1975	Singapore	30	7	30
1971	India	18	2	17

Source: C. Hakim (1979) *Occupational Segregation*, HMSO, London.

Table 2.5 *Cross-national comparisons of women's share of higher-level occupations*

Census year	Country	Per cent of women among		
		All professionals	Managers, administrators	Total labour force
	Western Europe			
1970	Denmark	55	17	37
1975	Norway	48	13	38
1975	Sweden	48	11	42
1971	Italy	46	6	27
1975	Finland	45	18	46
1968	France	43	12	35
1971	Great Britain	38	8	37
1971	Austria	37	20	39
1970	West Germany	34	14	36
1970	Spain	33	4	20
	Latin America (contd)			
1970	Argentina	55	7	25
1971	Panama	51	12	26
1970	Chile	50	17	23
1975	Venezuela	50	7	28
1973	Costa Rica	47	11	19
1975	Mexico	38	19	22
1972	Peru	33	5	21

negative aspects of success include the women's belief that they have been discriminated against and the usual time and social demands (to which men are also subject). Although their work is demanding, women who enter management are likely to obtain increasing satisfaction from their work.

Analysis of the management job

People are an essential element of any organization, and in many ways a description and analysis of the people is the natural starting-place in organizational psychology. However, most organizations are independent of the individuals in it — at least in the sense that the organization will continue to operate more or less efficiently even though some individuals have left and been replaced by new recruits. In this sense an organization is simply a set of positions which various individuals can fill. These positions are called *roles*. Considerable research effort has been spent investigating the activities involved in the management role.

Methods of studying management jobs

Many methods of analysing jobs exist (see Blum and Naylor, 1968; McCormick, 1976) but the analysis of management jobs is usually conducted by interview, surveys, observation or diary method. Each of these methods has its own set of advantages and disadvantages, but the observation method and the diary method are usually regarded as most accurate. For example, in a study by Lewis and Dahl (1976) university administrative estimated that they spent 47 per cent of their time in meetings, whereas diary recordings revealed that they spent 69 per cent of their time in that manner.

Two studies of managerial work

Rosemary Stewart (1967) used the diary method to analyse the way in which 160 British managers spent their time in a four-week period. The average manager worked 42½ hours per week, and three-quarters of this time would be spent in his own establishment. Indeed, half of the total time was spent in the manager's own office. An analysis of the time spent on various types of activities is shown in Table 2.6. Clearly, managers spend a great deal of their time with other people, and the way that they manage these interactions will have a strong influence on their over-all effectiveness. Thus the way that managers judge and communicate with other people and the way that they work in groups are crucial aspects of effectiveness. These issues are examined in greater detail in Chapters, 6, 7 and 8.

Table 2.6   *Average proportion of managers' time spent on various activities*

	Percentage
Informal discussions	43
Paperwork	36
Committees	7
Telephone	6
Inspection of others	6
Social activities	4

Source: R. Stewart (1967) *Managers and their Jobs*, Macmillan, London.

Although the way that managers distribute their time is important in understanding the managerial task, it fails to capture a number of essential aspects of management. Rosemary Stewart noted that managers often complain that 'it's one damn thing after another' and that there is no time to think. Her data supported these complaints. During the four-week period covered by the manager's diaries the average manager would only have nine interruption-free periods lasting half an hour or longer. The picture which emerges of a typical management day is one of an attempt to cover thirteen widely different tasks, punctuated by almost as many fleeting contacts with subordinates, colleagues and, occasionally, with superiors.

Of course, the averages conceal wide variations, and a number of different types of management job exist. In the same way that Mant was able to identify seven types of experienced managers, Stewart was able to identify five groups of management job:

Group 1: the Emissaries (28 per cent). These jobs require managers to spend a lot of time away from their companies, visiting other companies and attending conferences and exhibitions. The emissary jobs involve longer hours but the working day is less fragmented and less liable to interruption. Sales management jobs frequently fall into this group.

Group 2: the writers (21 per cent). These involve jobs where managers spend atypical amounts of time by themselves reading and writing (i.e. they spend half their time with others compared with other managers who spend up to three-quarters of their time with others). Writing jobs involve rather shorter hours and less pressure from day-to-day issues. Head office specialist jobs frequently fall into this group.

Group 3: the discussers (22 per cent). These are not particularly distinctive jobs but they do involve more contact with other people, especially colleagues.

Group 4: the trouble-shooters (21 per cent). Trouble-shooting jobs involve an exceedingly fragmented working day and much time is spent coping with crises and finding speedy solutions. The jobs involve considerable contact with subordinates. Typical trouble-shooting jobs are done by works managers and production managers.

Group 5: the committee men. These are managers whose jobs are distinguished by the wide range of internal contact and the time spent in discussions. Typically, these jobs occur in large companies and involve personnel matters.

The division of management jobs into various types raises a number of interesting questions. For example, we could ask why different types of management jobs occur? Is it the nature of the work, is it the other members of the group or is it the individual manager's personality which is the main determining factor? In any event the existence of different types of managerial work has profound implications for the ways in which managers are selected and trained.

A classic analysis of management jobs was conducted in

the USA by Mintzberg (1973) and it demonstrates the use of observational methods. Mintzberg observed each of five managers over a period of one week. The methodology involved structured observations, and his results confirm most of Stewart's findings, particularly the findings of brevity, variety and fragmentation of most managerial jobs. Mintzberg also noted that managers gravitate towards the more active elements of their work — the elements which are current, non-routine and specific. A related phenomenon is a manager's strong preference for verbal media, including the telephone, unscheduled meetings and factory tours. Many managers regard the written medium as second best and feel that by the time something is written, typed, checked and circulated, it is out of date. Consequently processing the incoming mail is often regarded as a chore (many studies have indicated that managers overestimate the time they spend on paperwork).

On the basis of his observations of five managers, Mintzberg looked at the components of the management role, and was able to identify ten separate roles which dealt with four types of content (see Table 2.7).

First, the manager is someone who has to deal with *people*. He is the figurehead of the organization and is obliged to perform duties of a ceremonial or legal nature. He is also the leader of people and should give his group an 'ethos' and sense of direction. Every group needs to relate to other groups of people, and usually this liaison is part of the manager's job. Besides dealing with people, a manager must deal with *information*, he must monitor information from the outside world and from within his own organization. Information that is relevant must then be disseminated to the appropriate people within the work-group. This communication aspect of the management job is discussed in Chapter 7. When the 'outside' world wants information about his work-group's activities, it is usually the manager who acts as a spokesman and gives this information. The third area identified by Mintzberg concerns *decision-making*, with the manager acting as entrepreneur, trouble-shooter and allocator. The fourth role concerns negotiation.

The works of Mintzberg and Stewart are only two examples of studies of managerial jobs. A review by McCall, Morrison

Table 2.7   *Mintzberg's managerial roles*

Interpersonal roles

1. Figurehead and symbol
2. Leader defining group's ethos
3. Liaison with other leaders

Informational roles

4. Monitor of information
5. Disseminator of information
6. Spokesman to others outside group

Decision-making roles

7. Entrepreneur
8. Disturbance-handler and trouble-shooter
9. Resource allocator

Negotiating role

10. Negotiator

Source: H. H. Mintzberg (1973) *The Nature of Management Work*, Harper & Row, New York.

and Hannan (1978) found twenty-two studies of management jobs which met the criterion of having used the diary and/or observation methods. The replicated results from all twenty-two studies reveal the following composite picture of management work.

Managers generally work long hours, and often this takes the form of desk-work done at home or business meetings and social events. The length of the work week tends to increase as rank increases, but managers with well-defined functions such as accounting tend to work shorter hours. During the time they are at work managers are very busy. This is especially true of low-level management, where foremen can attend to over 300 separate activities and 'sit' for only about one minute in an eight-hour day.

The work does not form an identifiable whole. It tends to consist of brief episodes which may last as little as two minutes for foremen or nine minutes for executives. The brief episodes do not even follow each other in a logical order. Problems are handled in rapid-fire order with little attempt to order the priorities of issues according to their importance. Interruptions rule the day. It is not unusual for an executive to have forty telephone conversations and thirty visitors in a day. To make matters worse, the content of managerial work is varied and includes paperwork, interpersonal episodes, formal meetings and tours of inspection.

Managers at all levels tend to spend most of their time within their own organizations, mainly within their own departments. Senior executives tend to spend less time on the shop-floor and more time either in their own offices or outside their department. Most of the manager's communications are oral, mostly face-to-face interactions at meetings. The nature of a manager's communications implies that he needs and uses a lot of contacts, and contacts with colleagues at the same managerial level tend to increase with management level. About one-third to two-thirds of a manager's time is spent with subordinates, and only a small proportion of time is spent with superiors.

Many people feel that planning is the essence of a manager's job. But in fact research has shown that few managers are careful, effective planners, and a part of the explanation lies in the fact that few managers have uninterrupted periods of time when planning is possible. Several studies suggest that managers only spend between 2 and 5 per cent of their time on planning activities.

Thus it appears that planning is *not* the essence of the managerial job; the key aspect of the manager's role seems to be the way he handles *information*. McCall *et al.* make a final point that managers are not very good at estimating how they spend their time. It appears, for example, that managers tend to overestimate the time they spend on production, paperwork, telephone calls and thinking, while they tend to underestimate the time they spend on meetings and discussions.

A pertinent note on which to end this chapter on the manager and his role in the organization is to pose the question 'How much control does the manager have over his own job?' Opinion is deeply divided, but Carlson (in 1951) wrote:

> Even had the executives wanted to change their behaviour, they did not have much chance to do so. The content of their working day is determined only to a small extent by themselves and it is difficult to change it without making considerable alterations in the organizational structure of which they are parts. Before we made the study, I always thought of a chief executive as the conductor of an orchestra standing aloof on his platform. Now I am in some respects inclined to see him as the puppet in a puppet show with hundreds of people pulling the strings and forcing him to act in one way or another.

References for Chapter 2

Acton Society Trust (1956) *Management Succession*, Acton, London.

Ashridge Management Research Unit (1980) 'Women and Management Project', paper delivered at one-day conference on Women in Management, April 1980.

Blum, M. L. and Naylor, J. C. (1968) *Industrial Psychology: Its Theoretical and Social Functions*, Harper & Row, New York.

Carlson, S. (1951) *Executive Behaviour: A Study of the Work Loads and the Working Methods of Managing Directors*, Strombergs, Stockholm.

Clark, D. G. (1966) *The Industrial Manager, His Background and Career Pattern*, Business Publications, London.

Copeman, G. H. (1955) *Leaders of British Industry*, Gee & Co., London.

Deeks, J. (1970), *The Owner-Managers and Managers of Small Firms*, Furniture & Timber Industry Training Board, High Wycombe, England.

Glover, I. A. (1974) 'The Background of British Managers: A Review of the Evidence', unpublished paper, British Institute of Management, London.

Guerrier, Y. and Philpot, N. (1978) 'The British Manager: Careers and Mobility', *Management Survey Report*, No. 39, British Institute of Management, London.

Larwood, L. and Wood, M. M. (1977) *Women in Management*, D. C. Heath & Co., Lexington, Mass.

Lewis, D. R. and Dahl, T. (1976) 'Time Management in Higher Education Administration: a Case Study', *Higher Education*, 5, 49—66.

McCall, M. W., Morrison, A. and Hannan, R. L. (1978) *Studies of Managerial Work: Results and Methods*, Center for Creative Leadership, Breensboro, North Carolina.

McCormick, E. J. (1976) 'Job and Task Analysis', in Dunnette, M.D. (ed.), *Handbook of Industrial and Organizational Psychology*, Rand McNally, Chicago.

Mant, A. (1969) *The Experienced Manager, a Major Resource*, British Institute of Management, London.

Melrose-Woodman, J. (1978) *Profile of the British Manager*, British Institute of Management, London.

Mintzberg, H. H. (1973) *The Nature of Management Work*, Harper & Row, New York.

Stewart, R. (1967), *Managers and Their Jobs*, Macmillan, London.

Super, D. E. and Hall, D. T. (1978) 'Career Development: Exploration and Planning', *Annual Review of Psychology*, 29, 333–72.

3
Motivation and Job Satisfaction

An intelligent reader likes a challenge and this chapter starts with the challenge to identify the common factor in the following industrial and commercial situations.

First, there is the multinational clothing firm making blue denim jeans. Every week, in every one of its factories, strung across the globe, the seamstresses take part in their factory's production competition. One week the prize is a gold pen, next week the prize is a weekend holiday, the following week the prize is a hi-fi system. The scheme has operated for many years without a repetition of prizes and there is speculation that somewhere, in some town, in the Mid West of the USA, there must exist a Vice-President of Prizes.

Second, a medium-sized car manufacturer spends millions of its precious venture capital developing a production system which is more expensive than the conventional tried-and-tested assembly line.

Third, there is the university Vice-Chancellor pondering how he can prevent his staff subconsciously adjusting the level of their effort to match the level of their recent pay award.

Fourth, there is the grants panel of the Small Firms Council, trying to decide which applicants have the necessary drive and energy to become successful entrepreneurs and thus qualify for financial support.

Fifth, there is the manager of a small french polishing firm in the West Riding of Yorkshire who bitterly complains that his profit margins are eroded because his craftsmen put too much care and effort into their work instead of achieving a higher volume of work at a quality which is just acceptable to the customer.

The common factor in all these cases is that management is confronted with a problem of worker motivation. Paradoxically, even the problem of the french polishers is a problem of motivation. Viewed from the bottom line of the profit-and-loss account, the craftsmen are over-motivated by their pride in their finished product and under-motivated by the Mernch incentive wages scheme recommended by a local firm of management consultants.

As the examples show, motivation of its members is one of the most critical tasks facing any organization. Unfortunately, the concept of motivation is probably the most confused, confusing and poorly developed concept in organizational psychology. The difficulty is not due to a failure to recognize the importance of the problem. For example, evidence from Keenan (1976) indicates that interviewers of university graduates regard strong motivation as one of the most important characteristics required from applicants. The difficulty lies more in the inability of organizational psychologists to develop a theory which gives a satisfactory explanation of the evidence obtained in a variety of situations. Indeed, there has been a fairly rapid turnover of motivational theories. Each theory has been held in vogue for a number of years before sufficient contradictory evidence has accumulated to cause abandonment of the theory. Probably the best way of making sense of the subject of motivation is to give a simple, chronological description of these theories. Additional information on each of these theories can be obtained from an excellent book by Steers and Porter (1979) or review by Korman *et al.* (1977), Grossman (1979) and Brody (1980).

Drive-reduction theories

At the turn of the century, psychologists such as McDougall believed that human effort was energized by various instincts, and by definition that these instincts were genetically determined and exhibited by all members of a species in the appropriate circumstances without the need for learning. For example, all healthy and mature male sticklebacks exhibit a mating response when confronted with the red belly of a gravid female stickleback. Evidence gradually accumulated that many of the so-called human instincts did not meet the requirements of the definition. For example, a significant proportion of healthy mature people derive more excitement from nude pictures of their own sex than nude pictures of the opposite sex. Similarly, many women show no maternal instinct. Eventually the instinct theory was abandoned, and in the 1920s the term 'drive' became accepted and the important concept of *homeostasis* was introduced during the 1930s.

Drive-reduction theory starts with a picture of the living organism in perfect balance with itself and its environment. But the activity of living upsets the balance: food is burnt up and waste products accumulate. Ultimately these changes would bring about the death of the organism. The environment may also change and upset the balance. For example, it may get hotter or colder. However these changes are caused, the organism detects them and is driven to take action to restore the balance. Many of the homeostatic actions are automatic body reactions such as shivering or a change in the rate at which body salts are excreted; other actions are deliberate, such as going in search of food or putting on extra clothing. Initially these deliberate homeostatic actions are often inefficient, but the organism gradually adapts its behaviour and learns to be more efficient. Drive-reduction theory is a good explanation of the *physiological* drives of hunger, thirst, warmth, etc. To an extent it also applies to sexual motives in animals. However, it is exceptionally difficult to explain many human motives in drive-reduction terms.

Maslow's hierarchy of needs

The 'social motivations' which lack a clear physiological cause were highlighted by Maslow (1943, 1954). Maslow identified five different types of need. He then placed them in hierarchical order in such a way that the needs at one level have to be satisfied before a person starts to move up the hierarchy and concentrate upon satisfying 'higher' needs.

The most basic needs are the *physiological needs* which

were identified by the drive-reduction theorists. If all needs are unsatisfied, the person will be dominated by his physiological needs, such as hunger, thirst, sleep and sex. But as soon as these needs are satisfied, the higher motivations come into focus. Maslow (1943) writes that 'It is quite true that man lives by bread alone — when there is no bread. But what happens to man's desires when there *is* plenty of bread and when his belly is chronically filled? At once, other (and 'higher') needs emerge and these, rather than physiological hungers, dominate the organism.'

Once the physiological needs have been satisfied, the *safety needs* emerge. The person motivated by safety needs wants to be free from extremes of temperature, murder and physical harm. In an industrial setting, a worker who is motivated by safety will value a job with tenure, security, and pension and welfare schemes.

Once the safety needs are satisfied, the *belongingness needs* come into prominence. The individual will want to be in the company of others — preferably the company of warm, accepting friends, and he will feel keenly the absence of sweetheart, wife or children.

Once the belongingness needs have been satisfied, a person starts to fulfil his *esteem needs*. Here he will strive to be held in esteem by others. He will want others to respect him for his achievements, strength or intellectual ability. There will be a desire for recognition and importance.

The highest need in Maslow's hierarchy is the need for *self-actualization*, for people to achieve their full potential. The nature of self-fulfilment will vary from one individual to another. In one person self-fulfilment arises from being a good and effective salesman. In another person self-actualization will arise from being an effective organizational psychologist! Writing in 1943, Maslow wrote: 'Since, in our society, basically satisfied people are the exception, we do not know much about self-actualization, either experimentally or clinically.' Almost half a century has elapsed since the gestation of Maslow's ideas. In that time there has been an unprecedented rise in the prosperity of people in Europe, Australia and North America, so it is likely that the motivators influencing individuals in today's organizations are quite different from those operating half a century ago.

Maslow's analysis of human motives has had an enormous influence in industry and his theory has generated considerable research. For example, Porter (1961, 1962, 1963) attempted to establish the degree to which managers' needs at the different levels of Maslow's hierarchy were met, and was able to produce a need-deficiency score at each level. As Figure 3.1 shows, the need deficiencies were related to a manager's level in the organization. Top-level managers had siginficant deficiencies at the self-actualization level but were moderately satisfied at the physiological and safety levels, while junior managers tended to have a need deficit at the esteem level.

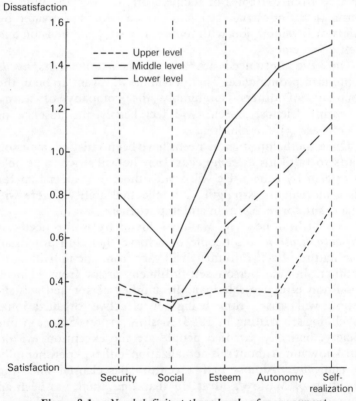

Figure 3.1   *Need deficit at three levels of management*

Source: L. W. Porter, E. E. Lawler and J. R. Hackman (1975) *Behavior in Organizations*, McGraw-Hill, New York.

Alderfer's (1969, 1972) thinking also followed the Maslow tradition, but Alderfer's hierarchy suggested three need levels: *existence* needs, which include both physiological and safety needs, *relatedness* needs and *growth* needs.

Although Maslow's hierarchy has been enormously influential, its empirical basis is not well established, and several key aspects have not been supported by research findings. Two particularly vulnerable aspects are the number of categories and their hierarchical arrangement. Psychologists frequently use factor analysis to determine the number and nature of underlying dimensions. Factor analysis is a statistical technique which starts with a data table containing numerical indices of how variables relate to one another. The statistics involved in factor analysis are sophisticated, but in effect the data table is scanned and the largest underlying trend is identified, and the effects of this trend are then extracted from the data and a lesser trend is extracted from the remainder. This process is repeated until no further trends are located. Consequently, if Maslow's hierarchy is true, five independent factors, each concerned with one level of motivation, should emerge from data concerning people's motives. In fact, this has not happened. After reviewing a number of studies of this type, Wahba and Bridwell (1979) conclude:

> None of the studies has shown *all* of Maslow's five need categories as independent factors. Only [one] study showed four independant factors reflecting four needs; the fifth need overlapped with an unrelated factor . . . it is not possible to assess from the studies reviewed whether self-actualization is, in fact, a need or simply a social desirability response resulting from certain cultural values. There is some empirical evidence to support this latter conclusion.

The second key element of Maslow's theory — the hierarchical arrangement of his need categories — is also under question. Luthans (1977) notes that there are many situations where the order of dominance among needs is not in accord with Maslow's theory. Common examples of this include celibacy amongst priests and fasting for religious and political causes, and Sorokin (1942) compiled estimates of the proportion of the population who would violate social mores under conditions of starvation (see Table 3.1).

Maslow's pioneering work evolved during the 1940s. During the 1950s two other approaches, Hertzberg's *two-factor theory* and McClelland's *achievement motivation*, were under development.

Hertzberg's two-factor theory and job enrichment

Hertzberg's two-factor theory has had an enormous influence on organizations and on the way that jobs have been structured. The two-factory theory arose mainly out of a study of some 200 engineers and accountants in Pittsburgh. Hertzberg *et al.* (1959) asked their engineers and accountants to give details of a time when they were especially *satisfied* with their job and to give details of a time when they were especially *dissatisfied*. The replies were then analysed and those replies which 'seemed to go together' were classified and frequent responses noted. Hertzberg *et al.* observed that certain factors tended to be associated with satisfaction while others tended to be associated with dissatisfaction. Poor company administration, for example, was often associated with dissatisfaction, but good administration was rarely associated with satisfaction. On the other hand, recognition was frequently associated with satisfaction, but lack of recognition was rarely associated with dissatisfaction. (See Figure 3.2.)

Hertzberg and his co-workers concluded that job satisfaction and job dissatisfaction result from different causes. Satisfaction depends on *motivators*. Dissatisfaction results from the *absence* of sufficient *hygiene factors*. Increasing the level of hygiene by increasing pay, improving supervision or improving company administration will prevent workers from becoming dissatisfied. But even very large increments in these factors will not produce the positive will to work. In industrial terms this means that poorly paid, poorly administered workers will leave the firm. If pay and other hygiene factors are high, workers stay with the firm but may not give their very best efforts. Hertzberg (1968) claimed that to obtain such positive motivation it is necessary to increase the

Table 3.1   *Approximate percentage of the population showing various behaviours under starvation conditions*

Activities induced by starvation	Percentage of population succumbing to pressure of starvation
Cannibalism (in non-cannibalistic societies)	Less than one-third of 1%
Murder of members of the family and friends	Less than 1%
Murder of other members of one's group	Not more than 1%
Murder of strangers who are not enemies	Not more than 2 to 5%
Infliction of various bodily and other injuries on members of one's social group	Not more than 5 to 10%
Theft, larceny, robbery, forgery and other crimes against property which have a clear-cut criminal character	Hardly more than 7 to 10%
Violation of various rules of strict honesty and fairness in pursuit of food, such as misuse of rationing cards, hoarding, and taking unfair advantage of others	From 20 to 99% depending upon the nature of the violation
Violation of fundamental religious and moral principles	Hardly more than 10 to 20%
Violation of less important religious, moral, juridical, conventional and similar norms	From 50 to 99%
Surrender or weakening of most of the aesthetic activities irreconcilable with food-seeking activities	From 50 to 99%
Weakening of sex activities, especially coitus	From 70 to 90% during prolonged and intense starvation
Prostitution and other highly dishonourable sex activities	Hardly more than 10%

Source: Pitirim A. Sorokin (1942) *Man and Society in Calamity*, E. P. Dutton & Co. Inc, New York, p. 81 (reprinted 1970, ed. Helen P. Sorokin).

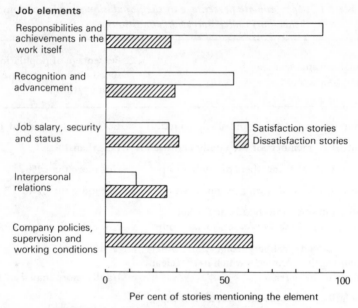

Figure 3.2   *Satisfiers and dissatisfiers at work*

Source: C. H. Smith and J. H. Wakeley (1972) *Psychology of Industrial Behavior*, McGraw-Hill, New York.

intrinsic interest in the job itself and to give an employee a sense of responsibility, recognition and achievement. Hertzberg's approach is clearly related to Maslow's hierarchy of needs, and the motivators can be classified as esteem and self-actualization satisfiers, while the hygiene factors can be classified as physiological and safety needs.

The job-enrichment movement grew out of Hertzberg's central conclusion that workers were motivated by a sense of achievement and challenging work. The job-enrichment movement claimed that the production-line system of manufacture is inherently demotivating. On a typical production line work is repetitive and production engineers have organized the work into a series of small, unskilled tasks which have little intrinsic interest. Under these circumstances it is hardly surprising if motivation is low. Improving the situation can be attempted in three ways: job rotation, job enlargement and job enrichment.

Job rotation usually involves the least change from the traditional production-line method. It simply involves scheduling a worker's time to ensure that he performs a variety of tasks. In a typical production line involving three distinct processes to manufacture an article, process A is performed by person X, process B is performed by person Y and process C is performed by person Z. In a job-rotation system person X will spend, say, a day on process A, then a day on process B and then a day on process C. The scheduling of employees' duties is carefully worked out to ensure that all processes are manned and working. Job rotation is a relatively cheap way of introducing variety to a job.

Job enlargement usually requires a bigger change. In job enlargement the production processes and methods of manufacture are changed so that an individual employee performs all the tasks required to produce one unit of work. In an enlarged job person X will perform processes A, B and C and at the end of the day he will derive a sense of achievement from seeing the goods that he has produced.

Job enrichment takes the process a stage further. In job enrichment the job is first enlarged and then many of the traditional managerial functions of setting targets, scheduling and deciding methods of working are left to the worker's own judgements. Job enrichment involves the greatest change from the traditional production-line system and it carries the greatest implications for managerial philosophy and practice.

The job-enrichment movement has had great influence. Factories have been specially designed and equipped in order to enrich the jobs of automobile workers (Gyllenhammer, 1977). Governments have financed research units to aid the implementation of job enrichment. Job enrichment has also been applied to more mundane levels of processing insurance claims and selling computer equipment. For example, Purcer Smith (1967) compared the motivation of sales forces in two companies and found that company A employees were more satisfied with their salaries, their training and their prospects, while in company B satisfaction was expressed more in terms of job security and employee benefits. She writes that in company A the expansionist company policy is a source of satisfaction, while 'short staffing, budget consciousness, the amount of work and its effects on home life rank among the most dissatisfying features. With the exception of the effects on home life, these receive little emphasis in company *B*. In both companies there is dissatisfaction with paper work and communications.' She also noted that sales executives in company *A* gave the amount of responsibility in their jobs rather more emphasis and that job satisfaction was related to the extent that managers were seen as showing trust in subordinates, giving them enough responsibility and inspiring them with enthusiasm.

In spite of the existence of many case studies which seem to show the advantages of job enrichment, many psychologists are sceptical about its effectiveness. A part of the scepticism arises from the realization that most workers are satisfied with their jobs. Gallup Polls cited by the US Department of Health, Education and Welfare (1973) indicate that 80 to 90 per cent of American workers are satisfied with their jobs. Sorenson (1973) suggested that 82 to 91 per cent of blue- and white-collar workers like their work, and when the workers were asked 'If there were one thing you could change about your job, what would it be?', only a very few workers said that they would make their jobs less boring or more interesting. A similar picture of satisfaction emerged from Britain. A survey reported by the Central Statistical Office (1973) revealed that, in 1971, 88 per cent of British workers were satisfied with their jobs. If current levels of satisfaction are already high, clearly there is limited scope for improvements from job enrichment.

A second source of scepticism about job enrichment concerns the impracticability of enriching some jobs. The very technology of our manufacturing processes imposes real constraints upon the degree of enrichment that is possible. Fein (1979) notes:

> Even in the highly praised experimental Volvo plant where a small team assembles an engine, the workers have no choice in the selection of parts to be installed and they must assemble the parts in a given sequence. Furthermore, to modify existing technology can involve considerable capital expenditure and higher labour costs.

He quotes a study in which a job-rotation scheme raised costs by 12.4 per cent and asks: 'Would the consumer be willing to pay the additional cost?'

A third concern about the job-enrichment movement focuses upon the scientific standing of the research data. Many of the studies have been poorly controlled, and consequently there is doubt about whether the reported conclusions are the result of job enrichment or some other cause. For example, since the early Hawthorne experiments in the 1920s it has been known that merely expressing interest in a group of workers tends to increase their productivity, and therefore any change, whether it enriches a job or not, has a good chance of improving production. Few job-enrichment studies have taken the 'Hawthorne effect' into account and several studies have ignored the effects of other changes. Thus in many widely quoted case studies of job enrichment the results may be attributed to other factors. Fein gives two classic examples. The first example is the widely quoted case of General Foods—Topeka, which introduced job enrichment and achieved improved performance. Unfortunately, the initial report of this study did not reveal that the sixty-three employees involved had been carefully selected using five interviews which included a personality test. Clearly the results could be a reflection of an improved selection procedure. Fein's second example dealt with a report of the job enrichment of cleaning and janitorial employees at Texas Instruments. Fein reveals that, in addition to enriching the job, the janitors' pay had been increased by 46 per cent and a better calibre of employee had been recruited. It is possible that the savings shown in the initial research report arose from the changes in the pay structure rather than the job redesign.

Yet another source of scepticism about the job-enrichment movement stems from the severe academic criticism which Hertzberg's study has received. A detailed exposition of these criticisms has been set out by Locke (1976), Wall, Stephenson and Skidmore (1971) and Wall (1973). Perhaps all academic criticisms of Hertzberg's work can be summed under two headings. First, there are the *methodological* issues which include the telling point that since Hertzberg used two different questions to obtain his responses (a question for satisfiers and a question for dissatisfiers), it is not surprising that he obtained two categories of replies (motivators and hygiene factors). In addition, the methodology of his analysis has been criticized. The second area of criticism concerns the *interpretation* placed upon the results. The emergence of two sets of factors could be an artefact of the defensiveness on the part of the employees. Because most people prefer to have a good image of themselves, they defend their self-images by attributing failure and dissatisfaction to tangible objects in their environment. Thus many argue that Hertzberg's two factors are merely a reflection of this tendency to attribute success to ourselves and to attribute failure to our environment.

McClelland's achievement motivation

At about the same time that Maslow was developing his hierarchy of needs, Murray (1938) was developing an alternative view of motivation. He saw motives largely as learned behaviours which are characterized by the object and the intensity. Murray felt that an individual's personality is subject to a large number of divergent needs, and he compiled a list of thirteen needs which included the need for achievement, the need for affiliation, the need for power, the need for succourance, the need for nurturance, etc. The achievement motive, the power motive and the affiliation motive have attracted considerable research attention. Without doubt, achievement motivation has attracted the lion's share of this attention, and as a consequence it is probably the most thoroughly researched aspect of organizational psychology. Furthermore, achievement motivation has a direct relevance to economic growth and prosperity.

McClelland (1961) starts with the example of Florence. He asks:

What produced the Renaissance in Italy, of which Florence was the centre? How did it happen that such a small population base could produce, in the short span of a few generations, great historical figures first in commerce and literature, then in architecture, sculpture and painting, and finally in science and music? Why have the countries of Northern Europe and North America accumulated wealth at a faster rate than ever before in history? [He also asked the darker questions] Why did Athenian civilization decline and why did the predominant medieval Spain lapse into obscurity?

According to McClelland, one of the most important causes of all these phenomena was the level of achievement motivation in relevant populations.

Achievement motivation is usually defined as the need to excel in relation to competitive or internalized standards. Two main components are usually differentiated: the hope for success and the fear of failure. In short, achievement motivation is the desire to do something better, faster, more efficiently or with less effort. When a society contains many individuals with high levels of achievement motivation, things start to hum and economic growth ensues. In order to test this proposition, McClelland and his co-workers developed methods of measuring the levels of achievement motivation in past societies. The main method takes a sample of the written culture such as children's stories or street ballads and carefully analyses the content or themes they contain. Themes which concern strivings to attain high standards are counted and an achievement score obtained. These achievement scores can then be compared with the economic indices of the day. For example, McClelland reports a study which analysed English street ballads between 1500 and 1800 and for each fifty-year period an achievement score was obtained. Of course, national economic indicators of today's sophistication are not available and one of the best available indices of economic development throughout this period was the level of coal imports to London. As Figure 3.3 shows, there is an impressive relationship between the level of achievement motivation and the level of economic activity fifty years later.

McClelland also reports a similar study, relating the achievement themes in American children's readers between 1800 and 1950 and the number of patent applications which, he claims, is an index of economic growth and innovation within

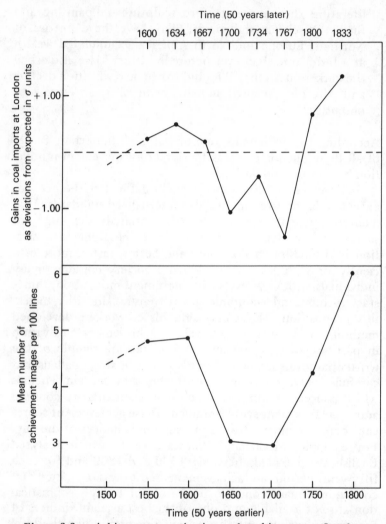

Figure 3.3 *Achievement motivation and coal imports at London*

Source: D. C. McClelland (1976) *The Achieving Society*, revised edn, Irvington Publishers, New York.

a society (see Figure 3.4). Although the precise details and methods of these studies vary, similar results have been obtained from investigations of medieval Spain, Athenian Greece and even pre-Incan Peru.

The results from all these studies are impressive, but on

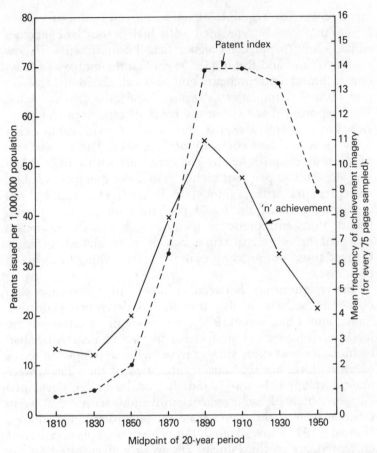

Figure 3.4 *Achievement motivation and US patents*

Source: D. C. McClelland (1976) *The Achieving Society*, revised edn, Irvington Publishers, New York.

their own they cannot be conclusive, because many alternative explanations are possible, and of course there are exceptions to the rule – it is difficult to explain either the economic rise of Japan or the economic decline of Argentina in terms of achievement motivation.

Fortunately, there have been studies linking achievement motivation to specific economic advances which, if repeated on a societal scale, would produce the effects indicated by McClelland. For example, Morgan (1964) obtained achievement scores for a sample of self-employed businessmen and found that the businessmen with high scores had incomes which were 73 per cent higher than businessmen with low scores. Wainer and Rubin (1969) studied the motives of fifty-one technical entrepreneurs and also calculated the growth rate of their companies in terms of the value of their sales. They reported that 'within the range of moderate to high *n*-Ach (*need achievement*) a very marked relationship exists between *n*-Ach and company performance. The growth rate of those companies led by entrepreneurs with a high *n*-Ach was almost 250 per cent higher than those companies led by entrepreneurs with a moderate *n*-Ach.' This finding was replicated in Australia by Morris and Fargher (1974), who found that entrepreneurs owning high-growth businesses obtained achievement scores which were almost twice as high as those obtained by entrepreneurs owning low-growth businesses.

The relationship between achievement motivation and economic activity is also true in less developed countries. Sinha and Chaubney (1972), for example, contrasted the levels of achievement motivation in villages near Allahabad in India. Two of these villages were highly developed in terms of agriculture, health, housing, etc.; two of the villages were underdeveloped. It was found that adults in the developed villages obtained achievement-motivation scores that were twice as high as the scores from the underdeveloped villages. Hundal (1971) investigated the achievement motivation of entrepreneurs in the Punjab. His work concentrated on the small-scale hosiery and metal industries and, once again, a significant relationship between achievement motivation and a fast rate of economic growth emerged. The consistency in all these findings is particularly surprising, as different investigators were using different methods to measure achievement motivation in different set-ups. These replications give extra confidence in the generality of the relationship between achievement motivation and economic advance.

Once the link between achievement motivation and economic growth has been firmly established, the next step is to build up a picture of individuals who exhibit high achievement motivation. Over the years an amazingly detailed picture of the high *n*-Ach individual has been established. He is likely to be non-conformist in his religious views and prefer sombre shades of blue and green over the more vibrant colours of red and yellow. The high *n*-Ach individual shows brisk, energetic, restless movements. He likes to travel, is a social climber and is acutely aware of the rapid passage of time. In many ways the high *n*-Ach individual shows characteristics of the *A*-type personality which is described in Chapter 5. However, the really distinctive feature of the high *n*-Ach individual is his attitude towards taking risks. The highly achievement-orientated individuals are not the 'butch' heroes of the business world taking high-risk decisions. Equally, they are not the timid cowards. One of his key characteristics is his preference for *moderate* risks. In low-risk and high-risk situations events are either determined by chance or determined by outside forces. The achivement-motivated individual chooses the area in between the extremes where his skills and his competencies have maximum room to take effect. The highly achievement-motivated person also wants immediate *feedback* which tells him how much progress he is making towards his goal. He will tend to prefer jobs in management positions where they are evaluated against specific performance criteria. Above all, such persons are task-orientated. They feel pressure to get the job done. Given the choice between working alongside a companion who will provide a congenial social atmosphere and working alongside an expert who will help complete a task, a person with high achievement motivation will almost certainly choose to work with the expert. When confronted with the task-process dilemma which faces the functioning of groups (see Chapter 8) the high *n*-Ach individual will probably concentrate on task issues.

Few other motives have been so extensively researched as achievement motivation. Consequently, we already know some of the influences which cause an individual to have a high level of achievement motivation. It is extremely doubtful whether achievement motivation is genetically determined, since achievement motivation within a society can rise or fall within a period of fifty years. This time period is far too short for significant changes in a nation's genetic pool. High achievement motivation seems to be caused by an individual's past experience in achievement situations. Experience during childhood seems to be particularly important. Research by Winterbottom (1958) and by Rosen and D'Andrade (1959) suggests that high achievement motivation is likely to be engendered by parents who expect their children to be self-reliant at an early age. These parents are warm and give praise. Interestingly the mothers tend to be authoritarian, but the fathers of the children with high achievement motivation are less dominant and authoritarian.

Of course, once it is established that experience plays an important part in the development of achievement motivation, it should be possible to manipulate experience and increase achievement motivation by appropriate training. Training courses have been developed which teach participants to think, talk, act and set goals like an individual with high achievement motivation (Alschuler *et al.*, 1970; McClelland, 1972). It may be that these training courses work because they give the individual the belief that he is the main influence in achieving success. Technically, this is known as *internalizing the locus of control*.

Some of the most recent research (e.g. Weiner, 1974) suggests that achievement motivation results from a particular cognitive outlook on life, and individuals with high achievement motivation believe that in moderately difficult but stable situations they are able to influence the outcome of events.

Process theories of motivation

The theories of motivation developed by Maslow, Hertzberg and McClelland deal with the *content* of motivation, such as self-actualization, hygiene factors or achievement strivings. Recent research on achievement motivation by Weiner seems to be looking at achievement motivation as a cognitive process and looks upon achievement actions as the results of decisions an individual makes about events. These decisions are in turn determined by the view the individual builds up of the world about him. Adams (1963, 1965) developed a process theory of motivation based on the assumption that *equity* is an important construct in most people's thoughts. Adams suggests that most people balance what they put into a situation with what they get out and they then compare the result obtained by other people in similar situations. If these comparisons are not equitable, the individual alters his behaviour to bring the rewards and costs into balance. Equity theory has direct relevance to the salaries which business organizations pay their members. The theory implies that if individuals are underpaid, they bring the cost–benefit equation into balance by *reducing* the effort they put into their work. On the other hand, if an individual is overpaid, he will bring the cost–benefit equation into balance by *increasing* the effort he puts into his work. Mowday (1979) reviews many empirical studies of payment and equity theory. In general, the results concerning underpayment conform to the results predicted by equity theory. However, the results concerning overpayment are contradictory and inconclusive.

Without doubt the most influential process theory of industrial motivation is Vroom's (1964) *expectancy* theory. According to this theory, motivation involves three phases. First, an individual has to believe that extra effort could help him attain a target. This is the effort–expectancy link and is typical of a management comment such as 'If I work hard and manage my team more effectively, I will obtain higher production figures for my unit by 20 per cent.' The second stage consists of a link between target and outcome, such as 'If production of my unit goes up by 20 per cent, I am more than likely to be promoted.' The third stage consists of an evaluation of the outcome: 'Promotion means more pay and more status, which I will enjoy.' If this chain is broken at any stage by such thoughts as 'even if I flog my guts out, production can't increase', or 'Promotion around here depends on seniority', or 'Promotion means longer hours for less thanks', then the manager will not be motivated.

A pragmatic approach to motivation

Earlier in this chapter it was said that motivation is one of the most confused and confusing aspects of organizational psychology with the possible exception of achievement motivation — we have seen that a succession of theories have failed to produce consistently accurate predictions. In the light of these inconsistencies many organizational psychologists have adopted a pragmatic approach in which a range of satisfiers are identified and then some kind of survey is used to identify which satisfiers are deficient in a specific factory or department. The list of possible satisfiers is enormous, and workers in the field usually group the satisfiers into *extrinsic* satisfiers and *intrinsic* satisfiers.

The extrinsic are those satisfiers which are outside the job and which can be readily altered without changing the basic nature of the work that is performed. The main extrinsic satisfiers concern pay, promotion prospects, co-workers, physical working conditions, job security and social status.

However, people may work hard at their job even though they receive no extra pay and their chances of promotion are not enhanced. They may work hard because they find the work fascinating. There is something in the job itself which motivates them. The satisfaction received from these factors is termed intrinsic satisfaction. A number of investigators have attempted to determine the components of intrinsic satisfaction. Jobs which are intrinsically satisfying will tend to have three characteristics: *variety* — workers will not be asked to perform the same operations all day and every day; *autonomy* — the work has a substantial degree of discretion in scheduling the work and in determining the procedures to be used in carrying it out; *feedback* — the worker will know from the job itself how well he is doing.

A great deal of effort has been expended to determine the relative importance of satisfiers. Typically, samples of workers have been asked to rank a list of satisfiers in order of importance. Table 3.2 shows the results from one study.

The main motivation for conducting surveys of the importance of various types of satisfiers is that if satisfaction can be increased an improvement in productivity can be expected to follow. At best this is only partially true, and it is perhaps wise to end this chapter on motivation by turning to the results obtained by Locke *et al.* (1979). Locke and his co-workers collected research reports containing the results of

Table 3.2 *Importance ratings for various satisfiers*

Job factors	Factory workers	Office workers	Management
Steady work	1	1	1
High wages	3	10	2
Pension	2	8	6
Not work too hard	8	14	14
Getting along with people	4	4	7
Getting along with supervisor	5	3	10
Chance quality work	7	5	4
Chance interesting work	10.5	2	3
Chance promotion	12	7	5
Good working conditions	10.5	6	9
Paid holidays	9	12	12
Good union	13	13	13
Good working hours	6	9	11
Good chance raise	14	11	8

Source: U. M Gluskinos (1970) 'Management and Union Leaders' Perception of Worker Needs as compared with Self-reported Needs', *Proceedings of the 78th APA Convention.*

attempts to alter productivity by changing motivational factors. They were careful to exclude any studies where the performance criteria were inadequate (for example, supervisors' estimates of performance were not acceptable), and they focused attention on four main categories of motivation: money, goal-setting, participation, job enrichment.

Their empirical results should have a sobering effect on many organizational and motivational theorists. The most effective way of motivating a work-force involves the use of pay as a motivator; a median improvement of 30 per cent was obtained. Goal-setting was the second most effective technique. This motivational technique involves setting specific, challenging goals and then providing relevant feedback so that an employee knows how he is progressing. Goal-setting achieved a median improvement in performance of 17 per cent. The motivational technique of job enrichment was particularly difficult to evaluate because, as noted earlier in this chapter, studies involving job enrichment are frequently confounded with other variables. Locke *et al.* comment that

> typical confounding variables in the so-called job enrichment studies included . . . changes in incentives, selection, training, manpower allocation and goal settings . . . If the most questionable studies are deleted from the calculations . . . the median improvement reduces to 8.75%. It is striking that some of the best controlled studies of job enrichment obtained the poorest results although some studies with seemingly good designs obtained substantial performance effects. The least effective motivational technique appears to be participation in decision-making, which obtained a median percent performance improvement of only one-half of one per cent.

However, it would be wrong to end this chapter on a totally iconoclastic note because many would argue that participation is a goal in its own right and that it may be related to other organizational goals such as reduced labour turnover or the organization's mental health.

References for Chapter 3

Adams, J. S. (1963) 'Toward an Understanding of Inequity', *Journal of Abnormal and Social Psychology*, 67, 422—36.

Adams, J. S. (1965) 'Inequity in Social Exchange', in Berkowitz, L. (ed.), *Advances in Experimental Social Psychology*, Academic Press, New York, vol. 2.

Alderfer, C. P. (1969) 'A New Theory of Human Needs', *Organizational Behaviour and Human Performance*, 4, 142—75.

Alderfer, C. P. (1972) *Existence, Relatedness and Growth*, Free Press, New York.

Alschuler, A. S., Tabor, D. and McIntyre, J. (1970) *Teaching Achievement Motivation*, Educational Ventures Inc., Middletown, Conn.

Brody, N. (1980) 'Social Motivation', *Annual Review of Psychology*, 31, 143—68.

Central Statistical Office (1973) *Social Trends*, HMSO, London.

Fein, H. (1979) 'Job Enrichment: a Re-evaluation', in Steers, R. M. and Porter, L. W. (eds), *Motivation and Work Behavior*, McGraw-Hill, New York.

Grossman, S. P. (1979) 'The Biology of Motivation', *Annual Review of Psychology*, 30, 209—42.

Gyllenhammer, P. G. (1977) 'How Volvo adapts Work to People', *Harvard Business Review*, July—August, 102—13.

Hertzberg, F. (1968) 'One More Time: How Do You Motivate Employees?', *Harvard Business Review*, 46, 53—62.

Hertzberg, F., Mausner, B. and Snyderman, B. (1959) *The Motivation to Work*, Wiley, New York.

Hundal, P. S. (1971) 'A Study of Entrepreneurial Motivation: Comparison of Fast- and Slow-progressing Small-scale, Industrial Entrepreneurs in Punjab, India', *Journal of Applied Psychology*, 55, 317—23.

Keenan, A. (1976) 'Interviewers' Evaluation of Applicants', *Journal of Occupational Psychology*, 49, 223—30.

Korman, A. K., Greenhaus, J. H. and Badin, I. P. (1977) 'Personnel Attitudes and Motivation', *Annual Review of Psychology*, 28, 175—96.

Locke, E. A. (1976) 'The Nature and Causes of Job Satisfaction', in Dunnette, M. D. (ed.) *Handbook of Industrial and Organizational Psychology*, Rand McNally, Chicago.

Locke, E. A. *et al.* (1979) 'The Relative Effectiveness of Four Methods of Motivating Employee Performance', paper presented to NATO conference, Thessaloniki, Greece, August, 1979.

Luthans, F. (1977) *Organizational Behavior*, McGraw-Hill, New York.

McClelland, D. C. (1961) *The Achieving Society*, Van Nostrand, Princeton, N.J. (revised edn 1976 published by Irvington, New York).

McClelland, D. C. (1972) 'What is the Effect of Achievement Motivation Training in the Schools', *Teachers' College Records*, 74, 129—45.

Maslow, A. H. (1943) 'A Theory of Human Motivation', *Psychological Review*, 50, 370—96.

Maslow, A. H. (1954) *Motivation and Personality*, Harper, New York.

Morgan, J. N. (1964) 'The Achievement Motive and Economic Behaviour', *Economic Development and Cultural Change*, 12, 243—67.

Morris, R. T. and Fargher, K. (1974) 'Achievement Drive and Creativity as Correlates of Success in Small Business', *Australian Journal of Psychology*, 26(3), 217—22.

Mowday, R. T. (1979) 'Equity Theory, Predictions of Behavior in Organizations, in Steers, R. M. and Porter, L. W. (eds), *Motivation and Work Behavior*, McGraw-Hill, New York.

Murray, H. A. (1938) *Explorations in Personality*, Oxford University Press, New York.

Porter L. W. (1961) 'A Study of Perceived Need Satisfaction in Bottom and Middle Management Jobs', *Journal of Applied Psychology*, 45, 1–10.

Porter, L. W. (1962) 'Job Attitudes in Management: I Perceived Deficiences in Need Fulfillment as a Function of Job Level', *Journal of Applied Psychology*, 46, 375–84.

Purcer, L. W. (1963) 'Job Attitudes and Management: II Perceived Importance of Needs as a Function of Job Level', *Journal of Applied Psychology*, 47, 141–8.

Purcer Smith, G. (1967) 'The Motivation of Sales Executives in Two Major Companies', *British Journal of Marketing*, 1(4), 10–20.

Rosen, B. C. and D'Andrade, R. G. (1959) 'The Psychosocial Origins of Achievement Motivation', *Sociometry*, 22, 185–218.

Sinha, D. and Chaubney, N. P. (1972) 'Achievement Motive and Rural Economic Development', *International Journal of Psychology*, 7(4), 267–72.

Sorenson, T. C. (1973) 'Do Americans Like Their Jobs', *Parade*, 3 June 1973, 15–16.

Sorokin, P. A. (1942) *Man and Society in Calamity*, Dutton & Co., New York (quoted by Luthans, 1977, p. 316).

Steers, R. M. and Porter, L. W. (eds), (1979) *Motivation and Work Behavior*, McGraw-Hill, New York.

US Department of Health, Education and Welfare (1973) *Works in America*, Report of a Special Task Force to the Secretary of Health, Education and Welfare, prepared under the auspices of W. E. Upjohn Institute for Employment Research, Cambridge, Mass., MIT Press.

Vroom, V. H. (1964) *Work and Motivation*, Wiley, New York.

Wahba, M. A. and Bridwell, L. G. (1979) 'Maslow Reconsidered: A Review of Research on the Need Hierarchy Theory', in Steers, R. M. and Porter, L. W. (eds), *Motivation and Work Behavior*, McGraw-Hill, New York.

Wainer, H. A. and Rubin, I. M. (1969) 'Motivation of Research and Development Entrepreneurs', *Journal of Applied Psychology*, 53, 178–84.

Wall, T. D. (1973) 'Ego-defensiveness as a Determinant of Reported Differences in Sources of Job Satisfaction and Job Dissatisfaction', *Journal of Applied Psychology*, 58, 125–8.

Wall, T. D., Stephenson, G. M. and Skidmore, C. (1971) 'Ego Involvement and Hertzberg's Two-Factor Theory of Job Satisfaction: An Experimental Field Study', *British Journal of Social and Clinical Psychology*, 10(2), 123–31.

Weiner, B. (ed.) (1974) *Achievement Motivation and Attribution Theory*, General Learning Press, Morristown, N.J.

Winterbottom, M. R. (1958) 'The Relation of Need for Achievment to Learning Experiences in Independence and Mastery', in Atkinson, J. W. (ed.), *Motives in Fantasy, Action and Society*, Van Nostrand, Princeton, N.J.

4
Personality and Learning in Organizations

Introduction

What is the personality? In 1937 one well-known psychologist (Gordon Allport) found fifty definitions in the literature. Today there would be many more. Not all writers think highly of the term. Brown (1964) calls it 'rather a regretable word'. And Lazarus (1971) says:

> When the layman thinks about personality, he is likely to view it as the impression one makes on others; he is likely to be concerned with such things as having a 'good' or 'effective' personality . . . When the psychologist thinks about personality, however, he sees it as the study of the stable psychological structures and processes that organize human environment.

The view of personality held by the manager influences how he interacts with people. It is particularly important when he tries to influence their behaviour: that is, how he tries to get them to learn behaviours that he thinks are appropriate for the organization. We will review some of the best-known theories and ideas about personality and relate them to the manager's understanding of behaviour in organizations. There is no one best theory of personality. Each theory makes a contribution towards understanding people.

The humanistic view of personality

The most modern group of psychologists, and the one most often associated with the subject of organizational behaviour, is the humanistic school. It is often called the third force in psychology because of its late arrival to a field already dominated by Freud's psychoanalytic view and Skinner's stimulus—response view (both of which will also be discussed).

One of the most important points in the humanistic view of personality is that it holds up an ideal of what the personality can be and it suggests various ways of achieving that ideal. In a sense it inspires people to look to the fullest potential of the personality.

A second important point for the humanistic view is the belief that personality has an internal urge to grow and develop. This is a safe urge which can be followed. Lazarus (1971) calls this the 'force-for-growth' model of personality.

A third characteristic of humanistic psychology is that it has opened up personality, and how it works, to everyone. The person is seen operating in a social setting with a great amount of freedom. Everyone is encouraged to be psychologically aware and contribute to each other's psychological growth and development.

Hall and Lindzey (1978) summarize the humanistic school as being

> more hopeful and optimistic about humans. It believes that the person, any person, contains within him or herself the potentialities for healthy and creative growth. The failure to realize these potentialities is due to the constricting and distorting influences of parental training, education and other social pressures. These harmful effects can be overcome, however, if the individual is willing to accept the responsibility for his or her own life.

Maslow (1968, 1970, 1973), whose ideas were explained and criticized in Chapter 3, is often thought of as the father of humanistic psychology because he self-consciously wrote on the subject and worked to develop it as a school of thought. He saw the ideal personality in its fullest potential as the *self-actualizing* personality. This is the apex of his hierarchy of needs discussed in Chapter 3. He shifted the emphasis in psychology from building up the deficient personality to seeing the personality as having the power to be whole, healthy, and the organizing centre of the individual. He saw this as 'a new philosophy of life, a new conception of man'.

Rogers (1969; and Rogers and Skinner, 1956) probably has the most developed concept of personality among the humanistic psychologists. For him the personality is seen in a process of becoming; 'it is a direction, not a destination' (Rogers, 1967). He calls this direction 'living the good life', which means to gain a psychological freedom in order to select behaviours that are good for the total organism. He calls the ideal personality the *fully functioning person*.

Rogers has described the person who is in the process of becoming fully functioning under four headings. The *first* one is that it is a personality that is open to experience. This is a movement away from defensiveness and 'becoming more able to listen to himself, to experience what is going on within himself'. *Second*, the becoming person has an increasing tendency to live each moment fully. This focuses on discovering the structure of experience rather than always having each moment controlled from some past experience. *Third*, Rogers sees the personality in the process of becoming a fully functioning person as increasingly trusting his total self. This means that the individual not only listens to the mind but also feelings of fear and joy, as well as messages from the physical body. *Fourth*, this ideal person takes responsibility for his actions. The individual is his own sifter of evidence, and is more open to evidence from all sources: 'He is completely engaged in the process of being and becoming himself, and thus discovers that he is soundly and realistically social.'

One of the natural and healthy ways to become more fully functioning is to utilize the resources of other people. Professional help is also useful and legitimate. Rogers (1951) developed a concept of helping people called the *client-centred approach*. In this approach the client changes and develops himself. The role of the counsellor is to assist and further the development by interacting with the behaviours of the other person in an accepting, feeling manner.

Rogers's concept of how learning takes place is directly related to the personality of the individual. This approach is called *student-centred teaching* and can be summarised under four points (Rogers, 1951). The first is that 'we cannot teach another person directly; we can only facilitate his learning'. The responsibility to learn is up to the student. While this is probably what most of us think true, as teachers, parents or managers we inevitably take it upon ourselves to get the student to learn *in order to suit us.*

The second point is: 'A person learns significantly only those things which he perceives as being involved in the maintenance of, or enhancement of, the structure of self.' To put this another way, people only learn those behaviours which they see as in their self-interest. Sometimes this is expressed as the 'felt-need' theory: people only learn when they feel a need. Again, many readers will find some truth in this, but will also spend a lot of time and energy making the learner feel a need to learn. As parents we often do this by bribing the child to learn: 'You will get a new bicycle if you pass your exams.' The most significant learning in one's life must ultimately serve one's own self-interest.

Rogers's third point about student-centred learning is that significant learning is resisted. This is based on his theory that the personality protects itself. If the person sees that the learning is going to require a reorganization of self, he will not open up the boundaries of the personality to include new behaviours until he feels that it is safe to do so and that the new behaviours are in his self-interest. This is the root of Rogers's theory of personality and has direct relevance to learning. It is a concept that has been hotly disputed by those who feel that the personality does not know when it is safe.

His fourth point is concerned with the learning setting. Rogers says that the situation that most effectively promotes significant learning is one in which (a) threat to the self of the learner is reduced to a minimum, and (b) learning is facilitated.

Rogers's framework forms the basis of much modern organizational behaviour advice to managers. Consultants in the organization development (see Chapter 13) field, trainers, personnel specialists, counsellors and others in the helping professions often use his concepts. Those who advocate involving the workers in decisions, participation, autonomous work-groups, developing the potential of the work-force, will often be speaking from the Rogerian view

Argyris (1957, 1971) has developed a concept of personality and its tendency to mature. He feels that organizations retard or hinder the development of the personality. The characteristics of organizations which inhibit the personality from reaching *maturity* (his term for the idealised person) are: (a) task specialization, where each person does only a limited, short and completely manageable task; (b) chain of command, where a pattern of tasks is held together under the direction of a few people; (c) unity of direction, which means that each specialization is in a separate unit (for greater efficiency); and (d) span of control, which means that the size of the work-group is determined by the numbers *one* person can control.

Against these characteristics of an effective organization, Argyris (1971) lists the tendencies of a personality as it develops to maturity:

1. Tend to develop from a state of passivity as infants to a state of increasing activity as adults . . .
2. Tend to develop from a state of dependence upon others as infants to a state of relative independence as adults . . .
3. Tend to develop from being capable of behaviour only in a few ways as an infant to being capable of behaving in many different ways as an adult . . .
4. Tend to develop from having erratic, casual, shallow, quickly dropped interests as an infant to having deeper interests as an adult . . .
5. Tend to develop from having a short time perspective as an infant to a much longer time perspective as an adult . . .
6. Tend to develop from being in a subordinate position in the family and society as an infant to aspiring to occupy an equal and/or superordinate position relative to their peers . . .
7. Tend to develop from a lack of awareness of self as an infant to an awareness of and control over self as an adult.

Comparing the lists may lead to the conclusions that organizations have a negative impact on the personalities of their employees. Argyris proposes that the conflict between the needs of the personality and those of the organization results either in the member leaving the organization quickly, or the development of a restricted personality and becoming a long-serving, dependent, child-like employee.

Some think that Argyris's predictions can be seen in Britain. Mant (1979) says, 'At some point, Britain had become predominantly a culture of Dependence — a drawn-in, reflective unambitious place, revering the female gods of existence rather than the masculine gods of action.'

Fromm is a psychologist who also focuses on the organization as a source of deprivation to the personality developing to its fullest potential:

Fromm is utterly convinced of the validity of the following propositions: (1) humans have an essential, inborn nature, (2) society is created by humans in order to fulfil this essential nature, (3) no society that has yet been devised meets the basic needs of human existence, and (4) it is possible to create such a society (Hall and Lindzey, 1978).

Fromm spent most of his working life investigating the problems of freedom: *The Fear of Freedom* (1960), *The Sane Society* (1963) and *To Have or To Be?* (1979). His theme is that as man has gained more freedom through the ages he has felt more lonely. He is fearful of freedom and therefore he puts together societies and work organizations which are meant to reduce that feeling of alienation. In one of his latest books, Fromm (1979) describes the distinctive qualities of the individual which will enable him to have a liveable life. His suggestion is to centre one's life around *being* rather than having and using. Fromm is a provocative critic of the failure of organizations to meet the basic needs of human existence.

Lewin is known for his concept of the dynamic personality, based on his *field theory*. Field theory states that behaviour takes place in a field of forces. The personality itself is a field of forces operating in a wider field of forces, the *situation*. De Board (1979) says: 'Each individual exists in a psychological field of forces that, for him, determines and limits his behaviour.' This is an example of *gestalt* psychology, where the situation in which the behaviour takes place is seen as the most important influence on the personality. Therefore, Lewin represents the external forces acting on the personality for change. He says, 'in other words, to understand or to predict behaviour, the person and his environment have to be considered as one constellation of interdependent factors' (Lewin, 1952).

Lewin (1966) conducted experiments on how housewives could be influenced to buy inexpensive, but seldom used, cuts of meats (offal). He found that more people changed buying behaviours when presented with the idea along with discussion than with lecture. (See Chapter 13 for the implications of this for changing organizations.) The process at work in this change can be related to the personality and change. Similar to Rogers's concept of the boundaries of the personality opening up when not under threat, Lewin found that greater change occurs when a group is allowed to identify change based on felt needs. One group of housewives had a lecture on the value of offal and another group discussed the idea: 'A follow-up showed that only 3 per cent of the women who heard the lectures served one of the meats, whereas after group decision 32 per cent served one of them' (Lewin, 1966).

Two of Lewin's characteristics of personality help explain why behaviours change through group discussion and decision more easily than through lecture. One of these is Lewin's concept of *life space*. Hall and Lindzey (1978) say that this is '*a space* consisting of *a person* surrounded by a psychological *environment*'. Each person will want to maintain a balance between his behaviours and his environment. The discussion and group decision method of learning shares life spaces of the participants, and the sharing allows new forces to enter an individual's life space. In the lecture method each individual is psychologically alone, which makes it more difficult for new forces to enter because of the tendency to maintain the equilibrium between the person and the environment.

The second point Lewin makes about change is that before a personality will allow new forces in, the habits of the quasi-equilibrium must be broken. As the threat is lowered by sharing and being psychologically closer to each other, the old habits will not be defended and a decision to adopt new habits can be taken.

Lewin considered that the field of forces in the personality also had forces which produce new behaviours. These would be the characteristics of the individual which are driving him to be knowledgeable, adventuresome, and to have something to contribute. But this, if left unchecked, would be so un-stabilizing (constantly new behaviours) that social interaction with other people would be impaired. Therefore, the healthy personality also has restraining forces at work. These forces give the personality stability and a high degree of predict-ability and they enable us to know the habits of an individual which makes us feel comfortable with him. Too many restrain-ing forces 'make Jack a dull boy'. Both sets of forces are required to weld the personality into a set of social habits which are known well enough to make interaction with others possible but containing just enough new behaviours to make social interaction interesting and worth while.

Lewin's ideas about personality and learning new behaviours are significant because they emphasize the environment and the role of the group in decision-making. Lewin, often called the father of social psychology, is also discussed in Chapter 13.

The humanistic psychologists, mostly Americans, have had a major impact on current thinking about personality. They see the personality as more free to determine its own charac-teristics and more influenced by the social setting of the individual than either the psychoanalytical or behaviourist psychologists, who will be discussed next.

Freud

Sigmund Freud is one of the most important figures in psy-chology. He thought that problems of behaviour were due to conflicts between the mind and the instincts in man. He stated that 'individual psychology is concerned with the individual man and explores the paths by which he seeks to find satisfac-tion for his instinctual impulses' (Freud, 1959). He dared to make a science of analysing the unconscious roots of observable behaviour. His concepts of the personality are well known and probably form that concept of personality that is held by most lay people. He saw the personality as being composed of three parts. The *ego* contains men's urges. It drives one to develop the self and focus on the uniqueness of the individual. The *superego* is the collective ego of others in the society which the individual values, or is influenced by. This aspect of personality pushes the individual to listen to the expectations society makes of him. The superego could have a moderating effect on the work of the ego. The *id* is the animal urge and, in a sense, works between the other two aspects of the personality to activate them and encourage engagement with other people.

Freud places great importance on the concept of the personality developing through various stages. The difficulties of gaining satisfactions and making the various aspects of the personality come together in harmony often produce traumas. These traumas can be pushed to the back of the mind and forgotten. Freud sees these forgotten experiences as determining much of the current activity of the personality. For example, if a child has a traumatic experience, this may have a strong influence on adult behaviour. Most psychologists (whether they are Freudian or not) see four areas where such difficulties might arise: learning to feed, and the implications of that intimate relationship and the breaking away from it; learning toilet habits; handling early sex urges; and training for the socially accepted control of anger and aggression. This means that if a person has had an overly clean emphasis during 'potty' training, for example, he may be overly tidy and obsessive about detail as an adult.

Dickson, in his book *The Psychology of Military Incompetence* (1976), uses this Freudian model to examine the impact of the personality of its members upon the efficiency of an organization. Dickson contends that the regimentation and orderliness of military life are attractive to those who have been made insecure by harsh 'potty' training. The emphasis on masculinity and orderliness helps to combat these feelings of insecurity, and promotion is obtained by executing established rules and procedures with great efficiency. However, battle conditions require flexibility, and many military disast-

ers can be traced to an overemphasis on procedure and tradition. Dickson notes that many successful military leaders
had a poor 'middle career' involving many brushes with the
military 'establishment'.

The Freudian psychiatrist emphasizes going back in the
unconscious mind in order to share experiences with a sympa-
thetic, qualified scientist who can interpret the symbolic
messages in the free associations (saying what comes to mind)
and dreams which are discussed during analysis.

Freud's work lies in the tradition of high 'scientism' which
held sway at the beginning of this century. He saw the personality in terms of activities of the mind which can be neatly
divided and named. A qualified outside scientist is required
in order to assist in the change or cure of illness of the mind.
This is done by analysis where the patient is passive, relaxed
and entreated to a trusting attitude to the doctor. Fromm
(1973) says the psychoanalyst 'offered a substitute for religion,
politics, and philosophy. Freud had allegedly discovered all
the secrets of life: the unconscious, the Oedipus complex, the
repetition of childhood experience; and once one understood
these concepts, nothing remained mysterious or doubtful.'

If a manager holds a Freudian view of the personality, what
influence does it have on his view of organizational behaviour?
The Freudian view of the personality may lead the manager
to underestimate the significance of personality and make it
a forbidden aspect of individuals. Four ideas about personality
from Freud may contribute to this: personality is about the
mind; personality is about instincts; current behaviour is
controlled by past events; and only doctors have the skill for
the treatment of personality.

When the personality is seen as something concerned with
the mind, it sounds like an invisible control centre of the
person. Brain-washing, mind-bending and other frightening
images are often associated with professionals working in
psychology. There is often a sense of risk about the mind
being healthy, not going crazy. The mind is the most private
part of a person and, to the Freudian, managers do not have a
brief to invade it.

If the personality is thought to be the focus of the conflict
between animal and human instincts, a tense aura surrounds

the subject. Animal-like urges may be less than desirable. They must be kept under control. People might be triggered into acting out these base instincts. The manager using a Freudian view of personality will see behaviour determined by the past. Members of the organization could think that there is nothing one can do about their own or any one else's behaviour. It is fixed back in childhood and one now has to live with it. The organization has no role to play in the development of the personality. Many of the feelings of hopelessness in an organization may result from this view: 'He's an awkward bugger', 'What can one do?', 'He's just that way, isn't he?'

Freud might be seen as the conceptualizer who brought the study of behaviour into scientific respectability. His ideas are still the everyday view of personality. He saw the energy of the personality being largely used to reduce tensions and had great confidence in the biological aspects of personality. Contrasting the humanistic psychologists and psychoanalytical views shows some of the roots of our current notions about personality (see Table 4.1).

Learning and the behaviourists

The way that a person learns new behaviour is of prime importance to any organization, and consequently learning has attracted considerable attention from psychologists. The behaviourists have much to teach the manager about how the person learns new behaviour.

Among the earliest to work in the field of conditioning of behaviour were Pavlov (1927) and Thorndike (1932). Pavlov is credited with developing classical conditioning, a passive learner with the stimuli for learning controlled by the experimenter. He discovered that a dog could be 'taught' to salivate at the ringing of a bell. He did this by ringing a bell followed by presenting food. After a few trials the ringing of the bell caused salivation without food: a conditioned reflex. Thorndike developed these ideas further. Most of his work was with animals, and he emphasized that reward and punishment are important in learning — 'the law of effect'. He also suggested

Table 4.1 *Summary of phrases which characterize psychoanalytic and humanistic schools of thought about personality*

Psychoanalytic	Humanistic
Focus on the unconscious control of behaviour	Focus on the conscious, the blind-spots, known to others, unknown to self
Behaviour is to be understood	Behaviour is to be incorporated, experienced, developed
Focus on mental life, mind, illnesses, thoughts, dreams	Focus on feelings, behaviours, interactions of total persons
Analysis is an esoteric experience	Therapy is more like a religious group, a gathering, a fellowship of seekers, warm, supportive
Analyst interprets	Helper reflects, observes, shares, tries to pull together
Analyst distant and scientific	Helper reacts, authentic responses, feedback
Go back to the roots of the problem (instincts/early traumas)	Present manifestations of behaviour
Analytical	Facilitative
Emphasis on analyst and qualifications	Emphasis on client, relationship and experience to discover
Scientific, rational, objective	Heuristic, holistic, involved, dynamic
Fragile holding together of personality which is dangerous under the surface	Robust personality, tough at rejecting unwanted interference, wants to grow and self-actualize under the surface
Reduce tensions	Release forces for growth

that learning was the result of trial and error. During this early period learning was essentially defined as linking a stimulus to an involuntary motor response. A positive reward given when this link is made is a reinforcement, and a reinforcement will tend to ensure that the link will be made again in a similar situation.

B. F. Skinner (1953, 1973), who may be the single most important psychologist living today, also belonged to the stimulus—response $(S-R)$ school of thought and developed the concept of *operant conditioning*, where the animal in the experiment (usually a rat) operates a lever which reinforces the behaviour with a reward. This 'Skinner box' has been the subject of continuing debate. For research purposes the experiment is ideal because the entire environment can be controlled. Skinner investigated how behaviour is learned, how long it will survive when not reinforced, and how it can be changed. The debate is over the application of the findings to everyday life.

The basic tenet of his thinking is that behaviour can best be understood by looking at one's history of reinforcements. It also emphasizes the importance of external stimuli from the environment. Some might say that the application of this approach to modern organizations makes a factory into an enormous Skinner box, with people pushing levers to get rewards. According to such a view, managers can change the reward system and therefore get different behaviour from the workers.

Control is a central theme for Skinner. He emphasizes external control of an individual's behaviour. It is the stimuli from the environment that are crucial. He says about control: 'The fundamental mistake made by all those who choose weak methods of control is to assume that the balance of control is left to the individual, when in fact it is left to other conditions' (Skinner, 1973). Speaking more directly about behaviour modification, he says: 'There are many varieties of "behaviour modification" and many different formulations, but they all agree on the essential point: behaviour can be changed by changing the conditions of which it is a function' (Skinner, 1973).

There is always the danger of making Skinner look like a simplistic manipulator. The student may broaden that view by reading *Waldon Two* (Skinner, 1948) and *Beyond Freedom and Dignity* (Skinner, 1973). A number of behavioural scientists working with organizations have taken his work seriously. Nord (1969) has discussed the application of operant conditioning to management. He refers to reward systems and management activities such as social approval as examples of Skinner's theories being applied. Skinner (1973) himself refers to pay as reinforcement: 'a person is paid when he behaves in a given way so that he will continue to behave in that way'. Luthans and Kreitner (1975) develop the idea of organizational behaviour modification. They discuss reinforcement schedules and the training of various levels of management to conduct them. The famous application of their work at the Emery Freight Company appears to have improved productivity greatly. Their work at Emery can be summarized in five steps:

1. Identify key performance and behaviours.
2. Measure these for operational significance.
3. Analyse how they can be changed.
4. Intervene with feedback of results of the employees' behaviours.
5. Evaluate them and show the findings, as well as continue reinforcement as required.

In contrasting the $S-R$ school of thought and the humanistic school (force for growth), it can be seen that the humanistic school emphasizes intrinsic rewards (Hertzberg, 1968) for controlling behaviour. Such writers are interested in the internal forces in personality on learning (felt needs, forces for growth, motivation, response to threat, and the assumption that individuals can be self-controlled). These interests result in emphasizing the role of the individual, the autonomy of the worker, increased personal responsibility, self-control, and tend to decrease the traditional role of the manager.

The $S-R$ advocates, on the other hand, emphasize external stimuli, whether operant or not (controlling the environment, extrinsic rewards, trial and error, reinforcement of desired behaviour and the assumption that individuals need to be controlled by the environment). They emphasize the role of manager, manipulating the environment, pay, advancement and other rewards for adapting individual behaviour to the environment.

An issue related to external stimuli is that of obedience. The words of Bendix (1963) might sound a little old fashioned today: 'Wherever enterprises are set up, a few command and many obey.' Yet Milgram (1973, 1974) has conducted extensive experiments in which ordinary people are willing to give 'learners' an electric shock when instructed to do so by an authority figure, such as a university experimenter. He conducted his experiments at Yale University. Advertisements asked for volunteers to participate in a study of memory and learning. Volunteers worked in pairs and one was designated as a 'teacher' and the other a 'learner'. The learner is actually an actor who is strapped into a chair while the teacher watches. The teacher is seated at a panel of thirty switches with labels ranging from 15 volts (or 'slight shock') to 450 volts ('danger — severe shock'). The experimenter tells the teacher to administer the learning test. When the learner gives an incorrect answer, the teacher is to give an electric shock:

> We have now seen several hundred participants in the obedience experiment, and we have witnessed a level of obedience to orders that is disturbing. With numbing regularity good people were seen to knuckle under to the demands of authority and perform actions that we call callous and severe. Men who are in everyday life responsible and decent were seduced by the trappings of authority. (Milgram, 1974)

In spite of the learner's screams and pleas to stop the experiment, ordinary people from all walks of life continued to administer shocks when told to do so by the authority present. Milgram's experiment indicates that people will go to extreme lengths in order to follow orders.

Epilogue

As an epilogue to this chapter on personality, we include our own version of personality development and its relation to learning to function in an organization. The person comes into the world with only inherited limitations and potentials of personality, as well as the basic needs for food, shelter, clothing and security. All other social behaviours are learned. There is a force for growth in the individual and continuous stimuli from the environment to control that growth.

The earliest learning comes with the first relationships,

usually with the mother and father. These relationships have the most important, but not deterministic, impact on the personality.

The second influence on behaviour is the 'primary group'. These include the people in the family, the neighbourhood and the first school: 'Primary groups are primary in the sense that they give the individual his earliest and completest experience of social unity' (Cooley, 1964). Our perception of self and our view of expected behaviour in groups begin with this experience. In this sense all other groups are 'secondary groups'.

The early learnings of the individual are very important, as Freud and others have said. One might think of the rest of life as being a learning experience to update and decide continually how much of these early experiences to keep and how much to discard. If one makes no effort to be aware and understand oneself, one is more likely to have the significant-other and primary-group experience continue to be the basis of one's self and other perceptions throughout life.

Organizations will tend to enrol people who seem to fit the organizations' needs. They do this partly by selecting whom they think is the right person. After the initial selection there is an on-going effort to inculcate the person with the values, attitudes and expectations of the organization. This process is termed *socialization:* 'Socialization refers to the learning by which the individual is prepared to participate in interpersonal relations by incorporating societal sentiments, knowledge, beliefs, and standards into his personality' (Lasswell, Burma and Aronson, 1965).

The personality is constantly pulled in two directions: response to the forces for growth from inside the person which push for autonomy, idiosyncratic behaviour; and external, tension-reducing, conditioning stimuli which are constantly trying to socialize the person into a compatible, functional, reliable, social partner.

References for Chapter 4

Allport, G. W. (1937) *Personality: a Psychological Interpretation*, Holt, New York.

Argyris, C. (1957) *Personality and Organization*, Harper & Row, New York.

Argyris, C. (1971) 'The Impact of the Formal Organization upon the Individual', in Pugh, D. S. (ed.), *Organizational Theory*, Penguin, Harmondsworth, England.

Bendix, R. (1963) *Work and Authority*, Harper & Row, New York.

Brown, J. A. C. (1964) *Freud and the Post Freudians*, Penguin, Harmondsworth, England.

Cooley, C. H. (1964) 'Primary Groups', in Caser, L. A. and Rosenberg, B. (eds), *Sociological Theory: a Book of Readings*, 2nd edn, Macmillan, New York.

De Board, R. (1978) *The Psychoanalysis of Organizations*, Tavistock, London.

Dickson, N. S. (1976) *The Psychology of Military Incompetence*, Cape, London.

Freud, S. (1959) *Group Psychology and the Analysis of the Ego*, translated and edited by J. Strachey, Norton, New York.

Fromm, E. (1960) *The Fear of Freedom*, Routledge & Kegan Paul, London.

Fromm, E. (1963) *The Sane Society*, Routledge & Kegan Paul, London.

Fromm, E. (1973) *The Crisis of Psychoanalysis: Essays on Freud, Marx and Social Psychology*, Penguin, Harmondsworth, England.

Fromm, E. (1979) *To Have or To Be?*, Sphere, London.

Hall, C. S. and Lindzey, G. (1978) *Theories of Personality*, 3rd edn, Wiley, New York.

Hertzberg, F. (1968) *Work and the Nature of Man*, Staples Press, London.

Lasswell, T. E., Burma, J. H. and Aronson, S. H. (1965) *Life in Society*, Scott, Foresman & Co., Glenview, Ill.

Lazarus, R. S. (1971) *Personality*, 2nd edn, Prentice-Hall, Englewood Cliffs, N.J.

Lewin, K. (1952) *Field Theory in Social Sciences*, ed. D. Cartwright, Tavistock, London.

Lewin, K. (1966) 'Group Decisions and Social Change', in Maccoby, E. E., Newcomb, T. M. and Hartley, E. L. (eds), *Readings in Social Psychology*, 3rd edn, Methuen, London.

Luthans, F. and Kreitner, R. (1975) *Organizational Behavior Modification*, Scott, Foresman & Co., Glenview, Ill.

Mant, A. (1979) *The Rise and Fall of the British Manager*, Pan Books, London.

Maslow, A. H. (1968) *Toward a Psychology of Being*, Van Nostrand, New York.

Maslow, A. H. (1970) *Motivation and Personality*, 2nd edn, Harper & Row, New York.

Maslow, A. H. (1973) *The Farther Reaches of Human Nature*, Penguin, Harmondsworth, England.

Milgram, S. (1973) 'Some Conditions of Obedience and Disobedience to Authority', in Leavitt, H. J. and Pondy, L. R. (eds), *Readings in Managerial Psychology*, 2nd edn, University of Chicago Press, Chicago.

Milgram, S. (1974) *Obedience to Authority*, Tavistock, London.

Nord, W. R. (1969) 'Beyond the Teaching Machines: The Neglected Areas of Operant Conditioning in the Theory and Practice of Management', *Organizational Behaviour and Human Performance*, 4(4).

Pavlov, I. P. (1927) *Conditioned Reflexes*, transl G. V. Anrep, Oxford University Press, London.

Rogers, C. R. (1951) *Client-Centred Therapy*, Constable, London.

Rogers, C. R. (1967) *On Becoming a Person*, Constable, London.

Rogers, C. R. (1969) *Freedom to Learn*, Charles E. Merrill, Columbus, Ohio.

Rogers, C. R. and Skinner, B. F. (1956) 'Some Issues Concerning the Control of Human Behavior: A Symposium', in Evans, R. I. (ed.), *Carl Rogers: The Man and His Ideas*, E. P. Dutton & Co., New York.

Skinner, B. F. (1948) *Walden Two*, Macmillan, New York.

Skinner, B. F. (1953) *Science and Human Behavior*, Macmillan, New York.

Skinner, B. F. (1973) *Beyond Freedom and Dignity*, Penguin, Harmondsworth, England.

Thorndike, E. L. (1932) *The Fundamentals of Learning* (reprinted 1971), AMS Press Inc., New York.

5
Stress at Work: The Manager

The complexity of industrial organizational life is a source of stress for managers. Brummett, Pyle and Framholtz (1968) suggest that managers are suffering extreme physiological symptoms from stress at work, such as disabling ulcers or coronary heart disease (CHD), which force them to retire prematurely from active work before they have had an opportunity to complete their potential organizational life. These and other stress-related effects (e.g. tension, poor adjustment, etc.) also affect the family, becoming potential sources of disturbance. Thus stress pervades the whole quality of managerial life. The mental and physical health effects of job stress are not only disruptive influences on the individual managers, but are also a 'real' cost to the organization, on whom many individuals depend: a cost which is rarely, if ever, seriously considered either in human or financial terms by organizations, but one which they incur in their day-to-day operations. In order to do something positive about sources of stress on managers at work, it is important to be able to identify them. The success of any effort to minimize stress and maximize job satisfaction will depend on accurate diagnosis, for different stresses will require different action. Any approach in the management of stress in an organization which relied on one particular technique (e.g. organization development, job enrichment, transcendental meditation) without taking into account the differences within workgroups or divisions would be doomed to failure. A recognition of the possible sources of management stress, therefore, may help us to arrive at suggestions of ways of minimizing its negative consequences. It was with this in mind that the research literature in the field of management and organizational stress is brought together in a framework that helps us identify more clearly the sources of managerial satisfaction and stress.

A survey of the management literature reveals a formidable list of over forty interacting factors which might be sources of managerial stress and satisfaction — those to be dealt with here are drawn mainly from a wider body of theory and research in a variety of fields such as medicine, psychology and management sciences. Additional material has been drawn from exploratory studies carried out by Cooper and Marshall (1978, 1979). Seven major categories of stress can be identified. Figure 5.1 is an attempt to represent these diagrammatically; in the text they will be dealt with in a natural progression from those related to the job, to the organization, and to the individual.

The job of management

Factors intrinsic to the 'job of management' were a first and vital focus of study for early researchers in the field (Stewart, 1976), and in 'shop-floor' (as opposed to management) studies they are still the main preoccupation. Stress can be caused by too much or too little work, time pressures and deadlines, having too many decisions to make (Sofer, 1970), working conditions, excessive travel, long hours, having to cope with changes at work and the expenses (monetary and career) of making mistakes (Kearns, 1973). It can be seen that every job description includes factors which for some individuals at some point in time will be a source of pressure. As Chapter 2 has shown, many of these factors are inevitable parts of the job of management.

One of the most important sources of stress on managers is their tendency to work long hours and to take on too much work. Research into work overload has been given substantial empirical attention. French and Caplan (1973) have differentiated overload in terms of *quantitative* and *qualitative* overload. Quantitative refers to having 'too much to do', while qualitative means work that is 'too difficult'. Miller (1960) has theorized that 'overload' in most systems leads to break-

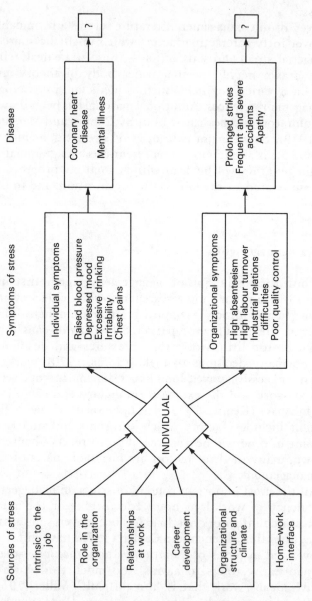

Figure 5.1 *Categories of stress*

down, whether we are dealing with single biological cells or managers in organizations. The concept of overload and the response to overload are discussed in greater detail in Chapter 7. In an early study, French and Caplan (1970) found that objective quantitative overload was strongly linked to cigarette smoking (an important risk factor or symptom of CHD). Persons with more phone calls, office visits and meetings per given unit of work time were found to smoke significantly more cigarettes than persons with fewer such engagements. In a study of 100 young coronary patients, Russek and Zohman (1969) found that 25 per cent had been working at two jobs and an additional 45 per cent had worked at jobs which required (due to work overload) sixty or more hours' work per week. They add that although prolonged emotional strain preceded the attack in 91 per cent of the cases, similar stress was only observed in 20 per cent of the controls. Breslow and Buell (1960) have also reported findings which support a relationship between hours of work and death from coronary disease. In an investigation of mortality rates of men in California, they observed that workers in light industry under the age of 45 who are on the job more than forty-eight hours a week have twice the risk of death from CHD compared with similar workers working forty or less hours a week. Another substantial investigation on quantitative work load was carried out by Margolis *et al.* (1974) on a representative national US sample of 1,496 employed persons, of 16 years of age or older. They found that overload was significantly related to a number of symptoms or indicators of stress: escapist drinking, absenteeism from work, low motivation to work, lowered self-esteem, and an absence of suggestions to employers. The results from these and other studies (Cooper and Marshall, 1978) are relatively consistent and indicate that quantitative overload is indeed a potential source of managerial stress that adversely affects both health and job satisfaction.

There is also some evidence that 'qualitative' overload is a source of stress for managers. French *et al.* (1965) looked at qualitative work overload in a large university. They used questionnaires, interviews and medical examinations to obtain data on risk factors associated with CHD for 122 university administrators and professors. They found that one symptom of stress, low self-esteem, was related to work overload, but that this was different for the two occupational groupings. Qualitative overload was not significantly linked to low self-esteem among the administrators but was significantly correlated for the professors. The greater the 'quality' of work expected of the professor, the lower the self-esteem. Several other studies have reported an association of qualitative work overload with cholesterol level: a tax deadline for accountants (Friedman *et al.*, 1958), and medical students performing a medical examination under observation. French and Caplan (1973) summarize this research by suggesting that both qualitative and quantitative overload produce at least nine different symptoms of psychological and physical strain: job dissatisfaction, job tension, lower self-esteem, threat, embarrassment, high cholesterol levels, increased heart rate, skin resistance, and more smoking. In analysing these data, however, one cannot ignore the vital interactive relationship of the job and manager which was outlined in Chapter 2, where the work of Rosemary Stewart and Henry Mintzberg were discussed; objective work overload, for example, should not be viewed in isolation but relative to the manager's capacities and personality.

Such caution is sanctioned by much of the American and some UK literature which shows that overload is not always externally imposed. Many managers (perhaps certain personality types, such as those with high achievement motivation, more than others) react to overload by working longer hours. For example, in reports on an American study (Uris, 1972) it was found that 45 per cent of the executives investigated worked all day, in the evenings and at weekends, and that a further 37 per cent kept weekends free but worked extra hours in the evenings. In many companies this type of behaviour has become a norm to which everyone feels they must adhere.

The manager's role in the organization

Another major source of managerial stress is associated with a person's role at work. A great deal of research in this area has concentrated on role ambiguity and role conflict, since the seminal investigations of the Survey Research Center of the University of Michigan (Kahn *et al.*, 1964).

Role ambiguity exists when a manager has inadequate information about his work role, that is, where there is *lack of clarity* about his work objectives associated with his role, about work colleagues' expectation of his work role and about the scope and responsibility of his job. Kahn *et al.* (1964) found that men who suffered from role ambiguity experienced lower job satisfaction, high job-related tension, greater futility, and lower self-confidence. French and Caplan (1970) found, at one of NASA's bases in a sample of 205 volunteer engineers, scientists and administrators, that role ambiguity was significantly related to low job satisfaction and to feelings of job-related threat to one's mental and physical well-being. This also related to indicators of physiological strain such as increased blood pressure and pulse rate. Margolis *et al.* (1974) also found a number of significant relationships between symptoms or indicators of physical and mental ill health with role ambiguity in their representative national sample ($n = 1,496$). The stress indicators related to role ambiguity were depressed mood, lowered self-esteem, life dissatisfaction, job dissatisfaction, low motivation to work, and intention to leave job.

Role conflict exists when an individual in a particular work role is torn by conflicting job demands or doing things he really does not want to do or does not think are part of the job specification. The most frequent manifestation of this is when a manager is caught between two groups of people who demand different kinds of behaviour or expect that the job should entail different functions. Kahn *et al.* (1964) found that men who suffered more role conflict had lower job satisfaction and higher job-related tension. It is interesting to note that they also found that the greater the power or authority of the people 'sending' the conflicting role messages, the more role conflict produced job dissatisfaction. This was related to physiological strain as well, as the NASA study (French and Caplan, 1970) illustrates. They recorded the heart rate of twenty-two men for a two-hour period while they were at work in their offices. They found that the mean heart rate for an individual was strongly related to his report of role conflict. A larger and medically more sophisticated study by Shirom *et al.* (1973) found similar results. Their research is of particular interest as it tries to look simultaneously at a wide variety of potential work stresses. They collected data on 762 male kibbutz members aged 30 and above, drawn from thirteen kibbutzim throughout Israel. They examined the relationships between CHD, abnormal electrocardiographic readings, CHD risk factors (systolic blood pressure, pulse rate, serum cholesterol levels, etc.), and potential sources of job stress (work overload, role ambiguity, role conflict, lack of physical activity). Their data were broken down into occupational groups: agricultural workers, factory groups, craftsmen and managers. It was found that there was a significant relationship between role conflict and CHD (specifically, abnormal electrocardiographic readings), but only for the managers. In fact, as we moved from occupations requiring great physical exertions (e.g. agriculture) to those requiring least (e.g. managerial), the greater was the relationship between role ambiguity and conflict and abnormal electrocardiographic findings. It was also found that as we go from occupations involving excessive physical activities to those with less such activity, CHD increased significantly. Drawing together these data, it might be suggested that managerial and professional occupations are more likely to suffer occupational stress from role-related stress and other interpersonal dynamics and less from the physical conditions of work.

Another aspect of role conflict was examined by Mettlin and Woelfel (1974). They measured three aspects of interpersonal influence – discrepancy between influences, level of influence, and number of influences – in a study of the educational and occupational aspirations of high-school students. Using the Langner Stress Symptom questionnaire as their index of stress, they found that the more extensive and diverse an individual's interpersonal communications network, the more stress symptoms he showed. A manager's role which is at a boundary – i.e. between departments or between the company and the outside world – is, by definition, one of extensive communication nets and of high role conflict. Kahn *et al.* (1964) suggest that such a position is potentially highly stressful. Margolis and Kroes (1974) found, for instance, that foremen (high role-conflict-prone job) are seven times as likely to develop ulcers as shop-floor workers.

Another important potential source of stress associated with a manager's role is 'responsibility for people'. One can differentiate here between 'responsibility for people' and 'responsibility for things' (equipment, budgets, etc.). Wardwell *et al.* (1964) found that responsibility for people was significantly more likely to lead to CHD than responsibility for things. Increased responsibility for people frequently means that one has to spend more time interacting with others, attending meetings, working alone and, in consequence, as in the NASA study (French and Caplan, 1970), more time in trying to meet deadline pressures and schedules. Pincherie (1972) also found this in their UK study of 2,000 executives attending a medical centre for a medical check-up. Of the 1,200 managers sent by their companies for their annual examination, there was evidence of physical stress being linked to age and level of responsibility; the older and more responsible the executive, the greater the probability of the presence of CHD risk factors or symptoms. French and Caplan support this in their NASA study of managerial and professional workers; they found that responsibility for people was significantly related to heavy smoking, raised diastolic blood pressure, and increased serum cholesterol levels – the more the individual had responsibility for 'things' as opposed to 'people', the lower were each of these CHD risk factors.

Having too little responsibility (Brook, 1973), lack of participation in decision-making, lack of managerial support, having to keep up with increasing standards of performance and coping with rapid technological change are other potential role stressors mentioned repeatedly in the literature but with little supportive research evidence. Variations between organizational structures will determine the differential distribution of these factors across differing occupational groups. Kay (1974) does suggest, however, that (independent of employing organizations) some pressures are to be found more at middle than at other management levels. He depicts today's middle manager as being particularly hard pressed:

1. by pay compression, as the salaries of new recruits increase;
2. by job insecurity – they are particularly vulnerable to redundancy or involuntary early retirement;
3. by having little real authority at their high levels of responsibility; and
4. by feeling 'boxed' in.

Interpersonal relations at work

A third major potential source of managerial stress has to do with the nature of relationships with one's boss, subordinates and colleagues. Behavioural scientists have long suggested that good relationships between members of a work group are a central factor in individual and organizational health (Cooper, 1976). Nevertheless, very little research work has been done in this area to either support or disprove the hypothesis. French and Caplan (1973) define poor relations as 'those which include low trust, low supportiveness, and low interest in listening to and trying to deal with problems that confront the organizational member'. The most notable studies in this area are by Kahn *et al.* (1964), French and Caplan (1970) and Buck (1972). Both the Kahn *et al.* and French and Caplan studies came to roughly the same conclusions, that mistrust of persons one worked with was positively related to high role ambiguity, which led to inadequate communications between people and to psychological strain in the form of low job satisfaction and to feelings of job-related threat to one's well being.

Relationships with the boss

Buck (1972) focused on the attitude and relationship of workers and managers to their immediate boss using Fleishman's leadership questionnaire on consideration and initiating structure. The consideration factor was associated with behaviour indicative of friendship, mutual trust, respect and a certain warmth between boss and subordinate. He found that those managers who felt that their boss was low on 'consideration' reported feeling more job pressure. Managers who were under pressure reported that their boss did not give them criticism in a helpful way, played favourites with subordinates, 'pulled rank' and took advantage of them whenever they got a chance. Buck concludes that the 'considerate behaviour of superiors appears to have contributed significantly inversely to feelings of job pressure'.

Relationships with subordinates

Officially one of the most critical functions of a manager is his supervision of other people's work. It has long been accepted that an 'inability to delegate' might be a problem, but now a new potential source of stress is being introduced in the manager's interpersonal skills — he must learn to 'manage by participation'. Donaldson and Gowler (1975) point to the factors which may make today's zealous emphasis on participation a cause of resentment, anxiety and stress for the manager concerned. It may produce the following stressors:

1. a mismatch of formal and actual power;
2. the manager may well resent the erosion of his formal role and authority (and the loss of status and rewards).
3. he may be subject to irreconcilable pressures — e.g. to be both participative and to achieve high production; and
4. his subordinates may refuse to participate.

However, for those managers with technological and scientific backgrounds (a 'things orientation'), relationships with subordinates can be a low priority (seen as 'trivial', 'petty', time-consuming and an impediment to doing the job well) and one would expect their interactions to be more a source of stress than those of 'people-orientated' managers.

Relationships with colleagues

Besides the obvious factors of office politics and colleagues' rivalry, we find another element here: stress can be caused not only by the pressure of poor relationships but also by its opposite — a lack of adequate social support in difficult situations (Lazarus, 1966). At highly competitive managerial levels it is likely that problem-sharing will be inhibited for fear of appearing weak; and much of the (American) literature particularly mentions the isolated life of the top executive as an added source of strain (see Cooper and Marshall, 1978).

Morris (1975) encompasses this whole area of relationships in one model — what he calls the 'cross of relationships'. While he acknowledges the differences between relationships on two continua — one axis extends from colleagues to users and the other intersecting axis from senior to junior managers — he feels that the focal manager must bring all four into 'dynamic balance' in order to be able to deal with the stress of his position. Morris's suggestion seems 'only sensible' when we see how much of his work time the manager spends with other people. In a research programme to find out exactly what managers do, Mintzberg (1973) showed just how much of their time is spent in interaction. In an intensive study of a small sample of chief executives he found that in a large organization a mere 22 per cent of a manager's time was spent in desk-work sessions, the rest being taken up by telephone calls (6 per cent), scheduled meetings (59 per cent), unscheduled meetings (10 per cent) and other activities (3 per cent). In small organizations basic desk-work played a larger part (52 per cent), but nearly 40 per cent was still devoted to face-to-face contacts of one kind or another (see Chapter 2).

Career prospects

Two major clusters of potential managerial stressors can be identified in this area:

1. Lack of job security; fear of redundancy, obsolescence or early retirement, etc.
2. Status incongruity; under- or over-promotion, frustration at having reached one's career ceiling, etc.

For many managers their career progression is of overriding importance — by promotion they earn not only money but also status and the new job challenges for which they strive.

In the early years at work, this striving and the aptitude to come to terms quickly with a rapidly changing environment is fostered and suitably rewarded by the company. Career progression is, perhaps, a problem by its very nature. For example, Sofer (1970) found that many of his sample believed that 'luck' and 'being in the right place at the right time' play a major role.

At middle age, and usually middle-management levels, career becomes more problematic and most executives find their progress slowed, if not actually stopped. Job opportunities become fewer, those jobs that are available take longer to master, past (mistaken?) decisions cannot be revoked, old knowledge and methods become obsolete, energies may be flagging or demanded by the family, and there is the 'press' of fresh young recruits to face in competition. Both Levinson (1973) and Constandse (1972) — the latter refers to this phase as 'the male menopause' — depict the manager as suffering these fears and disappointments in 'silent isolation' from his family and work colleagues.

The fear of demotion or obsolescence can be strong for those who know they have reached their 'career ceiling' — and most will inevitably suffer some erosion of status before they finally retire. Goffman (1952), extrapolating from a technique employed in the con-game 'cooling the mark out', suggests that the company should bear some of the responsibility for taking the sting out of this (felt) failure experience.

From the company perspective, on the other hand, McMurray (1973) puts the case for not promoting a manager to a higher position if there is doubt that he can fill it. In a syndrome he labels 'the executive neurosis' he describes the over-promoted manager as grossly overworking to keep down a top job and at the same time hiding his insecurity — he points to the consequences of this for his work performance and for the company.

Age is no longer revered as it was — it is becoming a 'young man's world'. The rapidity with which society is developing (technologically, economically, socially) is likely to mean that individuals will now need to change career during their working life. Such trends breed uncertainty, and research suggests that older workers look for stability (Sleeper, 1975).

Unless managers adapt their expectations to suit new circumstances, 'career development' stress, especially in later life, is likely to become an increasingly common experience.

Organizational climate

A fifth potential source of managerial stress is simply 'being in the organization' and the threat to an individual's freedom, autonomy and identity this poses. Problem areas such as little or no participation in the decision-making process, no sense of belonging, lack of effective consultation, poor communications, restrictions on behaviour and office politics are some of those with the most impact here. An increasing number of research investigations are being conducted in this area, particularly into the effect of employee participation in the work-place. Much of the research on participation is outlined in Chapter 12.

The research more relevant to this chapter, however, is the recent work on lack of participation and stress-related disease. In the NASA study (French and Caplan, 1970), for example, the authors found that managers and other professional workers who reported greater opportunities for participation in decision-making also reported significantly greater job satisfaction, low job-related feelings of threat, and higher feelings of self-esteem. Buck (1972) found that both managers and workers who felt 'under pressure' most reported that their bosses 'always ruled with an iron hand and rarely tried out new ideas or allowed participation in decision-making'. Managers who were under stress also reported that their bosses never let their subordinates do their work in the way they thought best. Margolis *et al.* (1974) found that non-participation at work, among a national representative sample of over 1,400 workers, was the most consistent and significant predictor or indicator of strain and job-related stress. They found that non-participation was significantly related to the following health risk factors: over-all poor physical health, escapist drinking, depressed mood, low self-esteem, low life satisfaction, low job satisfaction, low motivation to work, intention to leave job, and absenteeism from work. Kasl (1973) also found that low job satisfaction was related to non-participation in decision-making, inability to provide feedback to supervisors, and lack of recognition for good performance; and that poor mental health was linked to close supervision and no autonomy at work (Quinn *et al.*, 1971). Neff (1968) has highlighted the importance of lack of participation and involvement by suggesting that 'mental health at work is to a large extent a function of the degree to which output is under the control of the individual worker'.

To summarize, the research outlined above seems to indicate that greater participation leads to lower staff turnover, high productivity, and that when participation is absent lower job satisfaction and higher levels of physical and mental health risk may result.

Home—work interface stresses

The sixth 'source' of managerial stress is more of a 'catch-all' category for all those interfaces between life outside and life inside the organization that might put pressure on the manager: family problems (Pahl and Pahl, 1971), life crises (Dohrenwend and Dohrenwend, 1974), financial difficulties, conflict of personal beliefs with those of the company, and the conflict of company with family demands (Cooper, 1981b).

The area which has received most research interest is that of the manager's relationship with his wife and family. (It is widely agreed that managers have little time for 'outside activities' apart from their families. Writers who have examined their effects on the local community (Packard, 1975) have pointed to the disruptive effects of the executive's lack of involvement.) The manager has two main problems *vis-à-vis* his family:

1. That of 'time management' and 'commitment management'. Not only does his busy life leave him few resources with which to cope with other people's needs, but in order to do his job well the manager usually also needs support from others to cope with the 'background' details of house management, etc., to relieve stress when possible, and to maintain contact with the outside world.

2. The second, often a result of the first, is the spillover of crises or stresses in one system which affect the other.

As these two are almost inseparable we discuss them together.

Marriage patterns

The 'arrangement' the manager comes to with his wife will be of vital importance. Pahl and Pahl (1971) found that the majority of wives in their middle-class sample saw their role in relation to their husband's job as a supportive, domestic one; all said that they derived their sense of security from their husbands. Barber (1976), interviewing five directors' wives, finds similar attitudes. Gowler and Legge (1975) have dubbed this bond 'the hidden contract', in which the wife agrees to act as a 'support team' so that her husband can fill the demanding job to which he aspires. Handy (1978) supports the idea that this is 'typical' and that it is the path to career success for the manager concerned. In his sample of top British executives (in mid-career) and their wives he found that the most frequent pattern (about half the thirty-two couples interviewed) was the 'thrusting male-caring female'. This he depicts as high role segregation, with the emphasis on 'separation', 'silence' and complementary activities. Historically both the company and the manager have reaped benefits from maintaining the segregation of work and home implicit in this pattern. The company thus legitimates its demand for a constant work performance from its employee, no matter what his home situation, and the manager is free to pursue his career but keeps a 'safe haven' to which he can return to relax and recuperate. The second and most frequent combination was 'involved–involved' – a dual career pattern, with the emphasis on complete sharing. This, while potentially extremely fulfilling for both parties, requires energy inputs which might well prove so excessive that none of the roles involved is fulfilled successfully.

It is unlikely that the patterns described above will be negotiated explicitly or that they will in the long term be 'in balance'. Major factors in their continuing evolution will be the work and family demands of particular life stages. A

BIM report (Beattie *et al.*, 1974), for example, highlights the difficult situation of the young executive who, in order to build up his career, must devote a great deal of time and energy to his job just when his young house-bound wife, with small children, is also making pressing demands. The report suggests that the executive fights to maintain the distance between his wife and the organization, so that she will not be in a position to evaluate the choices he has to make; paradoxically he does so at a time when he is most in need of sympathy and understanding, Guest and Williams (1973) examined the complete career cycle in similar terms, pointing out how the demands of the different systems change over time. The addition of role-disposition and personality-disposition variables to their 'equations' would, however, make them even more valuable.

Mobility

Home conflicts become particularly critical in relation to managerial relocation and mobility. Much of the literature on this topic comes from the USA, where mobility is much more a part of the national character than in the United Kingdom (Pierson, 1972), and this argument is supported by the data given in Chapter 2. But there is reason to believe that mobility is an increasingly common phenomenon in Britain, too.

At an individual level the effects of mobility on the manager's wife and family have been studied (Cooper and Marshall, 1978). Researchers agree that, whether she is willing to move or not, the wife bears the brunt of relocations, and they conclude that most husbands do not appreciate what this involves. American writers point to signs that wives are suffering and becoming less co-operative. Immundo (1974) hypothesizes that increasing divorce rates are seen as the upwardly aspiring manager races ahead of his socially unskilled, 'stay-at-home' wife. Seidenberg (1973) comments on the rise in the ratio of female to male alcoholics in the USA from 1:5 in 1962 to 1:2 in 1973 and asks the question, 'Do corporate wives have souls?' Descriptive accounts of the frustrations and loneliness of being a 'corporate wife' in the USA and the United Kingdom proliferate. Increasing teenage delinquency and violence is also laid at the door of the mobile manager and the society which he has created.

Constant mobility can have profound effects on the life-style of the people concerned – particularly on their relationships with others. Staying only two years or so in one place, mobile families do not have time to develop close ties with the local community. Immundo (1974) talks of the 'mobility syndrome', a way of behaving geared to developing only temporary relationships. Packard (1975) describes ways in which individuals react to the type of fragmenting society this creates, e.g. treating everything as if it is temporary, being indifferent to local community amenities and organizations, living for the 'present' and becoming adept at 'instant gregariousness'. He goes on to point out the likely consequences for local communities, the nation, and the rootless people involved.

Pahl and Pahl (1971) suggest that the British reaction is, characteristically, more reserved and that many mobiles retreat into their nuclear family. Managers, particularly, do not become involved in local affairs, due both to lack of time and to an appreciation that they are only 'short-stay' inhabitants. Their wives find participation easier (especially in areas where mobility is common), and a recent survey (Middle Class Housing Estate Study, 1975) suggested that, for some, 'involvement' is necessary to compensate for their husband's ambitions and career involvement which keep him away from home. From the company's point of view, the way in which a wife adjusts to her new environment can affect her husband's work performance. Guest and Williams (1973) illustrate with an example of a major international company which, on surveying 1,800 of their executives in seventy countries, concluded that the two most important influences on over-all satisfaction with the overseas assignment were the job itself and, more importantly, the adjustment of executives' wives to the foreign environment.

The type-A manager

Sources of pressure at work evoke different reactions from different managers. Some are better able to cope with these stressors than others; they adapt their behaviour in a way that meets the environmental challenge. On the other hand, some managers are psychologically predisposed to stress, that is, they are unable to cope or adapt to the stress-provoking situations. Many factors may contribute to these differences – personality, motivation, being able or ill-equipped to deal with problems in a particular area of expertise, fluctuations in abilities (particularly with age), insight into one's own motivations and weaknesses. However, much of the research in this area has focused on personality and behavioural differences between high- and low-stressed individuals.

The major research approach to individual stress differences began with the work of Friedman and Rosenman (Friedman, 1969; Rosenman *et al.*, 1964, 1966) in the early 1960s which showed a relationship between behavioural patterns and the prevalence of CHD. They found that individuals manifesting certain behavioural traits were significantly more at risk. These individuals were later referred to as the 'coronary-prone behaviour pattern type A' as distinct from type B (low risk of CHD). Type A was characterized by extremes of competitiveness, striving for achievement, aggressiveness, haste, impatience, restlessness, hyperalertness, explosiveness of speech, tenseness of facial musculature and feelings of being under pressure of time and under the challenge of responsibility. It was suggested that 'people having this particular behavioural pattern were often so deeply involved and committed to their work that other aspects of their lives were relatively neglected' (Jenkins, 1971). In the early studies persons were designated as type A or type B on the basis of clinical judgements of doctors and psychologists or peer ratings. These studies found higher incidence of CHD among type A than type B. Many of the inherent methodological weaknesses of this approach were overcome by the classic Western Collaborative Group Study (Rosenman *et al.*, 1964, 1966, 1967). It was a prospective (as opposed to the earlier retrospective studies) national sample of over 3,400 men free of CHD. All these men were rated type A or B by psychiatrists after intensive interviews, without knowledge of any biological data about them and without the individuals being seen by a heart specialist. Diagnosis was made by an electrocardiographer and an independent medical practitioner, both of whom were not informed about the subjects' behavioural patterns. They found the following result: after 2½ years from the start of the study, type-A men between the ages 39—49 and 50—59 had 6.5 and 1.9 times respectively the incidence of CHD than type-B men. They also had a large number of stress risk factors (e.g. high serum cholesterol levels, elevated beta-lipoproteins). After 4½ years the *same* relationship of behavioural pattern and incidence of CHD was found. In terms of the clinical manifestations of CHD, individuals exhibiting type-A behavioural patterns had significantly more incidence of acute myocardial infarction and angina pectoris. Rosenman *et al.* (1967) also found that the risk of recurrent and fatal myocardial infarction was significantly related to type-A characteristics. Quinlan *et al.* (1969) found the same results among Trappist and Benedictine monks. Monks judged to be type-A coronary-prone cases had 2.3 times the prevalence of angina and 4.3 times the prevalence of infarction as compared with monks judged to be type B.

An increasingly large number of studies have been carried out which support the relationship between type-A behaviour and ill-health (Caplan, Cobb and French, 1975). From a management perspective, the most significant work has been carried out by Howard *et al.* (1976): 236 managers from twelve different companies were examined for type-A behaviour and for a number of the known risk factors in CHD (blood pressure, cholesterol, triglycerides, uric acid, smoking and fitness). Those managers exhibiting extreme type-A behaviour showed significantly higher blood pressure (systolic and diastolic) and higher cholesterol and triglyceride levels. A higher percentage of these managers were cigarette smokers, and in each age group studied type-A managers were less interested in exercise (although differences in cardio-respiratory fitness were found only in the oldest age group). The authors conclude that type-A managers were found to be higher on a number of risk factors known to be associated with CHD than were type-B managers.

The management of stress

Cooper (1981a) has argued that understanding the sources

of managerial pressure, as we have tried to do here, is only the first step in stress reduction. We must next begin to explore 'when' and 'how' to intervene. There are a number of changes that can be introduced in organizational life to begin to manage stress at work, for example:

1. To recreate the social, psychological and organizational environment in the work-place to encourage greater autonomy and participation by managers in *their* jobs.
2. To begin to build the bridges between the work-place and the home: providing opportunities for the manager's wife to understand better her husband's job, to express her views about the consequences of his work on family life, and to be involved in the decision-making processes of work that affects all members of the family unit.
3. To utilize the well-developed catalogue of social and inter-active skill training programmes to help clarify role and interpersonal relationship difficulties within organizations.
4. More fundamentally, to create an organizational climate to encourage rather than discourage communication, oppenness and trust — so that individual managers are able to express their mobility to cope, their work-related fears, and are able to ask for help if needed.

There are many other methods and approaches of coping and managing stress, depending on the sources activated and the interface between these sources and the individual make-up of the manager concerned, but the important point that we are trying to raise here is that the *cure* (intervention or training technique) depends on the *diagnosis*. It is important to encourage organizations to be sensitive to the needs of its managers and begin to audit managerial stress. As Wright (1975) so aptly suggests, 'the responsibility for maintaining health should be a reflection of the basic relationship between the individual and the organization for which he works; it is in the best interests of both parties that reasonable steps are taken to live and work sensibly and not too demandingly'.

References for Chapter 5

Barber, R. (1976) 'Who would Marry a Director?', *Director*, March, 60–2.

Beattie, R. T., Darlington, T. G. and Cripps, D. M. (1974) *The Management Threshold*, British Institute of Management, London.

Breslow, L. and Buell, P. (1960) 'Mortality from Coronary Heart Disease and Physical Activity of Work in California', *Journal of Chronic Diseases*, 11, 615—26.

Brook, A. (1973) 'Mental Stress at *Work*', *The Practitioner*, 210, 500—6.

Brummett, R. L., Pyle, W. C. and Framholtz, E. G. (1968) 'Accounting for Human Resources', *Michigan Business Review*, 20(2), 20—5.

Buck, V. (1972) *Working under Pressure*, Staples Press, London.

Caplan, R. D., Cobb, S. and French, J. R. P. (1975) 'Relationships of Cessation of Smoking with Job Stress, Personality and Social Support', *Journal of Applied Psychology*, 60(2), 211—19.

Constandse, W. J. (1972) 'A Neglected Personnel Problem', *Personnel Journal*, 51(2), 129—33.

Cooper, C. L. (1976) *Developing Social Skills in Managers*, Macmillan, London.

Cooper, C. L. (1981a) *The Stress Check*, Prentice-Hall, Englewood Cliffs, N.J.

Cooper, C. L. (1981b) *Executive Families under Pressure*, Prentice-Hall, Englewood Cliffs, N.J.

Cooper, C. L. and Marshall, J. (1978) *Understanding Executive Stress*, Macmillan, London.

Dohrenwend, B. S. and Dohrenwend, B. P. (1974) *Stressful Life Events*, Wiley, New York.

Donaldson, J. and Gowler, D. (1975) 'Prerogatives, Participation and Managerial Stress', in Gowler, D. and Legge, K. (eds), *Managerial Stress*, Gower Press, Epping, England.

French, J. R. P. and Caplan, R. D. (1970) 'Psychosocial Factors in Coronary Heart Disease', *Industrial Medicine*, 39, 383—97.

French, J. R. P. and Caplan, R. D. (1973) 'Organizational Stress and Individual Strain', in Marrow, A. J. (ed.), *The Failure of Success*, American Management Academy, New York, 30—66.

French, J. R. P., Tupper, C. J. and Mueller, E. I. (1965) 'Workload of University Professors', unpublished research report, University of Michigan.

Friedman, M. (1969) *Pathogenesis of Coronary Artery Disease*, McGraw-Hill, New York.

Friedman, M., Rosenman, R. H. and Carroll, V. (1958) 'Changes in Serum Cholesterol and Blood Clotting Time in Men Subjected to Cyclic Variations of Occupational Stress', *Circulation*, 17, 852—61.

Goffman, E. (1952) 'On Cooling the Mark Out', *Psychiatry*, 15(4), 451—63.

Gowler, D. and Legge, K. (1975) 'Stress and External Relationships — The "Hidden Contract" ', in Gowler, D. and Legge, K. (eds), *Managerial Stress*, Gower Press, Epping, England.

Guest, D. and Williams, R. (1973) 'How Home Affects Work', *New Society*, January.

Handy, C. (1978) 'The Family: Help or Hindrance?', in Cooper, C. L. and Payne, R. (eds), *Stress at Work*, Wiley, New York.

Howard, J. H., Cunningham, D. A. and Rechnitzer, P. A. (1976) 'Health Patterns Associated With Type A Behaviour: A Managerial Population', *Journal of Human Stress*, March, 24—31.

Immundo, L. V. (1974) 'Problems Associated with Managerial Mobility', *Personnel Journal*, 53(12), 910.

Jenkins, C. D. (1971) Psychologic and Social Precursors of Coronary Disease', *New England Journal of Medicine*, 284(6), 307—17.

Kahn, R. L., Wolfe, D. M., Quinn, R. P., Snoek, J. D. and Rosenthal, R. A. (1964) *Organizational Stress*, Wiley, New York.

Kasl, S. V. (1973) 'Mental Health and the Work Environment', *Journal of Occupational Medicine*, 15(6), 509—18.

Kay, E. (1974) 'Middle Management', in O'Toole, J. (ed.), *Work and the Quality of Life*, MIT Press, Cambridge, Mass.

Kearns, J. L. (1973) *Stress in Industry*, Priory Press, London.

Lazarus, R. S. (1906) *Psychological Stress and the Coping Process*, McGraw-Hill, New York.

Levinson, H. (1973) 'Problems that Worry Our Executives', in Marrow, A. J. (ed.), *The Failure of Success*, American Management Academy, New York.

McMurray, R. N. (1973) 'The Executive Neurosis', in Noland, R. L. (ed.), *Industrial Mental Health and Employee Counselling*, Behavioral Publications, New York.

Margolis, B. L. and Kroes, W. H. (1974) 'Work and the Health of Man', in O'Toole, J. (ed.), *Work and the Quality of Life*, MIT Press, Cambridge, Mass.

Margolis, B. L., Kroes, W. H. and Quinn, R. P. (1974) 'Job Stress: An Unlisted Occupational Hazard', *Journal of Occupational Medicine*, 16(10), 654—61.

Marshall, J. and Cooper, C. L. (1978) *Executives Under Pressure*, Macmillan, London.

Marshall, J. and Cooper, C. L. (1979) 'Work Experiences of Middle and Senior Managers: The Pressures and Satisfactions', *Management International Review*.

Mettlin, C. and Woelfel, J. (1974) 'Interpersonal Influence and Symptoms of Stress', *Journal of Health and Social Behaviour*, 15(4), 311—19.

Middle Class Housing Estate Study (1975), unpublished paper, Civil Service College, United Kingdom.

Miller, J. G. (1960) 'Information Input Overload and Psychopathology', *American Journal of Psychiatry*, 8, 116.

Mintzberg, H. (1973) *The Nature of Managerial Work*, Harper & Row, New York.

Morris, J. (1975) 'Managerial Stress and "The Cross of Relationships" ', in Gowler, D. and Legge, K. (eds), *Managerial Stress*, Gower Press, Epping, England.

Neff, W. S. (1968) *Work and Human Behavior*, Atherton Press, New York.

Packard, V. (1975) *A Nation of Strangers*, McKay, New York.

Pahl, J. M. and Pahl, R. E. (1971) *Managers and Their Wives*, Allen Lane, London.

Pierson, G. W. (1972) *The Moving Americans*, Knopf, New York.

Pincherle, G. (1972) 'Fitness for Work', *Proceedings of the Royal Society of Medicine*, 65(4) 321–4.

Quinlan, C. B., Burrow, J. G. and Hayes, C. G. (1969) 'The Association of Risk Factors and CHD in Trappist and Benedictine Monks', paper presented to the American Heart Association, New Orleans, Louisiana.

Quinn, R. P., Seashore, S. and Mangione, I. (1971) *Survey of Working Conditions*, US Government Printing Office, Washington, D.C.

Rosenman, R. H., Friedman, M. and Jenkins, C. D. (1967) 'Clinically Unrecognized Myocardial Infarction in the Western Collaborative Group Study', *American Journal of Cardiology*, 19, 776–82.

Rosenman, R. H., Friedman, M. and Strauss, R. (1964) 'A Predictive Study of CHD', *Journal of the American Medical Association*, 189, 15–22.

Rosenman, R. H., Friedman, M. and Strauss, R. (1966) 'CHD in the Western Collaborative Group Study', *Journal of the American Medical Association*, 195, 86–92.

Russek, H. I. and Zohman, B. L. (1969) 'Relative Significance of Hereditary, Diet and Occupational Stress in CHD of Young Adults', *American Journal of Medical Science*, 235, 266–75.

Seidenberg, R. (1973) *Corporate Wives – Corporate Casualties*, American Management Association, New York.

Shirom, A., Eden, D., Silberwasser, S. and Kellerman, J. J. (1973) 'Job Stress and Risk Factors in Coronary Heart Disease Among Occupational Categories in Kibbutzim', *Social Science and Medicine*, 7, 875–92.

Sleeper, R. D. (1975) 'Labour Mobility Over the Life Cycle', *British Journal of Industrial Relations*, 13(2).

Sofer, C. (1970) *Men in Mid-Career*, Cambridge University Press, Cambridge.

Stewart, R. (1976) *Contrasts in Management*, McGraw-Hill, New York.

Uris, A. (1972) 'How Managers Ease Job Pressures', *International Management*, June, 45–6.

Wardwell, W. L., Hyman, M. and Bahnson, C. B. (1964) 'Stress and Coronary Disease in Three Field Studies', *Journal of Chronic Diseases*, 17, 73–84.

Wright, H. B. (1975) *Executive Ease and Dis-ease*, Gower Press, Epping, England.

Much of the material used in this chapter was first published in the *Journal of Occupational Psychology*, 1976, 49(1), 11–28.

Section 2: The Group Within the Organization

6
Forming Judgements of Others

At 9.30 on a bright October morning, Peter Swartz is ushered into an office for an interview. He looks smart in his new suit, immaculate shirt and tie and his highly polished shoes. The research director who comes to greet him is dressed in jeans, a T-shirt and wears his hair long. Unfortunately for Peter, the research director has great confidence in his own ability to size up applicants as they walk through the door. At a glance the research director knows that Peter is too conventional and too materialistically orientated for the vacancy. Peter is not alarmed at the outcome of his first interview because later that day he has another interview for a very similar job.

The research director at the second interview also has the gift of being able to size up applicants as they walk through the door. Fortunately for Peter, the second research director wears a suit and tie and at a glance he knows that Peter will be a reliable, go ahead, well-motivated employee.

On his first day in his new job the research director lunches with Peter in the works canteen. The operatives on a nearby table conclude that he is the latest addition to the management team and that he looks just as ruthless and manipulative as the other managers in the company. Just before they finish their lunch, Peter is introduced to the union representative, and the research director makes a tactful exit. Another shift of operatives enter the canteen and, seeing Peter talking to the union representative, they conclude that he seems a sociable and friendly new operative who has radical political views.

Peter Swartz works hard and is also very lucky. Within

three months he produces a breakthrough in one of the company's major development projects — computer recognition of handwritten documents. Peter basked in the glory of his breakthrough for several years and no one noticed that his subsequent work was wasteful and unproductive.

The story of Peter Swartz emphasizes how the judgements which we make about one another alter the course of our lives; it also shows the many subjective factors which influence these decisions. This chapter describes these subjective influences in more detail and explains the basis of *social perception*.

The process of perception

Perception is the *process by which we become aware of, and make meaning out of, the world around us.* It is concerned with how we get and deal with information. At first sight it may appear that this is not a particularly complex process. We simply open our eyes and look (or, if we listen, we hear). It is, however, not quite so simple. Consider a trivial example. We look at a rectangular surface such as the top of a table or desk. We 'see' a rectangle despite the fact that the actual image on the retina of our eye is rarely rectangular. One reason for this is because we 'know' it is a rectangle and automatically interpret it as one. Our past experience is one of many influences on our present perception. Other evidence on the complexity of perception is provided by the fact that different witnesses of the same event will often give completely different accounts of it — all apparently quite honest descriptions of what they 'heard and saw' — and often it is impossible to establish exactly 'what happened' in events such as accidents. The fact that all our information about the world and all our communication is based on our perception makes it important to have some understanding of this process.

Factors in perception

There are a number of factors which determine what, and how, we perceive.

Perception is based on change

Perception starts with a stimulus, i.e. a change in the environment which can be detected by our senses. These changes are simply changes of pressure, temperature, chemical concentrations or light. For instance, pressure waves in the air created by someone speaking are detected by the tympanum or eardrum. The variations in light intensity reflected from the print and white paper of this book are detected in the retina of the eye. Usually, unless some change of this sort takes place, nothing is perceived. For example, we only become aware of temperature if it changes, particularly if it rises or falls beyond normal comfortable limits for the human body.

Perception is selective

The average human being could not possibly cope with all the sensory data which are available at any one time, so therefore some selection inevitably has to be made. This means we are normally unaware of many potential stimuli in the environment. For example, we are normally unaware of the stimulus of the feel of our clothes (sense of touch) until our attention is drawn to it in some way — such as through this sentence! As we continue with other activities, and our attention shifts again, we once more cease to be aware of our clothing. Attention can therefore be considered as a *focusing* process. In general, we only perceive that which we attend to, though we may also have some less precise awareness of things on the margin of attention.

Perception is an organizing and interpretative process

Without some organization even the relatively limited amount of stimuli selected by the process of attention would be a meaningless jumble of sense impressions. We do this organization according to a series of well-defined principles so as to make experience as meaningful as possible. A trivial example of this is illustrated by Figure 6.1. When asked to describe

Figure 6.1   *Organization in perception*

what they see in the figure most people reply 'A triangle of crosses.' In strict fact it is simply three crosses, as the viewer has imposed the organization of triangularity, possibly because this is just about the simplest figure into which it could be organized. Thus what is meant by saying that perception is organized is that people tend to organize stimuli into meaningful arrangements, or configurations, rather than accept them as unrelated separate units of information. This total configuration is referred to as a *gestalt*.

The fact that perception is organized in this way is, in general, helpful because it is a way of making the world and the messages we receive more meaningful. For instance, many of the verbal messages we receive consist of very jumbled incomplete sentences, which we interpret and organize. We usually do this without being consciously aware of our actions. Many people are very surprised by the incoherence of typed transcripts of discussions or spontaneous talks. However, as with many other useful processes, there are dangers. So satisfying is the process of achieving a completed gestalt that we will often *force* an interpretation on incomplete data so as to make sense of them. This is well illustrated by the work of Brunner (1965) with a device called an *ambiguator*. An ambiguator projects a picture on to a screen starting with a completely out-of-focus picture and gradually bringing it to complete clarity. In one experiment subjects watched the picture come into focus over a period of several minutes and were instructed to say what the picture was as soon as they could recognize it. Frequently it took as long as thirty seconds after the picture was fully focused before the correct interpretation could be seen. Brunner explains that our desire to interpret obscure messages leads us to make incorrect inter-

pretations. These incorrect interpretations then become hard
to correct and this prevents us seeing the picture for what it
really is. He refers to these as *incorrigible strategies*. Many of
our difficulties of interacting with other people are due to
the formation of 'incorrigible strategies'. This will be discussed
later.

Perception within a frame of reference

A characteristic of the way we organize perception is that
objects or events are normally perceived against some frame
of reference. Visually we normally use the surrounding space
as the frame and objects are seen against this. This is often
referred to as *figure* and *ground*. This is because the object
we are perceiving is seen to stand against the background. It
is this figure—ground phenomenon which enables us to pick
out a spoken message against the background noise. As with
all other perceptual phenomena, it is essential for understanding our world, yet it can also lead to misperception. If a
spot of light is projected on to a large screen and then the
screen is moved from side to side, most observers judge that
the spot is moving. A similar effect is sometimes observed
when hazy or broken clouds are blowing across the moon.
The spot (or moon) is taken as the figure and is assumed to
be moving against the ground. The significance of this in
more complex situations is that we often bring with us to any
situation our own frame of reference. If we have set ideas about
what ought to happen, events which do occur will stand out
in figure against this background and will be perceived in
relationship to it. Thus, for example, a person may appear
more or less co-operative according to our ideas about the
situation and what co-operation looks like.

An even more complex example of a personal frame of
reference are our attitudes, which also tend to determine
what we perceive in any given situation. Thus a comment
made by a person towards whom we have a favourable attitude
may seem like a light-hearted joke. The same comment from
someone we view negatively may be perceived as a sarcastic
criticism.

Perception is learnt

A final factor of some importance concerning perception is that it is a learned process. Convincing evidence of this comes from work in the clinical area with patients blind from birth because of cataracts of the lens of the eye. In some cases the cataracts can be surgically removed during adulthood. A number of such cases have now been studied and a common experience is that after the operation the person is quite unable to 'see' in the sense of recognizing and making sense of visual impressions although physiologically the visual system is now operating perfectly. The ability to recognize even simple objects usually takes a long time and requires experience of the object in different situations and against different backgrounds. These skills are normally learnt in the first few months of life but are perhaps not fully developed until the age of 4 or 5. Some patients confronted with this amount of learning as an adult give up and continue to live as 'blind' people, even though the operation is physically a success (Gregory, 1966).

A theory of perception

In order to really understand and conceptualize the above information about perception, it is necessary to organize it in some way. The following 'theory' of perception is intended to help the reader do just this. The danger is that, as noted above, our systems of organization are to some extent idiosyncratic. So that while what follows is meaningful and helpful (though not original) to the authors, it may not be to the reader, with his different conceptual system. The theory itself suggests that perception is a three-stage process:

1. The *reception* processes.
2. The *symbolic* processes.
3. The *affective* processes.

The reception processes

The concept of reception is used to refer to the purely physiological aspects of perception. For example, the reception processes consist, in the case of vision, of such things as focusing of light rays by the lens on to the retina of the eye. Light-sensitive cells in the retina set up pulses in the optic nerve which are conveyed to the brain. The parallel process in hearing is the sound waves in the air setting up vibrations in the tympanum or ear-drum. As a result, pulses from pressure-sensitive cells are conveyed to the brain via the auditory nerve.

These processes are not of great interest to the psychologist, as human physiology is fairly standard, and provided the physiological systems are functioning correctly there are no particular causes of individual variation in perception due to the reception stage.

The symbolic processes

When the nerve pulses from the receptors reach the higher centres of the brain some process must take place which enables the individual to interpret the information which they convey. For example, the pattern of pulses set up in the optic nerve as the eye scans this page must be interpreted by the reader as English language words conveying meaning of some sort. The ability to do this is obviously derived from past experience (i.e. it is learnt) and there must be something stored in the brain which enables the individual to do this. This 'something' is what is referred to as the symbolic processes. The symbolic processes are obviously learned, as without past experience of the English language it would be impossible to interpret these symbols. More refined experience is needed to go beyond simply reading the words to understanding fully the meaning of them.

It is the symbolic processes, therefore, which are learnt and account for the learning aspect of perception. It is also through the symbolic processes that we organize and interpret our perception. Since what we learn depends on our own individual experience, and as no two people have identical experience, we develop different symbolic processes. This accounts for individual variation in perception. Luckily most people within a particular culture have sufficient common experience to make similar interpretations of most essential everyday situations. Inter-cultural differences in perceptual interpretation often occur in the non-verbal areas of communication. Facial expressions, gestures, amount of physical contact, all vary between cultures. An individual from one culture confronted by someone from another is thus often either unable to interpret the other person's feelings and reactions, or he interprets them wrongly.

An important implication is that it is only possible to communicate between individuals who have some degree of common experience. Apart from the obvious need to speak the same language, the degree of knowledge of the language needs to overlap and some common experience of the concepts is necessary. For example, a book on psychology which refers all the time to concepts the reader has not met will not communicate. It is necessary to start with common experiences and develop the experience of new concepts. Because of the tendency to *closure* (the tendency to complete percepts so as to make sense) the real danger of miscommunication is that the individual interprets what he reads or knows in a way that is sensible for him and assumes that communication has been made. It may be, however, that his interpretation is quite different from that intended by the communicator. This is potentially more misleading than the situation where a communication is totally meaningless because the receiver has not the experience necessary to interpret it at all. Here, at least, it is clear that there has been a failure in communication.

The affective processes

The third aspect of perception is the affective stage. This refers to the fact that we normally have some feelings or emotions about what we perceive. These feelings are also dependent on our past experience; and as there is even more individual variation in our emotional experience than in the cognitive area, so there will be correspondingly greater variations in how people feel about what they perceive. The fact that people can have very different emotional reactions to an identical phrase or words is an important aspect of the process of communicating information (see Chapter 7).

Thus in reading this book all people with normal vision will receive the same pattern of visual impact. How they interpret and understand this will depend on how much experience of reading in general they have and how much knowledge of psychology and other relevant topics. As this knowledge varies, so will the interpretation of each individual reader. How each person feels will be even more varied. Some will be interested, some bored, others annoyed, etc. The actual feeling depends not only on knowledge but on attitudes and beliefs. It is important to note, of course, that although these processes have to be described sequentially, they in fact occur virtually simultaneously.

Application of the theory

Two examples of the application of this theory now follow. The first is a simple one, simply to illustrate the theory. The second is more complex and is intended to show how the theory can give insight into 'real-life' situations.

Consider, first, a man who arrives home to find his wife preparing a meal for him. Let us say that the meal is steak and chips. The *receptor* processes will detect sound waves from the frying fat, visual information and chemical information giving rise to smells. His past experience will enable him to interpret these stimuli and 'recognize' what is being cooked. This is the *symbolic* stage. How he *feels* will depend on many factors: how hungry he is; the state of his digestion; how often he has had steak and chips recently; and how much he 'likes' them anyway. Suppose, on the other hand, that his wife is trying out an exotic eastern dish from a recipe in a women's magazine; there will be similar sense impressions of sound, sight and smell but he may not have the experience to interpret them – producing the possible reaction of 'What on earth's that!' That is, he does not have the symbolic processes to deal with the input he is receiving. How he feels about this will depend on many factors. It will be affected by how he normally feels in situations of uncertainty. It will also depend on whether this is a common experience and if the results are usually pleasant-tasting or not.

The more complex example considers a situation which

frequently occurs in industry. Let us say that an industrial engineer has produced a new method for a particular job. This is shown to representatives of management. They have a set of symbolic processes which interpret the scheme in terms of reducing work, saving cost and increasing profits. Their affective processes are all positive, as (with their frame of reference) these all seem desirable. The scheme is now shown to shop-floor representatives, but they have quite different symbolic processes which produce such concepts as 'redundancy' 'reduction in earnings', 'loss of overtime', etc., with consequent negative feelings, leading to rejection of the scheme. There may then ensue quite a considerable dispute and even industrial action of some sort. The important point is that this is not a dispute over facts or information but over interpretation. What is often not realized is that the two parties are perceiving something quite different and are therefore not arguing about the same thing. Many industrial disputes seem to be of this nature.

One suggestion which has been made to deal with this is that no one in an argument or dispute should be allowed to contribute to the discussion until he has summarized and repeated the previous contribution in such a way that the previous speaker agrees that that is what he said. This is often used in training programmes and has the effect of forcing participants to concentrate on and resolve differences in interpretation, and it also encourages them to listen to one another, both of which can improve communication enormously.

Social perception

The general characteristics of perception show clearly in a number of common phenomena which occur when people perceive and judge others. As these phenomena frequently lead to inaccurate perception and misjudgements it is particularly important to be aware of them.

Stereotyping

One mechanism which involves all three characteristics of

selectivity, interpretation and effects of past experience is stereotyping. This occurs when we allow our judgement of an individual to be affected by our beliefs about the group of which we see him as a member. Generalized beliefs are often held about groups of people (e.g. all Scotsmen are mean, or all students are long-haired radicals). Sometimes people hold even more complex and all-embracing concepts as representative of a particular class or group. These concepts are usually generalizations on small samples of unreliable evidence and large amounts of cultural mythology. Although these beliefs may be held as representing a class as a whole they do not of course actually fit any individual member. This generalized concept representing a whole class is known as a *stereotype*.

Secord and Backman (1964) have pointed out that stereo-typing is a socio-cultural phenomenon, in that particular stereotypes seem to be common (or very predominant) in any particular culture and that it involves three distinct activities:

1. The identification of a group or category of persons (Scotsmen, students, army officers).
2. An agreement in attributing sets of traits or characteristics to that category or group.
3. The attribution of these characteristics to any member of the group in question.

Stereotypes can be generally either favourable or unfavourable, i.e. the attribution of a set of totally positive or negative characteristics to a liked or disliked category of people, though there is evidence that stereotypes frequently combine both positive and negative characteristics. An aspect of stereo-typing which has important implications for organizations is where characteristics which are unfavourably evaluated in one group are attributed to another group which, in turn, may accept them but express them in terms more favourable to themselves. In a study by Campbell and Levine (cited in Secord and Backman, 1964), for example,

the English describe themselves as *reserved* and *respecting the privacy of others* and describe Americans as *intrusive*, *forward* and *pushy*. But the Americans describe the English as *snobbish*, *cold* and *unfriendly* and describe themselves as *friendly*, *outgoing* and *openhearted*.

During a training programme for a mixed group of academic staff and university administrators, conducted by two of the present authors, each group was asked to briefly characterize themselves and the other group. The administrators saw themselves as helpful and facilitating the work of the academics, but were seen by the academics as bureaucratic and more concerned with following rules than getting things done. The administrators saw the academics as disorganized and administratively incompetent. The academics saw themselves as pragmatic and getting on with the job in hand by the most direct route. It should, perhaps, be recorded that there were also positive characteristics in the cross-perceptions of the two groups, though interestingly these tended to be in areas where the roles did not overlap.

There are many other examples of this crossing of perceptions between sub-groups in organizations. It occurs most frequently between departments (sales *vs* production), functions (line *vs* staff) and levels (management *vs* workers). Haire (1955) found that when a photograph of a man was labelled management representative it produced a quite different impression from when the same photograph was labelled union leader. Furthermore management and shop-floor workers formed different impressions, each tending to see their own grouping more favourably. What this illustrates is the tendency to use stereotyping as the framework for organizing perceptions of people.

This is a perfect example of both the necessity to organize our perception and the dangers of such organization. Stereotyping is a necessary activity. Many concepts (e.g. labels for categories) would have no meaning if they did not call to mind a stereotype. The danger lies in applying the stereotype to any particular individual in the category. This process underlies much of the inter-group conflict and poor communication which occurs within organizations. This can be improved by a technique, known as *organizational mirroring*, where in the 'safe' environment of the training room, groups clarify and share their perceptions of each other, and explore what lies behind them. This usually produces a reorganization of perception and more positive attitudes. A description of this process is given by Bennis (1969, pp. 4—6).

Halo effect

People's judgement of another person are often unduly affected by just one or two characteristics of that person. interviewees who speak fluently in standard English with a good vocabulary are often judged superior, by interviewers, on a whole range of quite unrelated characteristics, on warmth or intelligence, for example. Conversely, people with regional accents or poor speech and limited vocabulary are often under-rated. As there there seems to be some sort of 'blurring of the edges' of one characteristic with another, thus preventing either being clearly seen, the phenomenon is referred to as the *halo effect*.

In a study by Asch (1946) it was found that changing one word in a list of characteristics completely altered the impression created by the list. Given the description of a person as 'intelligent, skilful, industrious, determined, practical, cautious and warm' produced a quite different impression from when the word 'warm' was replaced by 'cold'. The rest of the list remaining the same. In a variation of this experiment (Kelley, 1950) a guest speaker was introduced to different groups using the same two lists of stimulus words. Judgements of the speaker's personality showed similar biases as in the original experiment.

Self-fulfilling prophesies and perceptual defence

These experiments clearly illustrate the danger of operating on first impressions. There is evidence that in selection interviews there is a tendency for the unskilled interviewer to make tentative judgements within the first four minutes and then to spend the rest of the interview collecting data to confirm his first impression (Springbett, 1958).

There are many other instances which produce *self-fulfilling prophesies*, or incorrigible strategies in our perceptions of people. Haire and Grunes (1958) have shown that individuals are able to select and distort data to maintain an existing view. They refer to this as *perceptual defence*. Another example of this can be seen in some management discussions when an individual presents an argument which is strongly held and is confronted with some conflicting information. Considerable effort may be made to distort the new information to fit the old argument.

Effect of environment

Soskin (1953) noted, among other things, that perception of others was likely to be unduly affected by the setting in which the assessed was seen. Thus the prestigious, well-furnished office enhances the prestige of its occupant. The consultant carefully selects the right environment in which to meet an important client. This is really, of course, a special case of the halo effect.

Projection and introjection

Our perception of the behaviour of others can also be affected by characteristics which are really our own. For example, a person who is afraid may interpret the behaviour of others as showing fear when, in fact, they are not afraid. This interpretation is made as a result of his own interpretation of the situation and the fear thus induced in himself. For obvious reasons this phenomenon is known as projection. A person who is anxious in the presence of his boss may, for example, perceive the behaviour of his colleagues as also showing anxiety in similar situations. Sears (1936) showed that people tend to attribute to others undesirable personality characteristics which are really their own. This was particularly so for people with little insight into their own personality.

Another phenomenon (which is, in effect, the converse of projection) is *introjection*. Introjection occurs when a person takes on himself characteristics which really belong to another.

He becomes anxious or afraid because he senses these feelings in others. Individuals may take on the characteristics and behaviour of well-liked managers or leaders. This will, again, have a distorting effect on their perception.

Improving social perception

People in organizations are, of course, perpetually making judgements about others. It is an essential part of social inter-action, and yet (as we have seen) it is fraught with difficulties. How much is it possible for these poblems of perception to be overcome? To some extent they never can be. The ever-present risk of misinterpreting the appearance and actions of others is part of the human condition. However, there are some things which can be done to at least minimize these dangers.

Zalkind and Costello (1962), from an examination of research, defined four factors affecting social perception:

1. Knowing oneself makes it easier to see others accurately.
2. One's own characteristics affect the characteristics likely to be seen in others.
3. The person who accepts himself is more likely to be able to see favourable aspects of other people.
4. Accuracy in perceiving others is not a single skill.

The implications of this are obvious. To perceive others accur-ately one must first accurately perceive oneself. As Zalkind and Costello go on to say:

The administrator (or any other individual) who wishes to perceive someone else accurately must look at the other person, not himself. The things that he looks at in someone else are influenced by his own traits. But if he knows his own traits, he can be aware that they provide a frame of reference for him. His own traits help to furnish the cate-gories that he will use in perceiving others. His characteris-tics, needs and values can partly limit his vision and his awareness of the differences between others. The question one should ask when viewing another is: 'Am I looking at him, and forming my impression of his behaviour in the situation, or am I just comparing him with myself?'

The interview

One context in which judgements of others are formally made is the interview, whether for selection or appraisal. It is obviously desirable to reduce as far as possible perceptual bias, and there are a number of ground-rules which (if followed) will help towards this end. Most of the points below apply equally to both the interviewer and the interviewee:

1. Be clear what information you require or wish to give during the interview both in terms of factual information and impressions. Hence in selection there is a need for a good job analysis and specification, or in assessment a clearly defined scheme or set of headings defining the areas to be covered.
2. Guard against 'halo effect' by being clear which characteristics are relevant and which are not. Then discount the irrelevant ones. The use of a scheme such as the *seven-point plan* (Rodger, 1952) or the *five-fold grading* (Fraser, 1957) is a great help here as this facilitates the precise definition of the relevant characteristics.
3. Guard against 'self-fulfilling prophesies'. This is best done by suspending judgement during the interview. Treat it as a data-collection (or exchange) exercise. Make decisions only after all the data available have been assembled.
4. Choose the setting with care so as to facilitate communication, i.e. a quiet, comfortable room. It is also a good rule that the interviewee should be treated in the same way as the interviewer. Both should be in armchairs or both seated at a table. It is not good for accurate interpersonal perception to place the interviewee in a small upright chair in the middle of the room, while the interviewer sits comfortably behind a large and impressive desk.
5. As far as possible be aware of your own prejudices, biases and fears so as not to project them on to the other.

6. Check continuously 'Am I seeing this person as fitting some particular category?' And 'Am I seeing him as like certain others?' This will help to avoid stereotyping.
7. Think about what you are going to wear. A person's style of dressing can introduce considerable bias into the way he is perceived by others. When deciding what to wear a good rule is to question 'Could this give an undesirable impression?' If the answer is 'Possibly yes', wear something else.
8. Guard against 'halo effect' (either positive or negative) from the other person's clothes, hair-style, etc., by being aware of your own prejudices and by consciously looking for additional data to either confirm or deny initial impressions.
9. Be alert for cues in the other's responses that indicate he is interpreting your communications in a different way from your intentions. These differences may be very subtle but are important.

What should be obvious from this chapter is that perception is determined as much by what is within us as by the external stimulus. This applies to the observation of simple physical objects but even more so to the perception of people. It is therefore impossible to be sure that our perception is accurate. It is in fact meaningless to think in such terms. All we can say is 'Right now this is how it seems to be.' The only defence is to be constantly aware of the possibility of other perceptions and to be always checking for other possible ways to look at the person or problem.

References for Chapter 6

Asch, S. (1946) 'Forming Impressions of Persons', *Journal of Abnormal and Social Psychology*, 60, 258–90.
Bennis, W. G. (1969) *Organization Development: Its Nature, Origins and Prospects*, Addison-Wesley, Reading, Mass.
Brunner, J. S. (1965) 'Some Observations on Effective Cognitive Processes', in Steiner G. A. (ed.), *The Creative Organization*, University of Chicago Press, Chicago.

Fraser, J. M. (1957) *Interview Case Studies*, MacDonald & Evans, London.

Gregory, R. L. (1966) *Eye and Brain: The Psychology of Seeing*, World University Library, London.

Haire, M. (1955) 'Role Perceptions in Labour—Management Relations: An Experimental Approach', *Industrial and Labour Relations Review*, 8, 204—16.

Haire, M. and Grunes, W. F. (1958) 'Perceptual Defenses: Processes Protecting an Original Perception of Another Personality', *Human Relations*, 3, 403—12.

Kelley, H. H. (1950) 'The Warm—Cold Variable in First Impressions of Persons', *Journal of Personality* 18, 431—9.

Rodger, A. (1952) *The Seven Point Plan*, National Institute of Industrial Psychology, London.

Sears, R. R. (1936) 'Experimental Studies of Perception: 1. Attribution of Traits', *Journal of Social Psychology*, 7, 151—63.

Secord, P. F. and Backman C. W. (1964) *Social Psychology*, McGraw-Hill, New York.

Soskin, W. E. (1953) 'Influence of Information on Bias in Social Perception', *Journal of Personality*, 22, 118—27.

Springbett, B. M. (1958) 'Factors affecting the Final Decision in the Employment Interview', *Canadian Journal of Psychology*, 12, 13—22.

Zalkind, S. S. and Costello, T. W. (1962) 'Perception: Some Recent Research and Implications for Administration', *Administrative Science Quarterly*, 7, 218—35.

7
Communication and Attitude Change

Practically everyone is familiar with the old, old anecdote from the First World War where the message transmitted from the trenches urgently asked for reinforcements for an impending advance, but the message received at company headquarters baffled all the brigadiers by asking for three and fourpence because the unit was going to a dance. The failure, of course, was a failure of communication. Similar failures occur during every minute of every industrial day: a microchip factory is brought to the edge of bankruptcy because the ventilating engineer fails to communicate the correct grade of air filters and the resulting atmospheric dust reduces the reliability of the chips to the point where their main customer withdraws his orders; an apprentice loses his right testicle because the safety officer's talk contained too many facts for him to assimilate; and an employee emerges from a disciplinary interview with the conviction that, despite actual words, his boss does not have any really serious objection to him arriving late for work. These are a few examples of failures of communication in industry.

Many other, classic, examples can be seen in organizations: the failure of the salesman to communicate important market changes to the production and design departments; the failure of the negotiator to make it clear that the offer really is final; and the failure of the chief executive who slows down his whole organization by insisting that all letters, reports, invoices and specifications are channelled through him. Mintzberg's analysis, which was described in Chapter 2, shows that communication is one of the most important activities a manager must undertake. In a formal sense a manager must communicate to both his superiors and to his subordinates.

Formal—informal and upwards—downwards communication

There is a natural tendency to think of *formal communication* as flowing *downwards* from the chief executive to the operative, along the channels shown in an organization chart. In a perfectly predictable, simple and static world, where chief executives know everything, formal downward communication might be all that is needed. But in a complex and changeable world where chief executives exhibit human fallibilities, *upward communication* is also important, otherwise higher management will continue to evolve an elaborate corporate strategy without realizing the existence of such 'minor' problems as below-target sales figures caused by a collapse of the motivation of the sales team when a zealous accountant introduces new administrative checks on their expense claims.

In addition to the upward and downward communication within the formal organizational structure, a manager must be aware of *informal channels* of communication. A great deal of a manager's information is obtained from people who, in a formal sense, have no obligation to him. Nevertheless, every organization has its grapevine which develops largely on the basis of personal friendships and proximity (see section on informal groups in Chapter 8). A particularly important aspect of these informal channels are the *lateral communications* between managers of similar rank. The lateral communications are important in co-ordinating the day-to-day efforts of the organization, and building up norms within groups of managers. Informal communication networks have two particular characteristics: they are quick, and they are inaccurate. Very often, the first news of redundancy within a firm is obtained not from the immediate superior but from a friend, or from the manager in the adjoining office. Indeed, a manager's superior may have received specific instructions not to divulge details of the redundancy until a later date. Managers develop their own informal channels of communication, in part because they are aware of the possibility of a premeditated block in the formal system of communication.

The basic communication process

Whatever the formality or the direction, the process of communication follows the basic pattern shown in Figure 7.1.

Information to ⟶ Decision to ⟶ Encoding ⟶
be communicated   communicate   of message

　　　　　　Transmission ⟶ Reception ⟶ Decoding ⟶ Action
　　　　　　via communication
　　　　　　channel

Figure 7.1   *Information-processing model of communication*

The decision to communicate

Communication starts with an idea or fact in a manager's mind. The manager has to recognize that these facts need to be communicated if the objectives of the organization are to be met. Many of the failures of communication occur at this stage. At a very banal level a manager may not realize that his secretary needs to know that twelve copies of the production plan are required. At a more serious level the ventilation engineer does not realize that he needs to instruct the apprentice on the specific grade of filter to be used in the air-conditioning system for a microchip production line. These two examples highlight two important reasons why messages are not transmitted — a manager may not be aware of all the people that need to know the information, and he may wrongly assume that people already possess the important facts.

In Chapter 1, it was established that a manager's job is very complex, varied and progresses at an unrelenting pace. It is simply not feasible for him to communicate everything to everyone, so he must decide what is to be communicated to whom, and (as other chapters have shown) these decisions will be constrained by his knowledge of other jobs and his perceptions of the abilities and knowledge of other people.

Encoding the message

Once a manager has decided that something needs to be communicated, he then needs to *encode* the information into a series of symbols which other people will understand. Unfortunately, symbols such as words or gestures can mean different things to different people (see section on process of perception in Chapter 6). Even within a closely knit group, words will take on different shades of meaning according to the individual's outlook and past experience. The differing shades of meaning are particularly important when considering the *emotional impact of symbols and words* (see Chapter 6). For example, a capitalist employer may talk of giving charitable donations to pensioners and use the word 'charity' in the sense of a benevolent, philanthropic, community-minded act of responsibility towards fellow human beings. He is surprised when he is upbraided by a militant communist who rejects his 'conscience' money on the basis of *his* meaning of charity as the return, by the exploiter, of a small part of his gains as a cunning attempt to distract the exploited from rising to lose their chains. Both the capitalist and communist agree on the factual meaning of the word 'charity' — the transfer of wealth from the rich to the poor. However, at an emotional level the word 'charity' has very different meanings. This difference in emotional meaning makes it impossible for the boss and the communist to communicate effectively with each other. Managers will rarely encounter differences of meaning on this scale, but they still need to choose their words with care and avoid those with ambiguous or emotional meanings. Whenever a manager wants to communicate to a different cultural group he needs to be particularly careful. There are often marked *cultural differences in meanings*. For example, the phrases 'give me a fag' and 'knock me up in the morning' have a certain meaning in Britain and quite a different meaning in the USA.

When encoding an idea or fact, it is important to use a method which produces a simple result. The golden rule is to use short words and short sentences. Good communication is the essence of the advertising industry. Many advertising agencies ensure that the texts of their advertisements are simple and clear by using formulae which measure the *readability of text* (see Grundner, 1978). Advertising agencies emphasize this short and simple approach because research indicates that people tend to avoid reading material which is long-winded and difficult to understand. There is specific research (Insko *et al.*, 1976; Calder *et al.*, 1974) which suggests that the law of diminishing returns operates rapidly and that long communications are less efficient than shorter ones. Furthermore, research by Eagly (1974) suggests that a communication which is difficult to understand may annoy the recipient and, because he is likely to blame this annoyance on the communicator, he is less likely to respond to the message.

In addition to attending to the hidden meanings of his words and the 'readability' of his arguments, a manager needs to take a number of strategic decisions when building up a complex communication such as a presentation or a report. He may need to decide whether to use fear as a part of his appeal, whether his case will be the first or the second argument to be heard, or whether he will draw explicit conclusions.

The controversy covering the use of fear in communications was initiated by research conduced in 1953 by Janis and Feshbach. They attempted to persuade three groups of fifty people to brush their teeth carefully and to adopt better oral hygiene. The first group of subjects listened to a horrifying presentation which dwelt upon the pain and secondary infections which could result from severe tooth decay. The third group received a factual account of results of tooth decay and recommendations on oral hygiene were made. In the intermediate group, the pain and diseases were made vivid and again recommendations for oral hygiene were made. A later follow-up study revealed that the high-fear appeal had produced a net change of only 8 per cent of people adopting the measures of improved oral hygiene, whereas the moderate and low-fear groups showed net changes of 22 per cent and 36 per cent. Many other investigations were able to substantiate the basic findings in areas as diverse as anti-smoking and vaccination for mumps (Haefner, 1956; Janis and Terwilliger, 1962; Krishner *et al.*, 1973).

Janis put forward defence-avoidance reaction as an explanation of the surprising finding that fear appeals were less effective. The defence-avoidance explanation maintains that fear produces anxiety and that anxiety is so unpleasant that people close their minds and ignore the issues which are causing the anxiety. In the mid 1960s, however, doubts about this hypothesis began to develop (Dabbs and Leventhal, 1966; Leventhal and Niles, 1965; Singer *et al.*, 1965). Dabbs and

Leventhal, for example, found that appeals involving high levels of fear about tetanus infections were more likely to lead students to obtain anti-tetanus injections. In practical terms these results suggest that a manager should play safe and avoid the use of fear appeals in his communications. If, however, he feels compelled to use an element of fear, he should make sure that it does not exceed moderate levels and that he also advocates a clear and credible way which his audience can follow in order to avoid the fearful circumstances depicted in his communication.

Managers often need to communicate in competitive situations. For example, as a result of the petrol crisis American car-makers in Detroit and British car-makers in Birmingham have showed increased interest in battery-driven vehicles. Because the traditional lead—acid batteries are unsuited to this application, battery manufacturers have developed alternative systems such as a nickel—zinc battery or a zinc—chloride battery. When the sales manager of a firm developing the zinc—chloride battery approaches any one of the major car manufacturers, he can be fairly sure that (around the same time) they will also be approached by the sales manager of a firm developing the alternative nickel—zinc battery. Competitive situations like this involve an extra decision: is it better to make your sales-pitch first or last? The theoretical arguments are finely balanced. The first side to make its case seizes the initiative and moulds the unformed climate of opinion in a way that is favourable. On the other hand, the side that makes its case last has the advantage that its arguments are fresh in the mind of the customer. The *primacy vs recency* conundrum was investigated by Miller and Campbell in 1959. Their conclusions are complicated and indicate that the delays between the various presentations and a decision play a vital role. In a situation where both presentations will be given to the same Board meeting in May, one in the morning and one in the afternoon, and a decision will be made at the following June meeting of the Board, a manager should manoeuvre to make his presentation in the morning. In other words, in a situation where the second argument immediately follows the first argument and then there is a substantial delay before a decision is made, the primacy effect is strongest. In a rather different case, where the first presentation is made to the Board at its May meeting, where the second presentation is made at the Board meeting in June and where the decision will be made later at the same June meeting, the manager should manoeuvre to be the last to make his case. In other words, where there is a delay between the first and second arguments and where a decision is made immediately after the second argument, the recency effect is strongest. In the balanced situations where both presentations and the decision are made without dealy at the same June meeting of the Board, or where other presentations are given to the May and June Boards and a decision is made at the July Board meeting, there seems to be no advantage in being either first or last.

A manager about to communicate with others needs to make a further decision. Should he concentrate on giving the facts and leaving the audience to *draw its own conclusions* or should he explicitly state the conclusions to be drawn? With an intelligent audience there is a temptation merely to present the facts in the belief that if an audience draws its own conclusions it is more likely to change its beliefs. Hovland and Mandell (1952) checked this conclusion by preparing two communications advocating the devaluation of the US dollar. The facts in both communications implied that the dollar should be devalued, but in the second communication this conclusion was explicitly stated. It was found that the communication explicitly drawing the conclusion was twice as effective in changing attitudes. Recently, however, Worchel and Cooper (1979) concluded that

> the weight of the evidence supports the view that messages whose conclusions are explicitly drawn are more persuasive than messages whose conclusions are left to the audience. However, messages of the latter type may be more effective *if* they can be comprehended and *if* the audience is sufficiently motivated to undertake the effort of arriving at the conclusions.

Channels of communication

Once a message has been encoded, the next stage is to transmit it via a *channel of communication*. Many different channels are available: lectures, meetings, gossip, memos, reports, letters, trade papers, videotapes. Each of the available channels has its own characteristics which may make it suitable for various types of message. One of the most important characteristics of a channel is its *capacity*. Managers, themselves, are channels of communication, and they differ in many respects. For example, they clear their intrays at different rates: one manager may be able to give comments on a report by his subordinate within a day of its submission, while another manager may take several weeks. Whatever channel is available, it is important not to overload the channel by exceeding its capacity. Whenever channel capacity is overloaded, the message is distorted and some of the meaning is lost. Indeed, the possible consequences of channel overload are well documented.

It is easy to imagine a manager acting as a communication channel and operating within his limits when suddenly things change so that he is bombarded with more information and his capacity is exceeded. In consequence this manager is subject to stress. (The personal impact of stress has been considered in greater detail in Chapter 5.) From the point of view of communication, when a manager has to react to a volume of information which exceeds his capacity, what can he do? The simplest response is to do nothing and *ignore* the additional information. In a more extreme case the overloaded manager can simply wash his hands of everything and take refuge at the golf course or in the bar. This reaction of escape is not very functional, and soon the organization will grind to a halt because a vital managerial role is not being performed. The reaction of escape or ignoring the overload information is seen only rarely, at moments of acute crisis and overload. Managers are more likely to respond to overload by *queuing information* and dealing with it in the order in which it arrived. This reaction ensures that no information is ignored, and if the overload situation is only temporary a long queue does not accumulate. In the long term, however, this strategy can be disastrous because while the manager is dealing with a long-standing, but trivial item, opportunities are lost because recent, important decisions await their turn.

Another frequent response to overload is a *reduction in the quality of response*. If he reacts in this way, a manager will spend less time checking his facts, less time making his decisions and less time preparing his arguments, and he will make many *ad hoc*, on-the-spot, decisions. Under this strategy he will inevitably make mistakes and then he will need to spend more time correcting his mistakes. Because he spends time correcting his mistakes, he has less time to deal with the incoming communications, so consequently he degrades the quality of his responses even further. Because reducing the quality of response quickly develops into a downward spiral, it is not a very satisfactory reaction to channel overload. So what should a manager do when he finds that his capacity to handle information is unequal to the demands made upon him?

Probably the best response is to *delegate* some of his work and in this way reduce the information he needs to process. In many cases, delegation is not possible and a manager should then *allot priorities* for dealing with matters that need his attention. Many management consultants point to the Pareto principle, also called 'the 80/20 rule', which suggests that 80 per cent of a manager's effectiveness is determined by the way that he handles 20 per cent of the most vital tasks. Provided that his method of allotting priorities is effective, all the important items will be handled efficiently and only the unimportant items will be left to form a queue.

Although we have dealt with the specific case of an overloaded manager as our channel of communication, the reactions of escape, queuing, loss of quality, delegation and prioritizing are general phenomena and can be seen in most overloaded communication channels — especially when people are involved in the communication channel. Indeed, it has been known for some time that people are rather inefficient channels of communication. One of the earliest investigations was conducted by Bartlett (1932). His investigations on serial reproduction involved telling a ghost story to one person, who then told the story to a second person, who then told the story to a third person, and so on. Bartlett's results are clearly relevant to many communication situations in industry. For example, the chief executive makes a decision and calls a meeting to inform the divisional executives. The divisional executives then call meetings and inform their factory managers. The factory managers call a meeting to inform their departmental heads. The departmental heads call a meeting to inform the supervisors and the supervisors call a meeting to inform the operatives. In this typical pattern of industrial communication the message is passed repeatedly through human communication channels.

Bartlett's findings show that as a message passes through the minds of several people it becomes severely distorted. Messages are not stored in a mechanical sense as they are on a tape recorder. Each person modifies the incoming message so that it will fit with his past experience and his other ideas. Then, when he needs to give the message to someone else, the modified message may be only partially remembered and it may be expressed inappropriately. Consequently, at the end of a chain of serial reproductions, the message will be heavily modified and may be very inaccurate. Bartlett noticed four common types of distortion: shortening, sharpening, levelling and irrelevant detail.

People's mental capacity is strictly limited. Research from a number of areas indicates that the average adult has a channel capacity of seven pieces of independent information at any given time. This estimate is remarkably constant from person to person. Most people will be able to process five pieces of simultaneous information and very few people will be able to process more than nine pieces. Indeed, this consistency gave rise to the saying 'The magic number, seven plus or minus two.' Because channel capacity is limited, people *shorten* long communications in order to fit the available capacity. In shortening the communication people tend to focus on what they believe to be the main point. This process is known as *sharpening* and it often involves the elimination of important contextual detail and important provisos. Because of this sharpening process, the chief executive's carefully worded, reasoned statement becomes a bald, blunt, provocative diktat by the time it reaches the ears of the operatives.

Often a communication contains several points which are more important than the other points. But by the time a message has passed from mouth to mouth, all points will be given equal prominence; this process is known as *levelling*. Although many details are lost in the shortening process, fairly dramatic but *irrelevant detail* can be inserted into the central issue of the communication and dramatically alter the message. For example, it is widely believed that the next industrial boom after the silicon chip will be the biogenetic boom where the genetics of bacteria are manipulated to produce organisms which will ferment in large industrial vats to devour waste products and produce single-cell protein material which can be used as animal feedstuff. Several large multinational companies already have pilot plants in operation. The product development manager of one of these companies called a meeting to review progress. It was a long and exhausting meeting. During the lunch recess the product development manager joked in a martini-induced mood of expansion that his expense account was under pressure and that perhaps they should be looking into ways to induce bacteria to produce cheap *pâté de foie gras*. The joke was an infinitesimal and inconsequential part of the day's proceedings, yet the irrelevant detail took on an immense importance. The message which filtered down to shop-floor level was that management was about to waste the company's investment capital in a genetic engineering project to develop bacteria that would convert the waste from paper pulp-making plants into caviar.

Although the human communication channel is not accurate, it is immensely persuasive and influential. A classic study by Katz and Lazarsfeld (1955) on *Personal Influence* showed that on most topics the comments made by our friends and relatives are much more influential than comments in the press, radio or advertising. They also discovered the existence of *opinion leaders*. In any group there are certain competent individuals who personify the values of their group and who have developed an expertise on a given topic. Very often these opinion leaders act as relay stations in the human communication system. They pay a great deal of attention to the media and current developments. They filter this information and then transmit what they see as the important information to the rank-and-file members of their group. Thus communication between managers and their work-force is rarely a direct, one-step approach. Almost always there are one or two levels of opinion leader to filter the message and there is at least a *two-step flow of information*.

One of the characteristics of an opinion leader is that he occupies a strategic position in the *communication network*. Leavitt (1951) investigated the ways in which certain types of communication 'networks' operate (see Figure 7.2). In the *star* communication network one person is at the centre of communications and the other members can only communicate with him. In the *chain* network communications pass from one person to another. In the *completely connected* network everyone is allowed to talk to everyone else.

These three basic networks can be modified to produce other forms, for example the *wheel* is formed by closing the chain and the *Y* is formed by combining a chain with a star. Leavitt and his co-writers found that the different communication patterns showed different characteristics. The star pattern is efficient at providing quick answers to simple problems; the person at the centre of the network tends to be satisfied with his role, while the other members of the group tend to the dissatisfied with theirs. On the other hand, in the case

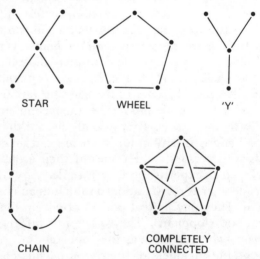

Figure 7.2   *Types of communication network*

of the completely connected pattern all members tend to be satisfied and complex problems are solved more effectively. But a group organized on this basis is often helpless at achieving simple objectives and solving simple problems. Leadership struggles often emerge in chain and Y communication networks. One of the implications of Leavitt's researches is that the communication network within a work unit should be chosen with care so that it matches the task at hand. In a research and development laboratory involving complex problems and where high morale is important, the completely connected network is probably most appropriate. In a purchasing department where the principal work is the application of routine procedures in a set sequence and where the work is easily checked, the star communication network may be most appropriate.

Earlier in this chapter it was noted that personal communication is often very influential and it was implied that written communication is *not* influential. These conclusions are supported by research by Hartman (1936) and Star and Hughes (1950). Hartman estimated that in the 1930s it took 10,000 leaflets to win between thirty and forty votes. In the early 1950s Star and Hughes found that in Cincinnati it took 150 broadcasts, 2,800 speeches to clubs and societies and almost 60,000 brochures to produce a 3 per cent improvement in the population's knowledge of the veto mechanism in the United Nations. Much more recently Chaiken and Eagly (1976) established that, for simple messages, videotape messages were 63 per cent more effective then written messages, while audiotape messages were 28 per cent more effective. For complex messages the results were quite different: video messages were 26 per cent *less* effective than written messages and audio messages were 51 per cent *less* effective.

This section on channels of communication has dealt with the problems of exceeding channel capacity, the human mind as a communication channel, communication networks and the efficiency of written and other methods of communication. Before leaving the topic of communication channels, it is essential to consider the concept of *noise*. In communication terms, noise means events that distort the message put into the communication channel. The noise may be the traditional auditory noise. Obviously, if the noise level is so high that the recipient cannot hear the message, it blocks communication, but in a much milder form, where the noise is merely distracting, it can help the communicator (Haslett, 1976; Keating and Brock, 1974). It seems that when people communicate to us we mentally argue against their point of view. Mild distraction interferes with the process of counter-argument, allowing the original message to get through.

A rather different type of noise in a communication channel consists of contradictory signals that confuse the recipient. A contradiction between the verbal and the non-verbal messages is a frequent cause of this type of confusion, and it is frequently seen in many industrial contexts. For example, many managers actively dislike disciplining subordinates and very few managers have received any training in this demanding activity. Because they are nervous, a large minority of managers are tempted to adopt a very casual approach. Thus the subordinate being disciplined receives non-verbal messages of an over-relaxed posture and smiling and friendly gestures. The general approach may have an affectation of spontaneity: 'Oh, by the way, I ought to mention that we are concerned at your time-keeping record.' The disciplinary point may be wrapped up in tangential and over-polite language. In a situation of this kind the non-verbal message is likely to override the verbal message and the interviewees will feel that the management has no real concern for punctuality of its employees.

Noise is likely to occur in almost every type of communication channel, and a good communicator needs to take action to combat the noise. The most effective way of counteracting the effects of communication noise is to increase the amount of redundancy contained in the message. Redundancy is the amount of repetition which the message contains and it is useful in overcoming the effects of communication noise because it is highly unlikely that the noise distorts the same part of the message each time it is repeated, and so the receiver is able to piece together the correct message. Redundancy is a well-established procedure in the transmission of data between computers. For example, one international bank regularly transmits information on the accounts held on the computer at its London branch to the computer at the New York head office via telephone lines and satellites. Because of the possibility of noise in the system, each set of data is transmitted twice and the computer in New York will only inscribe the data into its main memory bank if an identical message is received on both occasions. In this case the 100 per cent redundancy achieved by transmitting the message twice is an essential safeguard against distortion. In practically all human communication redundancy is essential and it is achieved either by repeating the message in a single channel, or using parallel channels such as 'phoning an order and then sending written confirmation'.

Receiving and decoding commnuciations

In a sense a manager has little control over how accurately a message is received and decoded. The reception and decoding links in the communication chain lie within the recipients, and it is *their* personality and *their* characteristics which are most important. Not only are these characteristics difficult to manipulate, they are also extremely numerous and include the processes of learning, perception and motivation dealt with in earlier chapters.

One important characteristic of the recipient is his present attitudes, because they set the *latitude of acceptance* and the *latitude of rejection*. The latitude of acceptance is the range of arguments which the recipient feels are valid and reasonable. Arguments which are outside the range of acceptance will be pooh-poohed and rejected out of hand. Clearly it is important to work within the latitude of acceptance but the difficulty lies in determining the width of the latitude. Research suggests that when the message involves a topic that is of deep concern to the recipient or where he already holds extreme views, the latitude of acceptance will be fairly narrow and it will be necessary to proceed in small stages. On the other hand, if the recipient is already inclined towards your point of view, his latitude of acceptance will be wide and you will be able to obtain the maximum favourable shift in his viewpoint by staging extreme arguments in your favour.

The concept of *cognitive dissonance* is closely related to the latitude of acceptance. Cognitive dissonance states that people try to be consistent in their attitudes and behaviour. When they are inconsistent, people experience dissonance and they will try to reduce this dissonance by changing either their beliefs or actions. For example, a worker who is induced to mislead another into believing that a repetitive operation is exciting will come to believe that the boring task is genuinely exciting. Most people feel that they are good guys, but since only bad guys mislead fellow workers, most people will experience dissonance. The dissonance is removed by a simple change of attitude towards the boring job. After this change of opinion they will be telling the 'truth' and this is consonent with the behaviour of a good guy. It is interesting to note that this kind of attitude change only occurs when the worker is not subjected to any pressure to make him mislead his co-workers. If he is offered a king's ransom as a reward for his deception, there will be no attitude change, because there is no dissonance — after all, even good guys have their price!

Cognitive dissonance is also relevant to the *credibility of the communicator* since if a communicator is perceived as being credible, dissonance will occur if his message is rejected. Early research by Hovland *et al.* (1953) cast doubt on the longer-term effect of this hypothesis and Wiess Hovland *et al.* (1953) found that a highly credible speaker was more effective than a speaker with low credibility when the audience was tested immediately after the communication. However, when the audience was tested four weeks later, the effect of the highly credible speaker had decreased and the effect of the speaker with low credibility had increased, so that, long term, there was little difference between their effectiveness. These changes were termed the 'sleeper effect'. Subsequent research has failed to replicate the effect (Cook and Flay, 1978; Gillig and Greenwald, 1974; Eagly and Himmelfarb, 1978); indeed, many studies have shown that if the recipient of a communication perceives the communicator in a credible light, the message has more influence. A very wide variety of characteristics such as speed of speaking, vocabulary, clothing, grooming and non-verbal cues have been found to influence the recipient's view of the communicator.

Taking action

Even when a message is carefully encoded, transmitted via a perfect channel and then faultlessly decoded, the effort will have been wasted unless the recipient takes action. Until recently many introductory psychology courses included a discussion of the 'La Piere effect', which indicates that attitudes do not affect actions and this implied that many communications designed to alter attitudes were a waste of time. La Piere (1934) wrote to restaurateurs in the USA explaining that he and his Chinese friends wanted to book a table for a special celebration. La Piere used the restaurateurs' replies as an index of their attitudes towards Chinese people. A little later he actually turned up at the restaurants with his Chinese friends and was able to compare the attitudes with the way the restaurateurs behaved. He concluded that there was no link between attitudes and actions: restaurateurs who refused the reservations nearly always served the 'Chinese party' when they arrived. In recent years, La Piere's study has been heavily criticized — judging attitudes from replies to a request to reserve a table is not a good method of measuring attitudes and the evaluation of the actions of the restaurateurs was also crude and La Piere's results may have been an artefact of his inadequate methods. Indeed, recent research indicates that there is at least a moderate relationship between attitudes and behaviour (Ajzen and Fishbein, 1977; Kelman, 1974).

An example of more recent research is the work by Ashton and Warr (1976). The study was carried out in the UK cities of Sheffield and Birmingham and questionnaires were handed out to drivers as they entered one of the cities' car-parks. Drivers wearing seat belts were handed one version of the questionnaire and non-users of seat belts were handed a slightly different version of the questionnaire. Both versions of the questionnaire measured the same two factors: attitudes towards wearing seat belts, and anxiety about having an accident. The major results indicate that there is a very strong relationship between attitudes towards seat belts and wearing seat belts among drivers who were *not* anxious about accidents. On the other hand, the relationship between attitudes and behaviour was much lower when drivers were anxious.

A possible explanation of these results is that anxiety tends to destroy the relationship between attitudes and behaviour. It is interesting to note that this explanation may also be relevant to the discussion of fear appeals earlier in this chapter. It may be argued that fear appeals arouse anxiety and the anxiety then destroys the link between attitudes and behaviour.

Once the link between attitudes and actions has been established, the question arises, how can this link be maximized? One clear suggestion is that communications should deal with *specific attitudes* and *specific behaviour*. It is generally accepted that general appeals for general improvements are not very effective (Weigel, Vernon and Tognacci, 1974).

Another suggestion involves using the *thin edge of the wedge* technique and first using a communication which asks for only a small change in behaviour. Subsequent communications can then ask for larger changes. For example, in one experiment by Freedman and Frazer (1966) 56 per cent of people agreed to comply with a large request when they had previously complied with a much smaller request, whereas only 17 per cent of people complied when they were faced with an outright request.

A third suggestion for improving the link between attitudes and behaviour is to harness the *social pressures* exerted by the groups to which people belong. The functioning of groups is discussed in more detail in Chapter 8, but the use of commitment and the importance of groups in the change process are particularly relevant here. Indeed, it has been said that attitudes and group pressures are the two most important factors which determine the way we behave.

This chapter has attempted to convey the complexity of each stage of the human communication process. The importance of communication means that it pervades every area of social and organizational activity and that there is hardly a facet of managerial life which does not involve communication of some type. Because communication is both complex and commonplace, it may be taken for granted, and so it is apposite to end this chapter with a warning note from Nichols (1962), who studied communication efficiency in 100 separate organizations:

there is a tremendous loss of information — 37 per cent — between the Board of Directors and the vice-Presidential level. General supervisors got 56 per cent of the information; plant managers 40 per cent; and general foremen received only 30 per cent of what had been transmitted downward to them. An average of only 20 per cent of the communication sent downward through the five levels of management finally gets to the worker level.

References for Chapter 7

Ajzen, I. and Fishbein, M. (1977) 'Attitude—Behaviour Relationships: A Theoretical Analysis and Review of Empirical Research', *Psychological Bulletin*, 84, 888—918.

Ashton, S. and Warr, P. (1976) 'Drivers' Use of Seat Belts as a Function of Attitude and Anxiety', *British Journal of Social and Clinical Psychology*, 15, 251—5.

Bartlett, F. C. (1932) *Remembering — An Experimental and Social Study*, Cambridge University Press, Cambridge, England.

Calder, B. J. Insko, C. A. and Yandrell, B. (1974) 'The Relation of Cognitive and Memorial Processes to Persuasion in a Simulated Jury Trial: *Journal of Applied Social Psychology*, 4, 62—93.

Chaiken, S. and Eagly, A. H. (1976) 'Communication Modality as a Determinant of Message Persuasiveness and Message Comprehensibility', *Journal of Personality and Social Psychology*, 34, 605—14.

Cook, T. D. and Flay, B. R. (1978) 'The Persistence of Experimentally Induced Change: An Evaluative Review', *Advances in Experimental Social Psychology*.

Dabbs, J. M. and Leventhal, H. (1966) 'Effects of Varying the Recommendations in a Fear Arousing Communication', *Journal of Personality and Social Psychology*, 4, 525—31.

Eagly, A. H. (1974) 'Comprehensibility of Persuasive Arguments as a Determinant of Opinion Change', *Journal of Personality and Social Psychology*, 29, 758—73.

Eagly, A. H. and Himmelfarb, S. (1978) 'Attitudes and Opinions', *Annual Review of Psychology*, 29, 517—54.

Freedman, J. L. and Frazer, S. (1966) 'Compliance without Pressure: The Foot in the Door Technique', *Journal of Personality and Social Phychology*, 4, 195—202.

Gillig, P. M. and Greenwald, A. G. (1974) 'Is it Time to Lay the Sleeper Effect to Rest?', *Journal of Personality and Social Psychology*, 29, 132–9.

Grundner, T. M. (1978) 'Two Formulas for Determining the Readability of Subject Consent Forms', *American Psychologist*, August, 773–5.

Haefner, D. (1956) 'Some Effects of Guilt Arousing Fear and Fear Arousing Persuasive Communications on Opinion Change', unpublished doctoral dissertation, University of Rochester.

Hartman, W. W. A. (1936) 'A Field Experiment on the Comparative Effectiveness of "Emotional" and "Rational" Political Leaflets in Determining Election Results', *Journal of Abnormal and Social Psychology*, 31, 99–114.

Haslett, D. M. (1976) 'Distracting Stimuli: Do They Elicit or Inhibit Counter Argumentation and Attitude Shift?', *European Journal of Social Psychology*, 6, 81–94.

Hovland, C. I. and Mandel, W. (1952) 'An Experimental Comparison of Conclusion-drawing by the Communicator and the Audience', *Journal of Abnormal and Social Psychology*, 47, 581–8.

Hovland, C. I., Janis, I. L. and Kelley, H. H. (1953) *Communication and Persuasion*, Yale University Press, New Haven, Conn.

Insko, C. A., Lind, E. A. and La Tour, S. (1976) 'Persuasion, Recall and Thoughts', *Reports of Research in Social Psychology*, 7, 66–78.

Janis, I. L. and Feshbach, S. (1953) 'Effects of Fear-arousing Communications', *Journal of Abnormal and Social Psychology*, 48, 78–92.

Janis, I. L. and Terwilliger, R. (1962) 'An Experimental Study of Psychological Resistance to Fear Arousing Communications', *Journal of Abnormal and Social Psychology*, 65, 403–10.

Katz, E. and Lazarsfeld, P. F. (1955) *Personal Influence: The Part Played by People in the Flow of Mass Communication*, The Free Press, New York.

Keating, J. P. and Brock, J. C. (1974) 'Acceptance of Persuasion and the Inhibition of Counter Argumentation under Various Distraction Tasks', *Journal of Experimental Social Psychology*, 10, 301–9.

Kelman, H. G. (1974) 'Attitudes are Alive and Well and Gainfully Employed in the Sphere of Action', *American Psychologist*, 29, 310–24.

Krishner, H. P., Darley, S. A. and Darley, J. M. (1973) 'Fear Provoking Recommendations: Intentions to Take Preventive Actions and Actual Preventive Actions', *Journal of Personality and Social Psychology*, 26, 2, 301–8.

La Piere, R. T. (1934) 'Attitudes vs Actions', *Social Forces*, 13, 230–7.

Leavitt, H. J. (1951) 'Some Effects of Certain Communication Patterns on Group Performance', *Journal of Abnormal and Social Psychology*, 46, 38–50.

Leventhal, H. and Niles, P. (1965) 'Persistence of Influence for Varying Durations of Exposure to Threat Stimuli', *Psychological Reports*, 16, 223–33.

Miller, N. and Campbell, D. (1959) 'Recency and Primacy in Persuasion as a Function of the Timing of Speeches and Measurements', *Journal of Abnormal and Social Psychology*, 59, 1–9.

Nichols, R. G. (1962) 'Listening is Good Business', *Management of Personnel Quarterly*, Winter.

Singer, R. P. *et al.* (1965) 'Effects of Fear Arousing Communications on Attitude, Change and Behavior', unpublished Ph.D thesis, University of Connecticut.

Star, S. A. and Hughes, H. M. (1950) 'Report on an Educational Campaign: The Cincinnati Plan for the United Nations', *American Journal of Sociology*, 55, 1–12.

Weigel, R. H., Vernon, D. T. A. and Tognacci, L. N. (1974) 'Specificity of the Attitude as a Determinant of Attitude–Behaviour Congruence', *Journal of Personality and Social Psychology*, 30, 724–8.

Worchel, S. and Cooper, J. (1979) *Understanding Social Psychology*, Dorsey Press, Homewood, Ill.

8
Working in Groups

Probably the most used and abused adjective which managers use about meetings with groups of colleagues at work is 'bloody':

> I've had one hell of a day — one bloody meeting after another.

> If only we could cut down the number of bloody meetings we have, I might be able to get some work done.

These statements, and sentiments like them, indicate the level of frustration and anger which many managers feel about the apparent ineffectiveness of the group activities in which they are involved. Furthermore, there is a feeling that meetings are an intrusion into the 'real' work which a manager is employed to perform. Yet a survey by Mintzberg (1973), which was mentioned in Chapter 2, showed that managers spend 69 per cent of their time in scheduled and unscheduled meetings which are crucial to the effective functioning of the organization: meetings within his own department to check progress, set objectives and solve problems; meetings with managers of other departments to set long-term strategies and co-ordinate operations; and meetings with managers from other organizations. An understanding of basic group processes and the development of skills in working in groups is therefore essential to a manager's personal effectiveness, and ultimately the success of his organization.

The purpose of this chapter is to examine some of the basic behavioural processes which occur in a group, some of the causes of frustration and satisfaction which members can gain from participation in groups, and some of the ways in which managers can develop skills in being more effective group members.

The basic problems confronting any work group

Any formally constituted group in an organization is brought together to complete a particular task or achieve a particular organizational objective. At one level the task may be the assembly of the components of a communication satellite, at a second level in the organization the task may be the co-ordination of the activities of the buying, production and sales functions, and at a third level the task may be the appraisal of the current state of the organization and planning for future developments in communication technology. The *task* provides the group's *raison d'être*, and the success with which the group fulfils its task will be one important measure of its effectiveness. The task therefore prescribes the job *content* or the required output from the group – in other words, *what* the job is all about.

But an understanding of the content of a particular task does not help us understand completely what is going on within the group. In order to gain more insight we need to examine the *processes* by which the group achieves its task. We need to look at *how* the group is operating, and to do this we need to look at the behaviour of the group members. The way in which group members relate to one another provides us with another measure of the group's effectiveness, i.e. the extent to which the group *maintains* itself as a cohesive, functioning unit. It involves the satisfaction members feel about their participation in the group. The quotations given at the beginning of this chapter reveal strong feelings of dissatisfaction with the group, and it would suggest that the group is being ineffective in meeting the needs of its members.

The two basic problems which confront any work group are therefore:

1. To achieve the *task* for which it has been set up.
2. To *maintain* itself as a cohesive unit so that its members feel part of a team.

Bales (1951) suggests that these two processes are separate and are mutually antagonistic. When a group is working on task activities it is creating problems for itself in remaining as a team. In the cut and thrust of argument, debate and disagreement, which are part of the life of any working group, the group is generating forces towards a fragmentation of the group. To overcome this fragmentation the group must devote some of its energy towards maintaining itself and repairing relationships between its members.

Equally when the group is working on maintenance issues such as resolving conflicts which have arisen during the task, it cannot sustain its progress towards its task objective, and, indeed, it will be incapable of working as an effective unit. The full implications of this suggestion will be considered when the stages of development of a group are examined, and the use of team-building programmes discussed.

Of course, not every group which forms in the work-place is assembled to perform some organizational task. People have social needs which they bring with them to work, and because of these needs spontaneous friendships develop with other colleagues. People who spend their lunch or tea breaks together, to discuss sport or the state of the nation, are examples of these *informal groups*.

Informal groups may not perform an organizational task but their importance to the organization should not be underestimated. Informal groups influence the attitudes of their members and, as Chapter 7 explained, attitudes strongly influence actions. Second, informal groups produce informal communication networks or 'grapevine' which can transmit rumours or work against the formal communication system.

To summarize, Figure 8.1 illustrates how a group task can be viewed in terms of its *content*, or *what* the task is that the group has to achieve, and in terms of its *process*, or *how* the group sets about achieving the task. The process is concerned with how group members behave in relation to one another, and this behaviour can be directed towards solving task problems or towards solving maintenance problems.

What is a 'group'?

So far the terms 'group' and 'team' have been used fairly ex-

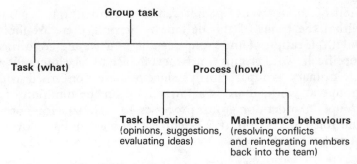

Figure 8.1 *A taxonomy of group activities*

tensively without any attempt being made to define what is meant by these terms. In particular we need to examine what makes a 'group' different from a 'collection of people' or a 'crowd' who happen to be in the same place at the same time. Indeed, some writers (e.g. Allport, 1924) have questioned whether such things as 'groups' as entities exist at all, or whether one can understand what is happening in a group in terms of what is happening to the individuals who comprise that group. Shaw (1971) considers these issues in some depth and examines the different emphases which group theorists have given to the definition of a group. He suggests that the motivation of group members to achieve certain goals may account for the *formation* of a group; group members may *perceive* themselves to be a group; a group may become organized in terms of the formation and development of roles and norms as a *consequence* of group processes, but the defining characteristic of a group is in terms of the interaction and interdependence of its members. Shaw (1971) offers the following definition of a group:

> A group is defined as two or more persons who interact with one another so that each person influences and is influenced by each other person.

A number of implications arise from this definition. The first is that a group is limited in size. In order for meaningful interaction to occur between members of a group an upper limit of about twenty people can be construed to be a group within the terms of this definition. Second, there are limits on the location of the group members, as we are concerned specifically with groups which meet in face-to-face interaction, i.e. primary groups. Finally, since we are concerned with groups at work, there is a lower limit on the duration of a group. In order for group processes to stabilize, for norms and roles to develop, it is essential that a group meets over a period of time.

The dynamics of the relationships between group members

Shaw (1971) suggests that the crucial defining characteristics of a group are interaction, interdependence and mutual influence between group members. One way of understanding the dynamics of the interaction and interdependency of group members is in terms of the satisfaction of the needs of each member by the other members of the group. This means that group members bring to the group certain needs which will have to be satisfied by the other participants in order for them to remain in the groups. These include the need to achieve the goals for which the group was set up, and also the social needs which members bring to the group as part of their personality. Of course, differences in personality reflect differences in the social needs of members. Both achievement motivation and social needs were discussed in more detail in Chapter 4.

Different members have different needs for certain styles of interaction with other group members. It may be that these differing needs are compatible, so that the satisfaction of one member's social needs leads to the satisfaction of another member's social needs. In this case there is interdependence of social need satisfaction. On the other hand, it may be that the needs are incompatible, in which case the group has the problem of finding a style of interaction which will optimize the satisfaction of all members' social needs. The dynamic of the interaction between members can be seen as members psychologically wrestling with one another to develop a style of interaction which will satisfy their own needs. This process has been graphically described by Schutz (1966) as the *interpersonal underworld*. Schutz suggests that in any work-group, beneath the overt task behaviour, there is an interpersonal struggle occurring between members of a group. The struggle is an attempt by each individual to find an acceptable level of interaction with the others on three crucial dimensions of interpersonal behaviour. The three dimensions are:

1. *Inclusion* – the extent to which a person feels *in* or *out* of the group.
2. *Control* – the extent to which a person feels *top* or *bottom* in the power hierarchy.
3. *Affection* – the extent to which relations will be *close* or *distant* in terms of warmth and intimacy.

The social needs members bring to the group can be thought of in terms of the extent they *express* needs to include, control or give affection to other group members, and the extent to which they *want* to be included, controlled and given affection by other members of the group. Schutz has developed a short questionnaire which attempts to measure the extent to which members express and want these needs, and this is called the Fundamental Interpersonal Relations Orientation– Behaviour (FIRO–B). He assumes that what we want from others on these dimensions is independent of our needs to express inclusion, control and affection to others. So it is possible, for example, for one manager to express a need to control others and want to be controlled by them, or for someone else to want to control others and not be controlled by them.

Within this framework the possibilities for compatible and incompatible interactions between group members can be seen. Schutz identifies two different types of interaction compatibility. The first type of compatibility is *interchange compatibility*, in which one person's needs are matched by similar needs in other members. Interchange compatibility occurs, for example, with the inclusion and affection dimensions, where one person's needs to express and want inclusion and affection are matched by similar needs in other group members. Interchange incompatibility occurs when one individual's needs for inclusion or affection are not satisfied by other members' desire to include or show him affection.

The second type of compatibility is *originator compatibility*, in which the needs of one person complement the needs of another. For example, on the control dimension there is compatibility when one person's desire to control is complemented by other members' desire to be controlled. Originator incompatibility occurs when two or more members have a high need to control others, and will result in a leadership crisis or power struggle within the group. Similarly, originator incompatibility also occurs where all members of a group have a desire to be controlled but no one wants to control the others. In this case the group has a power or influence vacuum.

Schutz (1966) has suggested that by the selection of members of a group based on FIRO—B profiles it is possible to create a group with compatible needs and whose members can work together harmoniously and productively. However, for many work-groups membership is based on skill, expertise or role within the organization, and not on FIRO—B profiles. In such cases highly compatible teams arise largely by chance. For most groups of managers there are incompatibilities which might initially create problems within the group. The problems then have to be worked through and resolved before the group can develop into a cohesive and productive unit.

The development of a group

Many theorists (Bion, 1961, Bennis and Shepard, 1956; Gibb, 1964; Schein, 1969; Schutz, 1966; and Tuckman, 1965) have attempted to understand how a group develops over time. In doing so they attempt to identify how the group changes from its early unclear, ambiguous and often unpredictable meetings, to the later meetings when the interaction between members has stabilized and norms, roles and behaviour patterns have developed. These theorists have used different frameworks to understand these changes in a group. But one unifying theme which is shared by them all is that the develop-

ment of a group follows a traumatic path. Within their
theories these writers have used concepts like 'crises', 'issues',
'concerns', 'conflicts', 'dilemmas', to describe the progress of
development of a typical group. Group development is therefore not seen as a smooth progression from an unintegrated
collection of people in its early stages to an integrated, cohesive, productive team as the group matures. The nature of
of these 'crises' can be viewed through Schutz's framework as
an incompatibility in members' needs. As the interaction
within the group progresses, some members will feel that
some of their preferred styles of interaction clash with other
members' preferred styles. They may feel that their behaviour
is going to be too closely controlled, or that others want an
interaction that is too close for comfort. The issues which
emerge in this way will probably be different for each individual, but it is essential that these issues are resolved if the
group is to develop as an effective team. The major problem
the group has to resolve is to find a method of interacting
which most members find comfortable. In this way the group
will develop norms, or implicit rules, about how they will
interact together which are shared and agreed by all members.

Phases of group development

A number of the theorists mentioned earlier have suggested
that a group develops through a fairly predictable sequence
of phases. Each phase has at its core a particular issue or concern, which the group must at least partially resolve before
moving on to the next phase when it works on a different
issue. Schutz has suggested that the first concern confronting
members in their early meetings is the issue of *inclusion* – to
what extent do I feel part of this group? When some resolution
of this concern has been achieved the group concentrates on
the issue of *control* – do I feel comfortable with the amount
of influence I have in this group? When this is resolved the
group concentrates on *affection* – do I feel comfortable with
the level of intimacy in the group? When this is resolved the
group recycles on to the inclusion issue again. With each cycle
the group reiterates the same sequence of phases in developing

a solution to these issues which the group members feel more and more comfortable with.

A slightly different approach is taken by Schein (1969), who suggests that the early meetings of any group are characterized by 'self-orientated' behaviour from most members. The term 'self-orientated' indicates that the members are initially more concerned about their own needs, and in particular their own identity and their own roles within the group, than they are about other members of the group or the group functioning as a total unit.

The principal self-orientated concerns identified by Schein are:

1. *Identity* — who and what am I to be in this group?
2. *Control* and *influence* — will I be able to control and influence others?
3. *Needs* and *goals* — will the group goals include my own needs?
4. *Acceptance* and *intimacy* — will I be liked and accepted by the group?

This initial self-orientated phase is characterized by high conflict and a rapid switching from one issue to another as different members raise their own particular concerns. There is little evidence of listening to other group members and offering help or support to them. At this stage very little attention is paid to the group task. Schein suggests that every group goes through this phase and that it cannot be short-circuited. Resolution of this phase is achieved when the members feel relatively comfortable with the identities they have managed to establish within the group and they feel content with the influence they have and the depth of intimacy they have managed to establish. It is at this point that the group can now begin to get down to work.

In this second phase, where the group begins to work on its task, Schein offers a classification of behaviour very similar to that of Bales (mentioned earlier). He sees contributions to the group being offered in the task or maintenance areas and offers the classification of roles which members might take up shown in Table 8.1.

Tuckman (1965), after an extensive review of the literature on group development, proposed a four-phase model of

Table 8.1   *Classification of members' roles within groups*

Task	Maintenance
Initiating activities	Harmonizing
Opinion-seeking	Compromizing
Opinion-giving	Gatekeeping (allowing members to have their say)
Information-seeking	Encouraging
Information-giving	Diagnosing
Clarifying task issues	Norm-setting
Elaborating	Norm-testing
Sumarizing	
Consensus-testing	

Source: E. H. Schein (1969) *Process Consultation: Its Role in Organization Development*, Addison-Wesley, Reading, Mass.

group development which can act as a useful summary of what has been said so far.

1. *Forming.* This stage is characterized by members experiencing uncertainty and anxiety. This anxiety is resolved by members testing out and finding an orientation to the situation both in terms of the task, and in terms of what is acceptable behaviour within the group. Guidance is often sought from the leader to resolve some of the uncertainties in this situation.

2. *Storming.* This stage is characterized by conflict and internal dissent between members. There is often resentment about the task which has been set for the group and the roles which each member feels he or she is being encouraged to adopt.

3. *Norming.* This stage is characterized by feelings of cohesion and satisfaction in being part of a 'group'. The group develops norms or standards of behaviour which are generally accepted. The task is approached in a realistic fashion and ideas and information openly exchanged.

4. *Performing.* This stage is characterized by a central concern with the completion of the task. The interpersonal
obstacles to dealing with the task have now been resolved,
and the roles and norms which have been established
in the previous stage enable the group to complete its
task successfully.

Group norms

We have seen that one of the crucial processes of a group's
development is the setting of group norms. A group norm is
an implicit rule, shared by the members of a group, which
identifies behaviour which is acceptable and expected from
each of the group members. By definition, norms also define
behaviour which is unacceptable from group members, and
can be seen as setting the limits within which a group member
can behave without upsetting others. If a group member
violates a norm, then he must expect some form of pressure
or sanction in order to bring him back into line. The pressures
and sanctions placed on deviants will be discussed in more
detail later in this chapter.

Group norms tend to develop around issues of central
importance to the group and have described by Schein (1974)
as *pivotal norms.* Cartwright and Zander (1968) suggest that
norms in general can be seen as serving the following functions
for the group:

1. *Task.* Certain norms develop about the ways in which
the group will accomplish its goals.
2. *Maintenance.* Other norms emerge which help the group
to remain as a cohesive unit.
3. *Defining relations with others.* These norms indicate
how group members should respond to significant figures
in the group's social environment, e.g. the boss, or other
departments in the same organisation.
4. *Help members test the validity of their opinions.* We live
in an uncertain world, and if other members of a group
agree with our opinions, there is some evidence that our
beliefs may be valid.

One of the most famous and seminal studies on the influence
of group norms on the behaviour of workers was conducted

as part of the research programme in the bank wiring room in the Hawthorne Plant of Western Electric by Roethlisberger and Dickson (1939). The group was involved in wiring up and soldering banks of telephone relays. The group was supervised by one supervisor, and their work checked by two inspectors. The main details of this study have been summarised by Schein (1972), but for our purposes we can look at some of the norms which developed in terms of the categories suggested by Cartwright and Zander.

(1) *Task*. A norm of 'a fair day's work for a fair day's pay' emerged. The production figure of 6,000 units satisfied management and because of the operation of a base rate and group bonus scheme the same production rate also satisfied the men's need for money. Deviants who produced more than this figure were known as 'rate busters' and social pressure was put on them to reduce output. Other deviants who produced less than 6,000 units but still received a share of the group bonus were known as 'chiselers' and pressure was put on them to increase output. The figure of 6,000 units was well below the production level which each worker might have produced if he had attempted to maximize his earnings. Schein comments: 'In that the men were colluding to produce at a level below their capacity, these norms taken together amounted to what has been called "restriction of output".'

(2) *Maintenance*. Within the total group two cliques of workers had become established. These cliques were mainly based on where the workers were located in the bank wiring room: one clique at the front of the room, and one at the back. Each clique had its own particular style of interaction and special games, which showed the contrasting ways in that the cliques maintained their own cohesiveness.

(3) *Defining relations with others*. The operatives had also developed a norm about the way in which those in formal authority, the supervisor and two inspectors, should behave. To quote Schein, the norm was 'those in authority must not act officious or take advantage of their authority position'. The supervisor and one inspector complied with this norm by letting the men trade jobs and report their own level of production. But the other inspector attempted to use his formal authority. The operatives played tricks on him and

made his life very unpleasant. Eventually he asked to be transferred from the department.

(4) *Help members test the validity of their opinions.* One of the two cliques tended to have a much higher rate of output than the other, and the members of the high-output clique regarded themselves as having higher status than the low-output clique. Since members of the high-output clique shared a similar attitude towards the low-output clique, there was support within the clique for the high opinions which the individuals had about their own status, and also for the low opinion they shared about the low-output clique. The support of other members of the high-output group therefore gave 'validity' to the view that the low-output group were 'chiselers'. As a consequence the high-output group nagged the low-output group into producing more. The low-output group, who felt insulted, decided to retaliate by lowering production even further. The opinion that the high-status group had, and the way they behaved towards the low-status clique, therefore caused or created the validity for that opinion and became what is known as a *self-fulfilling prophesy*. The self-fulfilling prophesy is a common phenomenon throughout the field of organizational behaviour — it was also mentioned in the context of individual perceptions in Chapter 6. It is also typical of the research conducted on inter-group conflict in which each group develops a positive stereotype about itself and a negative stereotype of the other group.

Not all norms are of course pivotal or central to the life of a group. Other *relevant norms* (Schein, 1974) can develop. These norms relate to aspects of behaviour which are not central to the existence of the group. The style of dress which a group typically adopts, or the amount of allowable 'bad' language, may become established as relevant norms. Violations of these norms may cause a few raised eyebrows, but they would not lead to the same expressions of disapproval which the violation of a pivotal norm would create.

Conformity to group norms

In a laboratory study of conformity Asch (1951) has demonstrated that a number of experimental subjects will make what they know to be an incorrect judgement of the length of a line after they have been influenced by listening to six other members of their group unanimously make the same incorrect judgement. They did not know, however, that the six other members of the group had been instructed earlier by the experimenter to give the same incorrect response. The subjects were therefore conforming to the group opinion despite the evidence of their own senses. Cartwright and Zander point out that this conformity occurs even within a group of strangers who were unlikely to meet again and where the judgement was of little intrinsic value to the subject. They suggest that 'one would surely expect these pressures [to conform] to be even stronger in more natural settings and with respect to matters having greater significance for the participants'.

In most groups, then, there are very strong pressures to conform to the group view, particularly where that view is seen as being the core to the existence of the group. Why is this? What are the pressures which act on people to make them conform? Deutsch and Gerrard (1955) suggest that there are two different types of pressure towards conformity in groups: *informational* pressure and *normative* pressure.

Informational pressure arises because we can never be completely sure that our beliefs and attitudes are absolutely correct. However, we can check if other people believe them. We thus use other people to validate our opinions, and if our opinions or beliefs about the 'facts' disagree with the majority view then this is evidence that we should modify our view and conform to the majority view.

Normative pressure arises because we want to be liked and accepted by other people, and we know that we put their acceptance of us at risk if we disagree with them on some issue of importance. We know that if we disagree, we still have to justify our view, to stand out as different from the other members of the group. Ultimately we know that if the differences are important and irreconcilable, we may have to leave the group, or be rejected by the group. So we conform in order to be acceptable to other members of the group.

Deviancy in groups

Of course, we realize that not every member of a group consistently conforms to group norms. Indeed, there seem to be some people who relish 'playing the devil's advocate' in a group, and who persistently violate group norms. Willis and Hollander (1964) have suggested that there are three basic types of response which an individual may show to normative pressures in a group (see Figure 8.2). The first two can be seen as opposite poles of a continuum of *conformity* to *anti-conformity*. Both responses are of course bound inexorably to the group norms. The conformist relies upon the group norms to structure his behaviour, whereas the anti-conformist rebels against group norms, but the individual's response is dependent upon the norms indicating what is required — so that they can do the opposite.

In contrast, the third reaction which members might show to group norms is that of *independence*. The person exhibiting the independence is aware of group norms but does not feel under strong pressure either to conform or rebel against the norms. He will take his own view of what is appropriate and this may involve some conformity or violation of group norms. Individuals may have a tendency to adopt one particular type of response to group norms persistently, but in general most members of a group will be at times conformist, at times anti-conformist and at other times act independently of the group norm.

Of course, different groups will be more or less tolerant of the deviant in their midst. But eventually in every group the member who persistently violates a group will come under increasing pressure to conform. This pressure is shown in

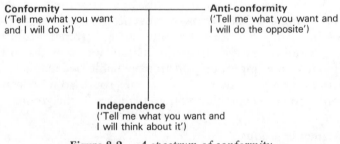

Conformity — Anti-conformity
('Tell me what you want   ('Tell me what you want and
and I will do it')   I will do the opposite')

Independence
('Tell me what you want and
I will think about it')

Figure 8.2   *A spectrum of conformity*

changes in communication to the deviant, and the communication changes in two ways, in terms of its *quantity* and in terms of its *quality*.

Schacter (1951) has shown that immediately after a deviant's view has been made public to the group there is a very rapid increase in the communication to him. The deviant becomes the focus of attention for both verbal and non-verbal interaction. The other members of the group are looking at him, and addressing most of their remarks to him. If he persists in his deviant view, this communication reaches a peak and then rapidly declines. The decline in communication is a sign that the deviant is being rejected by the group and is no longer considered as part of the group. This may even be said openly to the individual concerned. This change in communication to the deviant can be represented graphically (see Figure 8.3).

The change in the *quality* of communication has been described by Leavitt (1964). At first group members try to change the deviant's mind by using logical argument. If this fails, then calls are made on his loyalty to the group in order to get him to conform. If the deviant still persists, he may then be threatened or shown physical violence by other

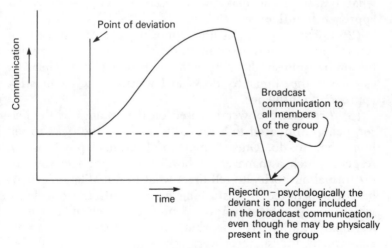

Figure 8.3   *Communications to deviants*

group members. 'Binging' or gently punching the upper arm of a deviant was one sanction used by workers in the Hawthorne studies. If this fails, then the deviant will be rejected by the group, shown in its extreme form as 'sending him to Coventry' or complete social ostracization of the deviant.

The bases of social power in groups

In looking at conformity we have been examining the group's power to influence and control the behaviour of its members. Group power is based on the social reward of acceptance, or social punishment by rejection of the deviant. But *individuals* in groups have power as well, and in order to understand some of the processes of interpersonal influence within a group we need to look at the possible basis of individual power.

French and Raven (1959) have identified five different kinds of individual power wielded inside a group:

(1) *Reward* power is based on the ability of the group member to satisfy some need in the person he is trying to influence. This might be achieved by money, praise, social acceptance, but its essence is the promise that 'if you do what I want, I can make life pleasant for you' — the carrot approach to influence.

(2) *Coercive* power is the opposite side of the coin of reward power and is based upon the ability of the influencing person to punish the person he is trying to influence. Its essence is the threat to 'do what I want or else' — the stick approach to influence.

(3) *Legitimate* power is based on the feelings of the person being influenced that the influencer has the *right* to tell him what to do. One example of legitimate power is the respect which a manager's subordinates might feel towards his formal authority to tell them what to do. Milgram (1974) has demonstrated in disturbing experiments the obedience which many subjects show to people perceived as having legitimate authority. In what was apparently a learning experiment the subjects were asked to give electric shocks when people learning a task made mistakes. On the instruc-

tions of a white-coated 'scientist' they were told to increase the voltage of the shock whenever the learner made the next error. The voltage increased, from mild through severe to dangerous levels, and although the 'learner' was not given a shock since he was a confederate of the experimenter, he behaved as if he had been shocked, by shouting, banging on the wall and pleading to be released from the experiment. This activity was followed by an ominous silence. Yet despite the learner's behaviour, and the obvious stress and anxiety which the subjects giving the shock were feeling many experimental subjects continued to shock the learner under the instructions of the 'scientist'.

(4) *Referent* power is based on the attractiveness of the influencing person to the person being influenced. Very often he will change his behaviour in order to become more like this attractive person. This may lead to 'apeing', mimicking the attractive person's behaviour, attitudes or gestures.

(5) *Expert* power is based upon the specialist skills or knowledge which the influencing person has. Because of these skills he may be put in the position of task leader and allowed to instruct, control and direct the activities of other group members.

Decision-making in groups

Many of the meetings which a manager is obliged to attend, including those meetings with their own teams, are meetings to make a decision concerning some aspect of the organization's activities. In addition to all the interpersonal processes which have been referred to earlier in this chapter, there are some important insights which social scientists can provide about the decision-making task itself. In particular, Thompson and Tuden (1964) have identified *two* basic dimensions of the decision-making task which groups will have to clarify and agree upon if their decision-taking is to be effective: they are *preferences about outcomes*, which means the *ends* or *goals* which the group is trying to achieve; and *beliefs about causation*, which are the *means* which the group will employ to achieve its goals. Thompson and Tuden suggest that it is possible for a group to agree or disagree about the goals which it wishes to pursue, and agree or disagree about the best means of pursuing these goals. Depending upon the nature of the agreement/disagreement, the group will need to pursue different strategies in order to reach a decision to which the group is committed. This is shown in Figure 8.4.

Where the group agrees about its goals and the means of achieving its goals (see box 1 in Figure 8.4), the decision more or less 'drops out', or is computed. For example, all members of the group may agree that they want to spend a luxury holiday on the Mediterranean and agree that the best means of getting there will be to take an air flight to the resort (means). In box 2 of Figure 8.4 the group disagrees about its goals – some people want the luxury holiday, others want a camping holiday in Brittany, but they do agree that whichever choice they make they would fly to the luxury hotel and take the cross-channel ferry for the camping holiday. In this case some of the group must *compromise*, perhaps by going camping this year and taking a luxury hotel next, or vice versa.

In box 3 of Figure 8.4 the group agrees its objective – luxury hotel – but some members of the group would prefer to drive rather than fly to the luxury hotel so that they have the use of the car for the holiday. In this case the group needs some *research* or *expert advice* into the comparative costs of flight and hire of car at resort and the financial and physical costs of driving from Britain to the luxury hotel.

In box 4 the group can neither agree on its goals nor the

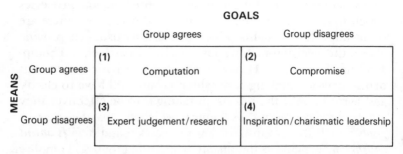

Figure 8.4 *Group decision-making*

means to achieve its goals. In ths case resolution of the disagreement can be reached by *inspiration*, one member
suggesting a walking holiday in Bolivia, which is a new and
attractive alternative to the group, or by a strong *charismatic
leader* who by the force of his personality gets the group to
agree to a canoeing expedition up the Amazon.

To reach a decision which has some support from all members of the group, the group must agree upon its goals and
the means to achieve its goals. To do this effectively members
must clarify which issues are creating disagreement, and concentrate their attention on one issue at a time. A trap shown
by many decision-making groups is having some members
talking about goal disagreement, only to have their attention
diverted by those considering problems of achieving the goals.
The discussion seems to go around in circles, the group is
unlikely to reach a decision and a lot of frustration and interpersonal hostility is generated in the process.

Training for effective participation in groups

In recent years one important concern for management
trainers has been the development of managers' skills in
working in groups, and in their interactions with work colleagues. One important development in this area has been the
T-group (training group), in which trainees assemble in small
groups with a qualified trainer. The features which characterize
T-groups are that participants are encouraged to reflect upon
what is happening in their relationships with one another,
and to share their reflections with other participants. This so-
called 'here and now' focus of learning is upon interpersonal
processes and feelings, and not upon the content of any discussion topic. In this situation participants are encouraged
to give feedback about how they see others and receive feedback about their impact on other people, and to experiment
with new styles of behaviour if these seem to be appropriate.
A vast amount of research has been conducted into the
impact of T-groups on participants and has been reviewed by
Smith (1980). In general terms the changes which participants
might experience have been summarized by Miles (1960) as

changes in:

> 'Sensitivity': the ability to perceive what is actually going on in social situations (including both behavioural events and the inferred feelings of other persons).

> 'Diagnostic Ability': the skill of assessing ongoing social situations in a way that enables effective action.

> 'Action Skill': the ability to intervene effectively in on-going situations in such a way as to maximise personal and group effectiveness and satisfaction.

Other programmes which have been designed to develop interpersonal skills in managers have taken a more structured approach to training than is implicit in the design of a T-group. The structure usually takes the form of a series of specific tasks which the group is required to perform, such as decision-making or a negotiation. Although the form of training may differ, the fundamental processes of a reviewing of the group's interactions, personal reflections, feedback and experimenting with new behaviour are common to all these types of group training.

Many group training programmes contain participants from different organizations who are total strangers at the beginning of the training. The organizational impact of such training therefore depends upon the development of each manager's individual skills. This has led Pugh (1965) to question the value of such training, since it does not affect the social milieu of the organization to which the manager must return after training. In recognition of this problem there is now an increasing emphasis on training the whole of a work-group, together, on the same programme. This *team-building* process can be tailored to the specific needs of the work-group and be focused on the 'real' interpersonal problems which confront that group as it sets about its tasks.

Summary

To review some of the points that have been made in this chapter let us return to the 'bloody' meeting which was referred to at the beginning. What kinds of attitudes do people have which help to create 'bloody' meetings?

— The crucial thing to remember is that the most important person at the meeting is me.
— The other members of the group are primarily there to listen to me and to come around to my way of thinking.
— People who have not got the guts to stand up for themselves and speak their piece should not be at the meeting, and certainly should not require to be helped into the discussion.
— If these people are not prepared to seek my advice, I do not see why I should have to force my opinions on them.
— The important thing is to concentrate on the task and not bother if people feel uncomfortable.
— Any conflict which develops between group members should be ignored and it will go away.
— Every member of a group should strictly adhere to group norms or face the consequences, apart, that is, from me, as I have an important role to play in stirring the group up.
— The most important skill in a group meeting is the ability to demolish the opposition's arguments and bring some rationality to bear on the issue.
— Training is something we do to operatives, as rational intelligent human beings; managers do not need to be trained to get on with one another.

These, of course, are only a few examples of the kind of attitudes which make group meetings frustrating experiences.

Perhaps if you look at your own attitudes, you will be able to add to the list?

References for Chapter 8

Allport, F. H. (1924) *Social Psychology*, Houghton Mifflin, Boston.
Asch, S. E. (1951) 'Effects of Group Pressure upon the Modification and Distortion of Judgements', in Geutzkow, H. (ed.), *Groups, Leadership and Men*, Carnegie, Pittsburgh.
Bales, R. F. (1951) *Interaction Process Analysis: A Method for the Study of Small Groups*, Addison-Wesley, Reading, Mass.

Bennis, W. G. and Shepherd, H. A. (1956) 'A Theory of Group Development', *Human Relations*, 9.

Bion, W. (1961) *Experiences in Groups*, Tavistock, London.

Cartwright, D. and Zander, A. (eds) (1968), *Group Dynamics*, 3rd edn,
Tavistock, London.

Deutsch, M. and Gerrard, H. (1955) 'A Study of Normative and Informational Social Influences upon Individual Judgements', *Journal of
Abnormal and Social Psychology*, 51.

French, J. R. P. and Raven, B. (1959) 'The Bases of Social Power', in
Cartwright, D. and Zander, A. (eds) (1968), *Group Dynamics*, 3rd
edn, Tavistock, London.

Gibb, J. R. (1964) 'Climate for Trust Formation', in Bradford, L. P. *et
al.* (eds), *T-group Theory and Laboratory Method*, Wiley, New York.

Leavitt, H. J. (1964) *Managerial Psychology*, 2nd edn, University of
Chicago Press, Chicago.

Miles, M. (1960) 'Human Relations Training: Process and Outcomes',
Journal of Counselling Psychology, 7.

Milgram, S. (1974) *Obedience to Authority: An Experimental View*,
Tavistock, London.

Mintzberg, H. (1973) *The Nature of Managerial Work*, Harper & Row,
New York.

Pugh, D. (1965) 'T-group Training from the Point of View of Organization Theory', in Whittacker, F. P. G. (ed.), *T-group Training: Group
Dynamics in Management Education*, Blackwell, Oxford.

Roethlisberger, F. J. and Dickson, W. J. (1939) *Management and the
Worker*, Harvard University Press, Cambridge, Mass.

Schacter, S. (1951) 'Deviation, Rejection and Communication', in
Cartwright, D. and Zander, A. (eds) (1968), *Group Dynamics*, 3rd
edn, Tavistock, London.

Schein, E. H. (1969) *Process Consultation: Its Role in Organization
Development*, Addison-Wesley, Reading, Mass.

Schein, E. H. (1972) *Organizational Psychology*, Prentice-Hall, Englewood Cliffs, N. J.

Schein, E. H. (1974) 'Organizational Socialization and the Profession
of Management', in Kolb, D. A. *et al.* (eds), *Organizational Psychology: A Book of Readings*, Addison-Wesley, Reading, Mass.

Schutz, W. C. (1966) *The Interpersonal Underworld*, Science & Behavior
Books, New York.

Shaw, M. E. (1971) *Group Dynamics: The Psychology of Small Group
Behavior*, McGraw-Hill, New York.

Smith, P. B. (1980) *Group Processes and Personal Change*, Harper &
Row, New York.

Thompson, J. E. and Tuden, A. (1964) 'Strategies, Structures, and Processes of Organizational Decision', in Leavitt, H. J. and Pondy, L. R. (eds) (1964), *Readings in Managerial Psychology*, University of Chicago Press, Chicago.

Tuckman, B. W. (1965) 'Development Sequences in Small Groups', *Psychological Bulletin*, 63, 384—99.

Willis, R. H. and Hollander, E. P. (1964) 'An Experimental Study of Three Response Modes in Social Influence Situations', *Journal of Abnormal and Social Psychology*, 69, 150—6.

9

Leadership and Supervision

They had something to celebrate, so it was quite a party. A small research team in the North-west had upstaged Silicon Valley and had given their company a competitive advantage with their refinement of the lazer zapping of silicon chips. They were also drinking to build up their Dutch courage, because they were about to endure a congratulation speech from a headquarter's executive. The speech took its predictable course: perfunctory appreciation; an acknowledgement of their position among the world leaders in lazer zapping; an acknowledgement of the lead they had shown to other research teams within the company. The executive knew little about the technicalities of lazer zapping but he considered himself an expert on the subject of leadership — the country needs more strong leaders . . . leaders are born not made . . . leaders must inspire awe in their followers . . . a leader must ruthlessly rivet everyone's attention on the strategy and objectives which he has identified.

The leader of the lazer zappers flushed with embarrassment because he knew that the reality of leadership is quite different. He knew that leadership often had to be learnt the hard way; he remembered the early days when his formal position as leader contrasted with his informal position, and he recalled that in leading his team he often needed to modify his leadership style according to the prevailing task and situation. He also recalled that, as leader, a great deal of his effort was spent ensuring that he had a cohesive team which could maximize the benefit from the experience of its members.

This account of the lazer zappers party indicates that leadership is particularly difficult to define. Most people would agree that it is concerned with influence and usually involves notions of power and authority derived either from the individual's position in the organization or from his personal characteristics. Coleman (1969) lists four main functions of a leader:

1. *Structuring the situation* — making it clear where the group is going and what has to be done.
2. *Controlling group behaviour* — creating and enforcing appropriate rules for guiding the behaviour of group members.
3. *Speaking for the group* — sensing and articulating (both internally and externally) the objectives and feelings of the group.
4. *Helping the group achieve its goals and potential* — mobilizing and co-ordinating group resources and decision-making.

This implies that leadership is related to group activity and requires the leader to be in close communication with the group members. This is summed up in the definition of leadership as 'interpersonal influence, directed through a process of communication, towards the attainment of group goals'. Traditionally leadership has been thought of as vested in one individual, usually formally so designated and with an appropriate title. Leadership can, however, be quite informal (groups can have both formal and informal leaders) and the functions of leadership can be widely shared among group members with different individuals exercising various aspects of it at different times.

It can now be seen that leadership is only one aspect of a manager's job. It occurs when he is actually influencing subordinates towards group and/or organizational goals. For many managers leadership may, in fact, be only a very small part of the job.

Trait theories of leadership

Many of the earlier studies of leadership were concerned with attempts to establish the characteristics of a good leader.

This approach is based on the assumption that leadership is an inherent quality of the individual and that the person who has that quality will tend to emerge as the leader in all situations. Unfortunately, there is very little consistency in the results of the dozens of studies which have attempted to define and measure those traits which distinguish leaders from their followers.

There may be a number of reasons for this. Personality traits are extremely difficult to define. There are an enormous number of words which describe traits, all with fine shades of meaning, so different researchers may have used different words for the same characteristic or the same word for slightly different characteristics. Even if definitions are precise, traits are hard to measure; many studies depend on ratings by other people, and these ratings may be wildly inaccurate. In any study it is impossible to measure everything, so consequently the investigator selects those characteristics which interest him most. If a particular trait is not measured, it cannot appear in the results. It may also be of course that leadership has very little to do with personal characteristics. There are certainly plenty of examples of highly successful leaders who do not fit any of the preconceived notions of what a leader should be like.

However, despite the above comments there are a few very general trends which emerge from the studies. Certain traits do appear with some consistency in many (but by no means all) investigations. Gibson, Ivancevich and Donelly (1979) mention the following:

1. Intelligence — one of the more consistent findings is that leaders are more intelligent than their followers.
2. *Personality* — some studies suggest that self-confidence, originality, alertness and initiative are important characteristics.
3. *Physical characteristics* — results in this area show no consistency; there seems no evidence for factors like height and weight having any influence.

Mainly because it has proved quite impossible to establish any accepted pattern of personality traits for effective leaders, studies of this type have now largely gone out of fashion.

Theories of leadership and management style

Another approach to the study of leadership has been to look at the actual behaviour of leaders and contrast the effects of different ways (or styles) of leading. One of the earliest studies in this field and one which has had considerable influence on subsequent thought is that of Lewin, Lippitt and White (1939), a good account of which is given by White and Lippitt (1960). In this study 10-year-old boys who were engaged in voluntary hobby activities were organized in small groups, each with an adult leader operating in one of three different styles:

1. *Authoritarian* — all decisions were made by the leader, who issued close instructions to each individual.
2. *Democratic* — decisions and control were carried out democratically by the group, encouraged and assisted by the leader.
3. *Laissez-faire* — everything was left to the group, with the leader virtually not participating at all.

The results were interesting. In general, the authoritarian groups showed considerable tension and hostility, both towards the leader and to each other, though some individuals took up a passive, uninvolved role. The democratic groups showed high cohesion and involvement and positive attitudes to the leader. The *laissez-faire* groups showed low cohesion and involvement and achieved little. As part of the experiment the leaders were 'rotated' so that each group experienced each style of leadership — with broadly the same results. This implies that group behaviour is a function of the type of leadership, different styles producing different effects. It would obviously be dangerous to generalize from studies of children to the behaviour of adults, so it is now necessary to look at some studies concerned with the style of supervision of actual work-groups.

The Ohio State studies

There are two sets of studies which have had considerable influence on ideas concerning the effectiveness of different styles of managing. The first of these to be considered here is the work of the Personnel Research Board of Ohio State University carried out, with the help of numerous co-workers, by Hemphill and Stogdill.

Data on the actual behaviour of supervisors were obtained from questionnaires completed by the supervisors, their subordinates and independent observers. Factor analysis of the data revealed two main dimensions which were independent of each other. That is, any particular supervisor could be high on one and low on the other, or high or low on both. The two dimensions were:

1. *Initiation of structure*, which refers to the extent to which a supervisor defines his own role and what is expected of the subordinate, and also defines the organization, objectives and pattern of communication.
2. *Consideration*, which refers to the extent the supervisor is supportive of his group and shows friendship, trust and respect for his subordinates.

Two important questions investigated by these studies are 'Why does the supervisor behave as he does?' and 'What effect do these factors have on performance?' Likert and Hayes (1957) summarize some of the main findings as follows:

1. The only positive connection indicating why a supervisor emphasized one or other dimension was that he tended to behave as his own boss did.
2. Subordinates preferred a supervisor who emphasized consideration.
3. Supervisors in production areas who got the best ratings from their superiors tended to emphasize the *initiation of structure* rather than consideration. In non-production areas the opposite was true.
4. Supervisors who were high on both dimensions were more likely to be accurately perceived by their subordinates as holding the position formally designated by the organization (40 per cent of the workers in this study did not correctly identify their boss as defined by the formal organization).
5. Emphasis on initiating structure was associated with higher absenteeism and more grievances — but it could be

that grievances tended to provoke an initiating structure from the supervisor.

While these studies have defined two major dimensions of supervisory style and given some indication of their effects on the behaviour of subordinates, they do not, unfortunately, tell us much about their effect on work output. Fortunately, the studies at the University of Michigan provide some answers to this question.

The University of Michigan studies

These studies were carried out at the Survey Research Center of the University of Michigan by Likert and his co-workers. The main effort was directed towards establishing the differences which existed in the supervision of high- and low-producing units. Carefully matched groups of high- and low-productivity teams were compared. One of the key factors to emerge was concerned with the style of the supervisor. From interviews with both the supervisors and their subordinates two distinct dimensions were established: a supervisor could be either primarily *production-centred* or *employee-centred*.

A *production-centred* supervisor tends to see his job in terms of organizing the physical production processes. When asked about his job he will tend to talk mainly about these processes, with less emphasis on the people involved.

An *employee-centred* supervisor sees his job more in terms of the human relations involved. He will tend to talk more about his subordinates and their needs when asked what his job involves.

The relationship between these dimensions and those of the Ohio State studies is obvious, and interestingly enough the high-producing groups tended to have employee-centred supervisors. Care should of course be taken in not necessarily interpreting this result to mean that the way to achieve high productivity is to take care of people. A correlation does not establish causality. It could be that when production is high supervisors have time to consider people, or alternatively it would not be surprising if when a supervisor has problems with output he tends to concentrate on production.

McGregor's theory X and theory Y

Another approach which sees managerial styles within two dimensions is that of McGregor. Unlike the previous two studies, his views are not based on empirical research but rather on the distillation of a life-time's experience as a manager, consultant and academic. In *The Human Side of Enterprise* (McGregor, 1960) he suggests that the way a manager manages will depend very largely upon the assumptions that he makes about the world in general and his subordinates in particular. He defined two possible sets of assumptions that managers might use. He labelled these *theory X* and *theory Y*. He chose these as neutral labels so as not to imply any value judgement between them, though in many ways McGregor's own value preference for theory Y shines clearly through his writing. The two sets of assumptions are summarized briefly below:

1. *Theory X assumptions*. The average person dislikes work and will avoid it if he can. Work is therefore a 'necessary evil'. Most people dislike responsibility, require direction and control, have little ambition and require security above all else.
2. *Theory Y assumptions*. These are more complex and include the beliefs that the average person is naturally active and enjoys achieving goals (particularly those he has set himself), that commitment to objectives is related to the rewards associated with their achievement, that ingenuity, imagination and creativity are widely distributed in the population, and that people will accept and seek responsibility.

It is important to remember that these are not statements of what 'man' is really like but statements of what managers may believe 'man' or their subordinates are like. The beliefs are not usually too consciously articulated by the manager, but can be inferred from his behaviour in the way he manages. A manager holding theory X assumptions will have a choice of either one of two styles, or he can use a mixture of both. Since in his view people do not want to work he can get them to produce by *coercion*, using threats and punishments (hard line X), or he can *seduce* people into work by offering 'bribes' or rewards, such as piece rates, bonuses and competitions (soft line X). Both these approaches are based on the same underlying assumptions and have much in common. Both require precise definition of the work to be done and close control and checks to ensure the required standards have been met.

Theory Y assumptions will give rise to a much more open and flexible style of managing. Since people are seen as active and co-operative, the manager's role is to ensure that work is co-ordinated, and that organizational goals are clear and compatible with those of the individual. It will, in general, be a much more participative style.

An important point made by McGregor is that theory X is an example of a 'self-fulfilling prophesy'. It gives rise to managerial styles which involve close supervision and control. The average person treated in this manner will tend to respond in one of two ways. He will either feel sufficiently resentful that he becomes unco-operative and antagonistic, doing (at best) minimal work, stopping when not directly supervised, and he may even become actively rebellious. Alternatively, he may passively accept the situation, doing what he is asked and no more, showing no initiative or creativity. Many readers will have experienced these feelings and responses in their own working lives and there is a vast amount of both formal and informal evidence that these behaviours do occur. Both responses simply serve to confirm the manager's original beliefs. In effect, theory X assumptions lead to a style of managing which only allows the subordinate to respond in a way consistent with the original assumptions. The key question is 'Are theory Y assumptions also self-fulfilling?' It seems likely that the answer is a tentative 'Yes', but as there are, at the time of writing, few documented examples of organizations managed on theory Y assumptions there is not yet enough evidence to be sure.

The managerial grid

One major piece of work which builds on all the previous studies is that of Blake and Mouton (1964). They have produced a theory which not only describes and explains managerial styles but can be (and is) used as the basis for improving managerial effectiveness. Perhaps because it has been very effectively marketed as the basis of a management and organizational development programme, this theory has had a very considerable impact on management thinking.

Blake and Mouton have taken the two dimensions of the earlier studies and relabelled them *concern for people* and *concern for production.* They then arrange them orthogonally as the two dimensions of a grid, as in Figure 9.1. Each axis is marked as a nine-point scale. Thus it is theoretically possible to identify any manager's style of relating to his subordinates

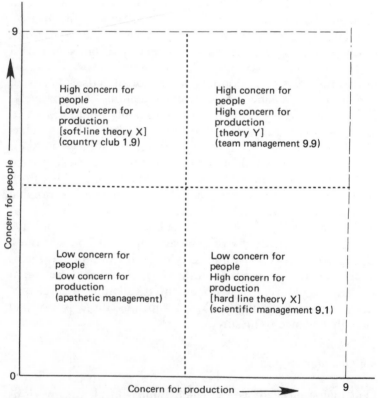

Figure 9.1 *Relationship between the managerial grid and theory X and theory Y*

with two co-ordinates indicating his position on the grid. They then identified and discussed certain extreme styles:

1.9 Management. This manager has a very high concern for people, but has a low concern for production. His assumption is that attention to the needs of people, the avoidance of conflict and developing good human relations will automatically encourage good work. Blake calls this *country-club* management since the objective is to keep everyone happy as in a country club. It is similar to soft line theory X in approach. The danger, he suggests, is that everyone is so busy being comfortable and happy that little production may take place.

9.1 Management. This manager has a high concern for production but a low concern for people. Blake calls him a *scientific* manager because he sees his role in terms of scheduling work and machines and will tend to be strongly influenced by 'scientific' techniques of production scheduling, such as critical-path analysis and operations research. He sees people as simply units in the production process. This style is similar to hard line theory X. The danger is that the high emphasis on production and control will produce high conflict and creativity to beat the system on the part of subordinates so that output will not, in fact, be optimized.

1.1 Management. This is the *apathetic* manager who shows low concern both for people and for production. His approach is simply to put in the minimum effort to meet organizational requirements. It is a style unlikely to produce high output. Some writers have typified this type of manager as a WIB (Weak, Inefficient, Bastard!).

5.5 Management. This is the *compromiser* who believes that the way to achieve success is to balance the needs of people against the need to produce. Blake's view is that while aiming for the best of two worlds he may, as is always the risk with compromise, end up with the worst. He may not put sufficient emphasis on people to achieve the loyalty inspired by the 1.9 manager, or sufficient emphasis on production to achieve the pay-offs of the scientific approach of the 9.1 manager.

9.9 Management. This Blake calls *team* management, where the approach is on achieving 'production through people'. The emphasis is on developing an interdependent team with high trust and commitment to organizational goals. This is very similar to McGregor's notion of theory Y management. The basic assumption, made by Blake, is that 9.9 is the best and most effective style.

When this model is used as a framework for management development, the manager is first helped to define his existing style or styles and then appropriate exercises are devised in order to help him develop towards a 9.9 style. The system can be used simply as a base for developing individual managers or as a complete organizational development programme, working from individual development through team and inter-group development to organizational goal-setting and attainment.

The strength of the managerial grid framework is that it is undoubtedly a powerful method of conceptualizing much of the earlier work on leadership styles in a way which has an appeal for managers. There is also some evidence that the system works in practice to an extent which will show in company profits (Blake, Mouton, Barnes and Greiner, 1964). On the other hand, there is not a lot of empirical support for Blake's views on the effectiveness of different styles, though intuitively they seem right and fit the experience of many managers. There is, however, the danger of making 'self-fulfilling prophesies' in accepting this type of evidence. An alternative view is that the effectiveness of a particular style depends on a combination of factors and hence that any style could be effective depending on the situation. Reddin (1970), discussed below, develops this idea.

Action-centred leadership

Before moving on to look at interactive theories of management, brief mention should be made of Adair's (1968) concept of *action-centred leadership*, which was also developed as a basis for training in leadership and his recommended ideal has much in common with theory Y and the 9.9 style.

Adair argues that for a group to be successful there are three types of need which must be met:

1. *Task needs*. The group exists to achieve a particular task

and certain things will need to be done in order to achieve this task.
2. *Group needs.* To achieve objectives the group requires to be a cohesive team who work well together. That is, there must be attention to group maintenance.
3. *Individual needs.* Each individual in the group will have a range of individual needs which he requires to meet via the group activity.

Since these needs overlap and interact with one another, they can be shown as a Venn diagram, as in Figure 9.2. Failure to meet task performance requirements, for example, may well lower group morale and in turn cause frustration of individual needs. All sorts of other interactions of both a negative and positive nature are obviously possible. The effective leader takes care to ensure that all three sets of needs are met. In this system the attention to task needs corresponds broadly to Blake's 'concern for production'. 'Concern for people' is split into the two areas of individual and group needs.

Figure 9.2 *Three sets of needs from action-centred leadership*

Source: J. Adair (1968) *Training for Leadership*, Macdonald, London.

Situational and interactive theories of leadership and management

It was noted above in the discussion on Blake's managerial grid that it is possible to criticize theories recomending one particular style of leadership or management on the grounds that different situations may call for different styles. Much of the thinking on these lines can be traced back to the work of Fiedler on *contingency theories* of leadership.

Fiedler's contingency theory

Fiedler (1967) suggests that there are three factors which influence a leader's effectiveness:

1. *Leader—member relations* — the degree to which the leader is liked and trusted by the group.
2. *Task structure* — the extent to which the group's goals and tasks are clear and well defined.
3. *Position power* — the amount of control the leader has over rewards and punishments in the group. Typically a senior manager in an industrial company would have strong position power, while that of a chairman of a voluntary committee would be weak.

Leader—member relationships can be good or poor. Task structure can be high or low and position power can be strong or weak. This gives rise to eight possible combinations, as shown in Figure 9.3. Fairly obviously the most favourable situation for the leader is number 1, with good relationships, high task structure and strong position power. The most unfavourable position is number 8, with poor relationships, low task structure and weak position power.

Fiedler's research in a wide range of organizations suggests that a different approach from the leader is required in situations with different combinations of these three variables. Very broadly, in situations 1, 2, 3 and 8 a more task-orientated approach is effective. In situations 4, 5 and 7 a more person/relationships-orientated   approach   may   be   more

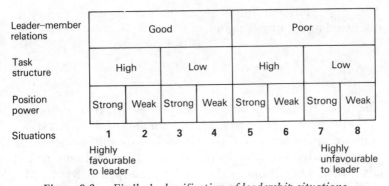

Leader–member relations	Good				Poor			
Task structure	High		Low		High		Low	
Position power	Strong	Weak	Strong	Weak	Strong	Weak	Strong	Weak
Situations	1	2	3	4	5	6	7	8

Highly favourable to leader   Highly unfavourable to leader

Figure 9.3   *Fiedler's classification of leadership situations*

Source: F. E. Fiedler (1967) *A Theory of Leadership Effectiveness*, McGraw-Hill, New York.

appropriate. Handy (1976) has well summarized these findings:

> When the task is clearly defined and the leader strong and well-respected he is expected to get on with the job and be fairly directive. When the task is ambiguous and he is in a weak position *vis-à-vis* the group his best strategy is still to be directive and structuring — to involve the group would then be seen as total abdication of leadership. On the other hand an ambiguous task confronted by a respected leader calls for a more supportive approach, if he is to draw out from his group all the contributions they can make.

In Fiedler's view the style the manager will adopt is deeply rooted in his personality, and so there is not much hope of inducing an individual to change his style. It is therefore better to look for an individual whose style suits the situation, or it may (perhaps) be possible to change the situation to suit the style of the incumbent manager. This may be done by structuring the task more, giving him more power, or changing the individuals in the group. The main implication of these views is of course that it is necessary to select as manager someone who already has the appropriate style for the situation in which he is going to work. Contrary to most other writers in this area, Fiedler does not believe that attempts to train managers to be more adaptable are likely to succeed.

The organizational implications of contingency theory is discussed in the next chapter.

The 3D grid

There are, however, a number of theories which arise from an opposite view and suggest that, as a number of different styles may be appropriate for coping with different situations, a truly effective manager would be adaptable and able to use any style. One framework has been proposed by Reddin (1970).

Reddin has, in effect, taken Blake's managerial grid and added an extra dimension, thus turning it into a three-dimensional grid, as in Figure 9.4. The extra dimension is *effectiveness*. The other two dimensions are *relationship orientation* and *task orientation*. On the near face of the cube, so formed, four *less-effective* styles are identified and on the far face

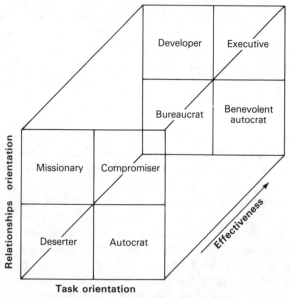

Figure 9.4   *The 3D grid*

Source: W. J. Reddin (1970) *Managerial Effectiveness*, McGraw-Hill, New York.

there are four *more-effective* styles. For a style to be more or less effective depends on whether it is being used in an appropriate or inappropriate situation. Thus a manager working on both low-task and low-relationship orientations could be a *deserter* and ineffective if he simply avoid issues and remains uninvolved. In an appropriate situation he would be an effective *bureaucrat* simply getting on running the system.

The manager using high-task/low-relationship orientations inappropriately is being directive where direction is not needed and hence becomes the *autocrat*. On occasions where direction is needed, emergencies or complex technical processes for example, the style is appropriate and is labelled *benevolent autocrat*. The high-relationship/low-task orientation used inappropriately is known as the *missionary* and describes the individual 'preaching' peace and harmony as an avoidance of conflict, where conflict may be necessary to healthy operation. On other occasions it may be necessary to place more emphasis on relationships in order to develop team or individual effectiveness — hence the *developer*. The final style, high-task/high-relationship orientation (equivalent to Blake's 9.9), obviously has value in long-term team management and is hence called the *executive*.

A continuum of managerial styles

Another way to conceptualize a variation in managerial styles has been provided by Tannenbaum and Schmidt (1958). They see the styles that a manager could use as ranged along a continuum (as in Figure 9.5) from a very authoritarian style (equivalent to theory X) at one end to an almost totally participative style (theory Y) at the other end. The styles are not seen as totally distinct entities but as merging into each other as movement is made along the continuum.

The principal variable, indicated by the diagonal line in the diagram, is the amount of authority and control which the manager either retains or shares with his subordinates. Thus the very authoritarian manager retains most of the control. The diagonal line does not go quite into the corners since in practice even with the most authoritarian manager there will

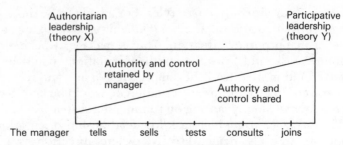

Figure 9.5   *A continuum of managerial styles*

Source: R. Tannenbaum and W. H. Schmidt (1958) 'How to Choose a Leadership Pattern', *Harvard Business Review*, 36, 95–101.

always be some area of discretion for the subordinate, even if very small. The most participative manager at the other end of the continuum will share most of his control with subordinates but the realities of the world will require that he retains some final authority. There may come the occasion when as a last resort and in order to fulfil his organizational obligations he will have to take a final decision and issue instructions.

Although the continuum is represented as a steady variation from one end to the other, it is possible to identify a number of distinct styles along the scale. These are defined in terms of the manager's approach to his subordinates. In a somewhat simplified and abbreviated version of the original, five such styles are described:

1. *The manager tells.* This is the most authoritarian style. The manager sees himself as having all the control, with the necessary information and power simply to issue instructions. The role of the subordinate(s) is to follow these instructions.

2. *The manager sells.* It is arguable whether this is really any less authoritarian than the 'telling' style. The manager still sees himself as the decision-maker and controller, but instead of simply issuing instructions will consider the best way to present his wishes to the subordinate so as to get reasonably willing compliance. One popular method is to present the situation in such a way that the subordinate actually suggests for himself the desired action, thus thinking it is own idea. It is a distinctly manipulative style which has something in common with McGregor's soft

line theory X. The 'tells' style is nearer to hard line theory X.

3. *The manager tests.* In this style the manager will still define the situation and possible courses of action, and will then ask the subordinate(s) for comments and opinions on the alternatives offered, reserving the right to accept or reject such comments as he (the manager) feels appropriate.

4. *The manager consults.* Here is the beginning of a more participative approach. In this style the manager presents the situation and asks for suggestions from the subordinate(s). The manager still reserves the right to accept or reject ideas on his own judgement. The essential difference between the 'testing' and 'consulting' styles is that in 'testing' the subordinate is only able to comment on possible actions already defined by the manager, whereas in 'consulting' he can put forward his own proposals. 'Consulting' is the first point in the continuum at which information and ideas from the subordinate can be incorporated into the final solution or action.

5. *The manager joins.* This is a totally participative style. The manager and subordinate(s) jointly review the situation and reach a decision on appropriate action. When a 'joining' style is being fully operated discussion continues until total agreement is reached. Many managers express reservations about such total participation on the grounds that it involves a loss (even abdication) of control. This is not really so, as the manager does not have to accept suggestions with which he disagrees. It does mean, however, that he will not impose decisions with which his subordinates disagree. The 'contract' is to keep working until agreement is reached. The potential cost, of course, is that it may take considerable time to reach such an agreement. The potential pay-off is better decisions (since all available information and expertise is utilized), to which there should be total commitment. This style involves McGregor's theory Y assumptions.

In this system the effective manager is the individual who can move up and down the continuum as the situation demands, operating at different points at different times. The question then arises: 'how does the manager identify which style is appropriate in a given situation?' Tannenbaum and Schmidt suggest that there exists a set of *forces* which will tend to push the manager in one direction or the other along the continuum. The manager who is sensitive to these forces will allow himself to move along the scale until he arrives at the point of balance between opposing pressures, and will thus be able to define an appropriate style. They suggest that there are three main sources of these forces:

1. *Forces in the manager.* These consist mainly of characteristics of the manager himself: his personality, his value system and his beliefs about people and how they should be managed. Other factors are his sense of security, his tolerance of ambiguity and the level and type of his social skills. Thus a manager with theory Y assumptions, feeling secure and with beliefs about the value of participation, who is able to tolerate the uncertainty of delaying a decision, will move towards the 'joins' end of the continuum. A manager with theory X assumptions who believes that management is about quick decisions and firm leadership will stay nearer the 'tells' end.

2. *Forces in the subordinate(s).* These include similar personal characteristics as those listed for the manager, but also involve factors such as their knowledge and understanding of the situation, their commitment to the goals of the organization or group, their degree of dependence or readiness to assume responsibility and their expectations. Thus a manager with a highly expert and committed group which is prepared to accept responsibility and to participate will have no difficulty in moving towards joining. A dependent group of low expertise and with low commitment to the task in hand will force the manager towards the telling end of the continuum.

3. *Forces in the situation.* The most obvious of these is time. If time is short, a lengthy participative discussion is automatically precluded. Other factors include the importance of the decision, who is going to carry it out and the way the organization, in general, tends to operate. Thus, where there is plenty of time for a decision which involves

a number of people in its implementation in a very participative organization, 'joining' would be the appropriate
style. An emergency in an authoritarian organization
requiring a quick decision by one man followed by rapid
action is a clear case for 'telling'.

One criticism which has been levelled at this approach is
that it will cause confusion if a manager continually changes
his style. This is based on a belief that people need consistency,
which is, in itself, a theory X assumption. Precise data on this
point are hard to come by, but there seems plenty of evidence
from everyday observation that a manager's change of style is
acceptable provided it is clear why he has changed, that is,
that the change is related to circumstances. Arbitrary changes
dictated simply by the manager's own feelings are the cause
of problems. Many fire services, for example, operate right
across the continuum. When fighting a fire the style is authoritarian, when making decisions back in the fire-station the
style is participative. Units in the army are reported to work
very participatively when planning an operation, but in combat conditions move to a 'telling' style. Equivalent examples
exist in industry.

There is another problem with which Tannenbaum and
Schmidt do not deal fully. Their system analyses the forces
which will move a manager towards any particular style and
gives some indication of the direction in which these forces
operate, though there are cases where even the direction is
not clear. They do not, however, provide sufficient precision
to enable a manager to decide exactly what style he should
use. This is still very much a matter of intuition and individual
judgement. Perhaps it always will be. Nevertheless, an attempt
has been made by others to provide some more precise guidelines, at least in the area of how a manager might best handle
decision-making.

A leadership decision model

Vroom and Yetton (1973) developed a model of managerial
decision-making processes which is based on the assumption

that different leadership styles are appropriate in different situations, and which is intended to provide a guide for managers and leaders as to what style to adopt in any given situation. The model emphasizes that a manager must be concerned with two distinct aspects of a decision:

1. *Decision quality*, which refers to those aspects of a decision which have a direct impact on performance. Decisions about the production process which have a direct bearing on output will, for example, be made differently from more peripheral decisions, about, say, the colour scheme of the washrooms.
2. *Decision acceptance* is concerned with the necessity, or otherwise, of high commitment from subordinates. A technically correct decision may well fail in implementation because of low commitment or outright opposition from those who have to carry it out. In general, if high commitment is required, a more participative approach is indicated.

The model involves a further distinction between *group problems* and *individual problems*. If the solution adopted has potential effects on all immediate subordinates, or some identifiable sub-set of them, it is classified as a 'group' problem. If the solution affects only one of a manager's subordinates, it is called an 'individual' problem. This distinction is important because it determines the range of decision-making processes available to the manager. From this basis the model provides a classification of management decision styles (summarized in Table 9.1) that are descriptive of common procedures used by managers.

The processes include *autocratic* (A), *consultative* (C), *group* (G) and *delegative* (D). Each process is identified by a letter which signifies the basic process and a roman numeral which follows the letter indicating a particular variant of that process. Thus AI represents the first variant of an autocratic process and AII the second variant. The processes shown in Table 9.1 are arranged in columns corresponding to their applicability to either group or individual problems, and are arranged in order of increasing opportunity for the subordinate to influence the problem. That this model is quite compatible with the Tannenbaum and Schmidt (1958) continuum

Table 9.1 *Management decision-making processes*

	Individual problems		Group problems
AI	The manager makes the decision himself, using information he has available	AI	The manager makes the decision himself using information he has available
AII	The manager obtains information from the subordinate, then decides for himself. The role of the subordinate is simply to provide information; he is not involved in the decision	AII	The manager obtains information from subordinates, then decides for himself. The role of subordinates is simply to provide information, they are not involved in the decision
CI	The manager shares problem with, and obtains ideas from, the subordinate, then makes the decision, which may or may not include influence from the subordinate	CI	The manager shares the problem with, and obtains ideas from, relevant subordinates individually, then makes a decision, which may or may not include influence from the subordinates.
GI	The manager shares the problem with the subordinate and after open discussion they arrive at a joint decision	CII	The manager shares the problem with, and obtains ideas from, relevant subordinates in a group meeting and then makes the decision, which may or may not include influence from the subordinates.
DI	The manager delegates the problem to the subordinate to solve, giving him any necessary support	GII	The manager shares the problem with subordinates or a group and co-ordinates discussion to reach a group decision. The manager supports and implements any decision which has the support of the entire group

Source: V. H. Vroom and A. G. Jago (1974) 'Decision Making as a Social Process', *Decision Sciences*, 5, 745–9.

of managerial styles is readily apparent. One apparent difference is the inclusion of 'delegation', which although not mentioned in the above discussion was, in fact, included as a possibility in Tannenbaum and Schmidt's original formulation.

The Vroom–Yetton model was designed as a guide for managers to regulate their choices among the decision styles in order to maximize the effectiveness of their decisions. The effectiveness of a decision is seen within the model as dependent on a number of dimensions of the situation in question. These include the quality requirement, leader and subordinate information, problem structure, likelihood and importance of subordinate acceptance, goal congruency, conflict and number of subordinates involved. These situation dimensions or problem attributes are related to the selection of a management decision style by a set of ten rules that are designed to ensure both quality and acceptance of the decisions. A convenient form of presenting these rules is by using a decision tree. The latest version of both the rules and the decision tree is presented in Vroom and Jago (1974).

Referring back to the account of the lazer zappers' party with which this chapter opened, it should by now be obvious that the views expressed by the company executive are much too simple to account for the complex process that is leadership. The chances are that leaders are 'made' not 'born' and the effectiveness of the leader depends on a complex mix of interacting factors, rather than just his personality. To be effective a manager or supervisor needs to be sufficiently adaptable to adopt any one of a range of possible styles and sufficiently sensitive to a wide range of factors to be able to determine which style he needs. Defining a range of styles seems to be relatively easy. It is much harder to define the factors which determine the effective style in any situation. For the practising manager this is still largely a matter of 'experience' and 'intuition'.

References for Chapter 9

Adair, J. (1968) *Training for Leadership*, Macdonald, London.

Blake, R. R. and Mouton, J. S. (1964) *The Managerial Grid*, Gulf Publishing Co., Houston.

Blake, R. R., Mouton, J. S., Barnes, L. B. and Greiner, L. E. (1964) 'Breakthrough in Organization Development', *Harvard Business Review*, 42, 133–55.

Coleman, J. C. (1969) *Psychology and Effective Behavior*, Scott, Foresman, Glenview, Ill.

Fiedler, F. E. (1967) *A Theory of Leadership Effectiveness*, McGraw-Hill, New York.

Gibson, J. L., Ivancevich, J. M. and Donnelly, J. H. (1979) *Organizations, Behavior, Structure, Processes*, 3rd edn, Business Publications, Dallas.

Handy, C. B. (1976) *Understanding Organizations*, Penguin, Harmondsworth, England.

Lewin, K., Lippitt, R. and White, R. K. (1939) 'Patterns of Aggressive Behaviour in Experimentally Created Social Climates', *Journal of Social Psychology*, 10, 271–301.

Likert, R. and Hayes, S. P. (1957) *Some Applications of Behavioural Research*, UNESCO, Paris.

McGregor, D. (1960) *The Human Side of Enterprise*, McGraw-Hill, New York.

Reddin, W. J. (1970) *Managerial Effectiveness*, McGraw-Hill, New York.

Tannenbaum, R. and Schmidt, W. H. (1958) 'How to Choose a Leadership Pattern', *Harvard Business Review*, 36, 95–101.

Vroom, V. H. and Jago, A. G. (1974) 'Decision Making as a Social Process', *Decision Sciences*, 5, 745–9.

Vroom, V. H. and Yetton, P. (1973) *Leadership and Decision Making*, University of Pittsburgh Press, Pittsburgh.

White, R. and Lippitt, R. (1960) 'Leader Behaviour and Member Reaction in Three "Social Climates" ', in Cartwright, D. and Zander, A. (eds), *Group Dynamics: Research and Theory*, 2nd edn, Tavistock, London.

10
Structures of Organizations

Introduction

The structures of organizations can be thought of as falling into two categories: micro and macro. The *micro* aspect of organizational behaviour deals with the behaviour in organizations of individuals, groups and inter-group activities (Chapters 2—9). These areas are often thought to be the special domain of the psychologist. The *macro* aspects of organizational behaviour, the central concern of this chapter, deal with the global behaviour of an organization as a social system. These aspects include the structure, the influence of the technology used by the organization, and the relationship of the organization to the environment.

The chapter is arranged chronologically, beginning with the classical proponents of the value of structure, such as Weber, Taylor, Fayol and Urwick, who laid down some of the basic concepts of organizational structure and described the behaviours expected to take place within them. They were committed to a rational understanding of organizational behaviour. Later, largely based on the work of Mayo, the human-relations school focused its attention on the social needs of the members of the organization. In recent years much work has been done on a contingency model of organizations. This is a more relativistic model where the behaviour of an organization is viewed as highly influenced by its setting, the technology in use, and its structure. One of the current views of organizations is a *systems* view which draws attention to the relationships between organizational structure and environment. Finally, it is necessary to look to the future to try to anticipate the forms which organizations of tomorrow might take.

Weber and Michels

One of the earliest classical thinkers was Max Weber, who tried to understand why capitalism was becoming the dominant mode of production in Europe. He was searching for a rationale for bourgeois capitalism. In *The Protestant Ethic and the Spirit of Capitalism* he identified the 'elective affinity' between Protestantism and capitalism where the virtues esteemed by the Protestants (hard work, sobriety, loyalty, frugality, etc.) serve the needs of capitalism. Weber traced this affinity to the Reformation, when he thinks the rational ascetism of the monastery moved to the work-place. Of Protestantism he says, 'Sebastian Frank struck the central characteristic of this type of religion when he saw the significance of the Reformation in the fact that now every Christian had to be a monk all his life' (Weber, 1930). This is the origin of the Protestant work ethic, which is often referred to as fuelling modern organizations with energy. He referred to this commitment as a 'calling', in the religious sense of that word. Once he had solved the problem of why people make a commitment to organizations, Weber went on to develop an idealized bureaucracy from his observations of the emerging organizations of the day.

Weber saw *bureaucracy* as rational behaviour. Gerth and Mills (1958) make an interesting comparison between Marx and Weber on the point of rationality in organizations:

> For Marx, the modern economy is basically irrational; this irrationality of capitalism results from a contradiction between the rational technological advances of the productive forces and the fetters of private property, private profit, and unmanaged market competition. The system is characterized by an 'anarchy of production'.

> For Weber, on the other hand, modern capitalism is not 'irrational'; indeed, its institutions appear as the embodiment of rationality. As a type of bureaucracy, the large corporation is rivalled only by the state bureaucracy in promoting rational efficiency, continuity of operation, speed, precision, and calculation of results.

These are the same benefits which the modern manager values in a rationalized organization.

Weber abstracted a set of five characteristics of bureaucracy which contribute to efficiency and quantification. First, bureaucracies operate by the principle of fixed and official areas of jurisdiction governed by rules. Each area has official duties, with the authority to give commands delimited to that area. Weber's second principle is that the higher levels of graded authority have command over all offices below. Weber's third principle says that all of the work of the official must be recorded in written documents. This is to promote the separation of private and public (or company) money. Many of the characteristics of the bureaucracy were an attempt to get away from the patronage of the 'old boy network' dating from the feudal system.

Another emphasis of bureaucracy from the start was to protect the members of the organization from the indiscriminate authority of officials. The fourth principle is that each office presupposes thorough and expert training, and is full-time work. Lastly, Weber sees the ultimate protection against individual privileges and sacred tradition in the principle that all rules can be learned. It is easy to see how modern management education and its attention to certificates is indebted to Weber.

Whereas Weber saw bureaucracy as the most efficient and predictable type of organization he did not value the bureaucrat:

> He deplores the type of man that mechanization and the routine of bureaucracy selects and forms. The narrow professional, publicly certified and examined, and ready for tenure and career. This type of man Weber deplored as a petty routine creature, lacking in heroism, human spontaneity, and inventiveness (Gerth and Mills, 1958).

Weber felt that if these drab bureaucrats did their jobs in a totally conscientious way the organization would grind to a halt:

> it is still more horrible to think that the world could one

day be filled with nothing but those little cogs, little men clinging to little jobs and striving towards bigger ones ... men who need 'order' and nothing but order, who become nervous and cowardly if for one moment this order wavers, and helpless if they are torn away from their total incorporation in it (Mayer, 1969).

The *charismatic* leader rises up from time to time and energizes the bureaucratic world. He is the direct opposite of the bureaucrat: direct and interpersonal, creative, spontaneous, gifted, imaginative, and people will follow him in spite of the fact that he has no qualifications or authority.

Michels (1962) was working about the same time as Weber. He focused on voluntary organizations such as trade unions. His best-known principle modulates the rational starkness of Weber's bureaucracy. His principle is called the 'iron law of oligarchy'. This states that even a bureaucracy with all the Weberian safeguards is actually run by a few leaders. They will put their own interests first and work to preserve the bureaucratic procedures which have all the character of efficiency and certification, and which keep them at the top. He showed that, frequently, persons of liberal, reforming views succumb to compromise and bureaucratic preservation after being in office for a while.

Early writers on management

Other writers were also trying to rationalize the work of the modern industrial world, though they were not directly concerned with structures. They include Taylor, Fayol, Follet and Urwick. Taylor is known as the father of scientific management. He, too, emphasized a blend of science and capitalism in his value system: 'The principle object of management should be to secure the maximum prosperity for the employer, coupled with the maximum prosperity for each employee' (Taylor, 1923). He argued that the typical rule-of-thumb operations needed to be replaced with a science of work behaviours. In order to accomplish this objective, management had four new duties (Taylor, 1923):

First.   They develop a science for each element of a man's work, which replaces the old rule-of-thumb method.

Second.   They scientifically select and then train, teach, and develop the workman, whereas in the past he chose his own work and trained himself as best he could.

Third.   They heartily co-operate with the men so as to insure all of the work being done is in accordance with the principles of the science which has been developed.

Fourth.   There is an almost equal division of the work and the responsibility between the management and the workmen.

Taylor gave managers a legitimacy which they had not had before, and laid down a concept of rational, scientifically based behaviour. Many managers today are still striving to get their organization to this degree of rationalization.

During the early decades of this century Henri Fayol (1967) was producing in France a more detailed manual for managers. He divides his book into principles of management and elements of management. The fourteen principles have a rational tone to them and still sound current. He discusses such principles as division of work, discipline, subordination of individual interest to general interest, remuneration, and *esprit de corps*. His five elements of management are planning, organizing, command, co-ordination and control. Fayol was a manager in a French mining company before the turn of the century and had a very successful career in management as well as publishing a number of articles and books on mining and management. Thus his books are full of advice such as 'avoid red tape'!

Mary Parker Follet was an American pioneer in the concept of management before the First World War. She generated the new idea that the *situation* was the real source of direction. She taught open, honest discussion of differences in creative group settings, and her work has been called the first to use psychology in management. Her collected works were published after her death.

Urwick was a prolific British author, director of the International Management Institute in Geneva, and head of a large firm of consultants in London. He was well informed about the work of Fayol, Taylor and Follet, building on them and trying to find a distinctive approach for the European manager. In 1933 he drew many of his ideas together in his book *Management of Tomorrow*. He adopted a rational view of work and lamented the reliance on American expertise in management: 'There is a third difficulty with the majority of the systems of foreman training which have hitherto been described. They hail from the United States. . . inapplicable directly to European conditions' (Urwick, 1933).

One of the lessons that can be learned from a review of the earliest thinkers in management and organizaitonal behaviour is that much of the elementary thinking had been done by the 1930s. Yet many managers still find the points made by these writers novel and new to them. For further reading and paraphrasing of and extracts from their works, we suggest Pugh, Hickson and Hinnings (1971) on *Writers on Organizations*, Pugh (1971) on *Organization Theory* and Burns (1969) on *Industrial Man*.

Structure and social behaviour

Several behavioural scientists have been concerned with the relationship between the informal and formal structure. Roethlisberger and Dickson (1939) report the research of Elton Mayo at the Hawthorne Plant of the Western Electric Company (the manufacturing company for the American Telephone & Telegraph Company). The original purpose of the research was to test the effects of lighting on fatigue and production. After having raised and lowered the lighting levels under rigorous conditions, and noting that production continued to rise in the experimental as well as the control areas, they concluded that it might be the workers' reaction to the presence of researchers that was the main cause of the change (often referred to as the 'Hawthorne effect'). From this, and other findings about group behaviour, they suggested: 'The point of view which gradually emerged from these studies is one from which an industrial organization is regarded as a social system' (Roethlisberger and Dickson, 1939). Their empirically based findings gave rise to the 'human-relations' approach to organizational behaviour. Their significant contribution was to make a case for the importance of informal behaviour on formal structures.

Selznick (1964) followed on from the Hawthorne studies and identified three hypotheses:

A.   Every organization creates an informal structure.
B.   In every organization, the goals of the organization are modified (abandoned, deflected, or elaborated) by processes within it.
C.   The process of modification is effected through the informal structure.

He was the first to demonstrate clearly that the functions performed by the members of organizations help to determine the structure. He also, along the way, developed the case-study method as a recognized research method. Following the ideas and methods of Selznick, the researcher, usually a sociologist, can examine the functions of the organization and thus understand its structure. This is usually done by comparing case studies and searching for the natural history and logic of the organization. One of the findings which often results is evidence of organizational goals being subverted by the personal goals of the leaders. This is similar to Michels's iron law of oligarchy (discussed earlier), except that Selznick paints the results of the lack of strong management leadership. Organizational goals may also be subverted by collusion between powerful groups in and outside the organization, the co-opting of the organization by political interests, routinizing the function to the easier but less ideologically based task, and being more concerned with perpetuity than achieving the goals of the organization. In general, these studies expose the abuse of power. Selznick (1949) obtained these results in his seminal work which discussed the Tennessee Valley Authority, and Perrow (1972) reviews a number of studies supporting the same findings in organizations such as an association for the blind, judical organizations, the YMCA and the military.

This period, before and following the Second World War, might be thought of as a period in which the study of structures of organizations was moving progressively in the macro direction. The human-relations school is concerned with how individuals and groups affect the structure. Selznick focuses more on how the functions are performed in relation to outside forces and how that influences structures. Since that time the study of the structures of organizations has been heavily influenced by contingency theory.

Contingency theory

In recent years many behavioural scientists have focused on 'contingency theory'. This is a relativist view of the organization and is based on the assumption that there is no universal structure for organizations. The structure of the organization depends upon many factors. Here we will discuss some of those factors, such as the environment, the technology, the task, the willingness to innovate, and the best fit between technical and social needs.

Joan Woodward (1965) conducted a series of investigations into a large number of firms in the South of England to see if classical management theory (span of control, layers in the hierarchy, etc. discussed earlier in this chapter) could be equated with organizational success. After some difficulty in finding any correlation between management theory and success, the researchers shifted their emphasis to the technology being used. To Woodward technology means not only the machines being used but also the technological process at work. She found that the characteristics of an organisation were contingent on the technology it used. She divided the organizations in her sample into three types of production technology:

1. *Small-batch (or unit) production*, where the product was either made to the customer's order or several were made when an order was obtained.

2. *Large-batch (or mass) production*, where the product was made to a warehouse order based on projected sales and usually in some form of assembly-line method.
3. *Process production*, where production was in a continuous flow, e.g. chemicals or petroleum.

The Woodward research found that there were structural characteristics of firms associated with the three types of technology. For instance, she found that the unit production firms began the production cycle with the marketing function, while product development was the first stage in process and mass-production firms. Small-batch production had the most subordinates per supervisor, while mass production had the next most and process had the least. They found no significant relationship between the size of a firm and the type of technology used. The mass-production firms appeared to be the least flexible and have more paperwork: 'The details are less important than the major point being made. In the Woodward studies, evidence was presented that questioned the idea that there is one best way to organize. Different structures are required for different technological demands' (Duncan, 1978).

Lawrence and Lorsch (1969) put forward their concepts of *differentiation* and *integration*. They examined the behaviour of managers in manufacturing, sales and research and development departments in a number of firms in the plastics, packaged-food and standardized-container industries. They examined the goal orientation, time orientation, interpersonal orientation and the formality of structure of the managers. They found that firms with highly differentiated departments but who also had committees or *ad hoc* groups to work for integration of the system were the most successful. This result is consistent with contingency theory. Each department has a structure contingent on its task in terms of time, goals, interpersonal needs and degree of formality. For example, there is usually a considerable difference in the time horizon of people in a research and development department, who are often thinking years ahead, and, say, the production department, where current productivity is the overriding concern.

Lawrence and Lorsch found that the degree of successful integration of units was a result of the way in which conflicts were resolved. In effective companies the managers who were good at resolving conflicts had key items of information, and were in functional areas most closely related to where the key competitive advantage could be gained for the organization. Communication tended to be open and confrontive rather than avoiding or suppressing conflict. Decisions tended to be pushed down to a lower level and conflict tended to be resolved more at these lower levels. Lawrence and Lorsch's findings on differentation refute the notion that an organization has a structure and style of operating that is consistent throughout all departments of the organization.

The work of Woodward and of Lawrence and Lorsch helps towards an understanding of the fact that there is no *one* best way to organize, nor is there *one* best style of leadership, decision-making, goal and time orientation which is suitable for all organizations, or even for an individual organization. These aspects of organizational structure are contingent on the task to be accomplished and the technology used.

Another British research team, Trist and Bamforth (1951), developed a concept to make the best fit between the social needs of the members of the organization and the technical needs of the system. They see organizations as *socio-technical* systems. They did their early work in the coal mines of England. The traditional way of coal mining was for two colliers to make a contract with the mine and usually hire a boy trimmer to work with them. This work arrangement also carried over into the social life of the village. They performed all the tasks of getting the coal out from a short wall at the coal face. When modern equipment was installed to increase production and efficiency it was for a long wall face. The jobs were rationalized with up to forty miners working together at one face. The mines experienced a high rate of disturbances due to upsetting the community of workers both below and above ground.

Trist and Bamforth examined the situation and introduced changes. The long wall method, which was better for the machines was retained but the work was performed in smaller groups with a greater degree of autonomy for each worker. Since the initial study, the concept of a socio-technical system has been used to organise work in many modern sites where complex technical demands and the needs of people involved are both considered. One of the best-known examples in Great Britain in the Shell Oil UK refinery at Fawley (Hill, 1971).

Structure and the environment

In the most macro sense, *systems theory* focuses on the organisation and its environment. One influential approach has been that advocated by Katz and Kahn (1966), who conceptualized an organization as an open system. Energy, information, raw materials and other resources are taken in from the environment, processed in various ways to produce goods which, together with information (e.g. advertisements), are exported into the environment in such a way as to generate the input of further raw materials and resources. The pattern of exchange between system and environment is seen as a cycle of events.

Katz and Kahn describe a set of five formal sub-systems necessary for the survival of such an open system: (i) *production* or task accomplishment, which is the conversion of raw materials and energy into products; (ii) *maintenance* of working structure, whose function is to mediate between task demands and human needs to keep the structure in operation; (iii) *boundary systems* are in two types—the first one is called the production-supportive system and includes the procurement of materials and manpower and product disposal, while the second is the institutional system which obtains and maintains social support and legitimation for the organization from its environment; (iv) *adaptive sub-systems* are concerned with the intelligence of the system, such as research and development and planning; and (v) the *managerial sub-system*, which is seen as having three main duties—resolving conflicts between hierarchical levels, co-ordinating and directing the other sub-systems, and co-ordinating external requirements and organizational resources and needs.

The open systems approach directs our attention in particular to the nature and control of transactions between an organization and its environment. Emery and Trist (1965) place special emphasis on the characteristics of environments: 'the characteristics of organizational environments demand consideration for their own sake'. They further suggest that a comprehensive understanding of organizational behaviour requires some knowledge of:

1. Processes within the organization (for example, wage negotiations, technological innovation, investment in new plant).
2. Exchange between an organization and its environment (for example, advertising campaigns, requirement to implement new safety regulations).
3. Processes through which parts of the environment become related to one another (for example, price increases in petroleum arising from the formation of OPEC, investment in Third World countries' manufacturing industries, formation of the EEC).

Emery and Trist identify and describe four idealized types of environment: a 'Placid randomized' environment, a 'placid clustered' environment, a 'disturbed reactive' environment, and finally 'turbulent fields'. They argue that the nature of the environment has a strong influence on the size, structure and survival strategy of organizations within it.

The 'placid randomized' environment is so named because goals and repellants (or 'goods' and 'bads') are relatively unchanging in themselves and randomly distributed. This environment is like a surface over which the organization can move, seeking out the goods and avoiding the bads (like looking for mushrooms in a field with bulbs in it!).

In a 'placid clustered' environment the goods and bads occur together in certain ways. For example, coal is usually found together with gas. Therefore, production methods need to be developed for extracting the coal without the miners being gassed. Because of the increased complexity and structure of the environment, organizations need specialized expertise to deal with its various aspects, or increased use of *boundary systems*, to use Katz and Kahn's phrase. Organizations in a placid clustered environment tend to be larger than those in a placid random environment.

A 'disturbed reactive' environment is described as being a placid clustered environment in which there is more than one organization of the same kind. Indeed, the existence of a number of similar organizations can become the dominant characteristic of an environment. Then organizations have to make decisions and choose actions that will 'draw off' competitors. One organization attempts to influence what its competitors do in a way that is favourable to itself. Here, the competition between the great trading nations for natural resources from the non-industrialized world provides a striking example of the disturbed reactive environment.

When the Third World countries begin to seek independence and control over their own resources we move into the fourth type of environment, known as 'turbulent fields'. In turbulent fields the dynamic properties arise not simply from the interaction of the component organizations but also from the total field itself. The 'ground' is in motion.

When the motions and interactions become large enough and sufficiently persistent they induce a response in other agencies. For example, the increase in oil prices led to an investment in research to develop less energy-intensive devices. These devices had military uses and in turn they influenced the arms race. The arms race increases the degree of uncertainty of the whole field:

What becomes precarious under type 4 condition [turbulent field] is how organizational stability can be achieved. The emergence of *Values that have overriding significance for all members of the field* as coping mechanisms that make men seek rules . . . to provide them with a guide and ready calculus. So far as effective values emerge the character of the richly joined turbulent fields changes in a most striking fashion. The relevance of large classes of events . . . is given directly by the ethical code . . . a field is created which is no longer richly joined and turbulent but simplified and relatively static. Such a transformation will be regressive, or constructively adaptive, according to how far the emergent values adequately represent the new environmental requirements. An appropriate response in a turbulent field requires a strategy which maximises co-operation and recognizes that no one organization can take over the role of the other and become paramount (Emery and Trist, 1965).

As understanding the nature of organizations and their environments increases, the idea of designing organizations begins to gain currency. Design can take the form of starting up a new organization or changing an existing one. One line of thought has involved the attempted classification of organizational structures together with assessment of their appropriateness to survival in various types of environment.

For example, Burns and Stalker (1958) have looked at organizational structure in view of how it responds to the external environment. They looked at electronics firms in Scotland and identified two ideal types: the mechanistic and the organic. The mechanistic is similar to the classical rational organization where jobs are broken down to well-defined small parts (as described earlier in this chapter). In such a case only the top management knows everything that is going on. There is much emphasis on inter-departmental work going through superiors only. A subordinate talks to his superior, who talks to his peers, who then relay the message back down to their subordinates. The system operates like a machine which makes control, precision and quantification easy. They also concluded from their study that the mechanistic system was more stable and appropriate for a stable environment.

For Burns and Stalker the organic system has less well-defined jobs where many of the interactions are handled directly between those concerned. Functions and responsibilities have to be constantly refined through discussion. More members of the organization have a large view of it. It is more demanding, with less appropriate traditional guidance and training available. They found that the organic system is more easily adaptable and therefore can respond to an unstable environment more readily.

Pugh (1976), in discussing Burns and Stalker, has put forward three dimensions which need to be considered in designing an organization. He presented dimensions in terms of *continua* (see Figure 10.1). Pugh viewed the poles as conflicts, and the organization designer's tasks a striking of a balance between them.

He cited Burns and Stalker's description of an organization located at the left-hand end of the three dimensions (that is,

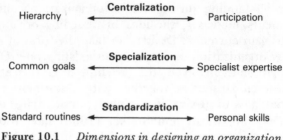

Figure 10.1　*Dimensions in designing an organization*

high on all three characteristics) as being *mechanistic* and an organization at the right on all three dimensions as being *organic*. The value of using terms like 'mechanistic' and 'organic' is that they provide readily understandable models on which to base our thinking about organizations. But such models, by virtue of their simplicity and coherence, can be misleading.

For example, the organic analogy can be taken too far. An organization that is like an organism (say, an animal or a plant) tends to:

1. seek to maintain its given structure;
2. change only in response to environmental change (and then only in limited ways);
3. evolve so that all its parts are functionally necessary (everything has its purpose);
4. have parts that are unself-conscious and passive, functionally specialized and non-interchangeable;
5. have parts which operate in harmony;
6. have the over-all goal of survival; and
7. be largely centrally controlled (only one brain).

Clearly this is not a description of an ideal organization. The main disadvantage of the organic model is that it does not handle internally generated change very well. In organisms the internal source of change is mutation. Mutations are relatively rare and most of them are disastrous. In organizations the main source of change is people. Inevitably different individuals or interest groups have differing interpretations of what is going on in organizations and of what should happen. Conflict is endemic in organizations and attempts to cope with conflict result in change. Various visions of what might be, as well as creativeness, are other sources of internal organizational change. People are not passive and unself-conscious parts of an organization (though they can behave as such if they feel it necessary).

Buckley (1967) has severely criticized proponents of both mechanistic and organic models of organizations on the grounds that they do not handle change adequately. He suggests a third model, the 'socio-cultural' system. Socio-cultural sytems are unique to man and have no analogy. Each socio-cultural system has a language of its own with its own symbolism. It has a past and a view of the future which influences its present behaviour. It understands itself as self and also in relation to the world around it. The tensions that exist within or between the system and the environment may be energy-producing. Table 10.1 is a summary of the main characteristics of mechanistic, organic and socio-cultural systems as described by Buckley.

Organizations of the future

What sorts of organizational structure can we expect in the future? A number of writers predict the demise of bureaucracies. Bennis (1969), for example, asserts that 'The key word will be "temporary"; there will be adaptive, rapidly changing temporary systems . . . People will be differentiated, not vertically according to rank and role, but flexibly and functionally according to skill and professional training.'

Perrow (1972) develops Bennis's point and suggests three reasons for anticipating decentralization, increased participation and more adaptive responses:

(1) *The increasing professionalization of management.* However, the rate of increase in professionalization is questionable. For example, Warman (1980) found in a survey for the Business Graduates Association of 10,000 senior managers in local government in Great Britain that barely a dozen had been to business school. Most modern British managers still learn about organizations through experience – a finding which confirms the diagnosis made in Chapter 2.

Table 10.1 *Buckley's mechanistic, organic and socio-cultural systems*

Characteristic	Mechanical systems	Organic systems	Socio-cultural systems
1. System parts	Simple, very stable and largely unaffected by being part of the system (e.g. a pendulum in a clock)	More complex, less stable and somewhat affected (e.g. organ in an animal)	Highly complex, relatively unstable and considerably affected by virtue of their membership of the system (e.g. a human psyche in a group)
2. System relations	Based on energy flow, spatial and temporal proximity; interaction is physical	Based on energy and information flow, with spatial and temporal proximity being less important. Interaction as largely physiological	Based largely on information flow, spatial and temporal proximity of parts much less important. Interaction is largely through symbolic communication

3.	Openness of system	Relatively closed — responds to changes in the physical environment	Open to physical and natural environment	Very open to social, symbolic environment
4.	System tension: sources of action and interaction of parts	Energy, attraction and repulsion, inertia, etc.	Inherent 'irritability of protoplasm' tension, or stress in animals	Psychic energy or motive power in men Tension manifested as strivings, frustrations, enthusiasms, aggressions, creativity, production, construction, destruction
5.	Characteristic development	Equilibrium — tending through mutual interactions of parts (and entropic processes)	Goal-seeking (homeostatic) through adaptation to environment using mainly negative feedback Change in structure (morphogenesis) largely through mutation and natural selection	Purposive and morphogenetic, self-directing, using (negative and positive) feedback for selective decision-making (about itself and its environment)

Source: adapted from W. Buckley (1967) *Sociology and Modern Systems Theory*, Prentice-Hall, Englewood Cliffs, N.J.

(2) *Rapid technological change.* It is interesting to note that the type of technology currently believed to be the most potent source of change — namely, micro-processors — is essentially an information-processing technology. It can be argued that the organizing principle of a bureaucracy is the control of information. The advent of micro-processors provides the biggest challenge yet to bureaucracies. The battle for access to information and for the right to interpret it and make decisions is still going on.

(3) *The increasingly turbulent environment as a source of organizational change.* Toffler (1970) is one of the prophets of the breakdown of bureaucracy:

> We are, in fact, witnessing the arrival of a new organizational system that will increasingly challenge and ultimately supplant bureaucracy. This is the organization of the future. I call it 'Ad-hocracy' . . . Instead of being trapped in some unchanging, personality-smashing niche, man will find himself liberated, a stranger in a new free-form world of kinetic organization. In this alien landscape, his position will be constantly changing, fluid and varied. And his organizational ties, like his ties with things, places and people, will turn over at a frantic and ever-accelerating rate.

Toffler is clearly envisaging a situation likely to produce additional stress in managers (see Chapter 5).

But is Toffler right? Although few people would disagree that the world has become increasingly turbulent, are organizations going to adapt? Emery and Trist (1965) argue, for example, that turbulent fields can become transformed into 'simplified and relatively static' fields by the 'emergence of values that have overriding significance for all members of the field'. During the last few decades we have seen the emergence of coalitions in turbulent fields. On the international scene we have NATO and the Warsaw Pact, OPEC, the grouping together of countries from the Third World, multinational organizations, and so on. Newly emerging common values bring these parties together. At the time of writing in 1981 common values for the whole world have yet to emerge (and in an age of virtually instantaneous communication the whole world is the environment of most organizations). But perhaps the resolution of the East—West and North—South polarizations will produce acceptance of a set of global values that will ensure stability. As Emery and Trist (1965) suggest, however, 'such a transformation will be regressive, or constructively adaptive, according to how far the emergent values adequately represent the new environmental requirements'.

People have always had to organize to achieve their goals. Their success has depended on how they worked together and on the environment in which they worked. Increasing our understanding of human nature, of the possible varieties of human organizations and of the characteristics of organizational environments, open up the possibility of consciously choosing how to achieve common goals. The development and use of such knowledge may yet turn out to be the most significant influence on the future structures of organizations.

References for Chapter 10

Bennis, W. G. (1969) *Organization Development: Its Nature, Origins and Prospects*, Addison-Wesley, Reading, Mass.

Buckley, W. (1967) *Sociology and Modern Systems Theory*, Prentice-Hall, Englewood Cliffs, N.J.

Burns, T. (1969) *Industrial Man*, Penguin, Harmondsworth, England.

Burns, T. and Stalker, G. M. (1958) *The Management of Innovation*, Tavistock, London.

Duncan, W. J. (1978) *Organizational Behavior*, Houghton Mifflin, Boston.

Emery, F. E. and Trist, E. L. (1965) 'The Causal Texture of Organizational Environments', *Human Relations*, 18, 21—3.

Fayol, H. (1967) *General and Industrial Management*, Pitman, London.

Gerth, H. H. and Mills, G. W. (1958) *From Max Weber: Essays in Sociology*, Oxford University Press, New York.

Hill, P. (1971) *Towards a New Philosophy of Management*, Gower Press, Epping, England.

Katz, D. and Kahn, R. L. (1966) *The Social Psychology of Organizations*, Wiley, New York.

Lawrence, P. R. and Lorsch, J. W. (1969) *Organization and Environment: Managing Differentiation and Integration*, Irwin, Homewood, Ill.

Mayer, J. P. (1969) 'Some Consequences of Bureaucratization (Weber)', in Cosser, L. A. and Rosenberg, B. (eds), *Sociological Theory: A Book of Readings*, Macmillan, New York.

Michels, R. (1962) *Political Parties*, Free Press, New York.

Perrow, C. (1972) *Complex Organizations: A Critical Essay*, Scott, Foresman, Glenview, Ill.

Pugh, D. S. (1971) *Organization Theory*, Penguin, Harmondsworth, England.

Pugh, D. S. (1976) 'Organization Design', visiting lecture, Department of Management Sciences, UMIST, Manchester, England.

Pugh, D. S., Hickson, D. and Hinnings, J. (1971) *Writers on Organizations*, Penguin, Harmondsworth, England.

Roethlisberger, F. J. and Dickson, W. J. (1939) *Management and the Worker*, Harvard University Press, Cambridge, Mass.

Selznick, P. (1949) *TVA and the Grass Roots*, University of California Press, Berkeley.

Selznick, P. (1964) 'An Approach to a Theory of Bureaucracy', in Coser, L. A. and Rosenberg, B. (eds), *Sociological Theory: A Book of Readings*, Macmillan, New York.

Taylor, F. W. (1923) *The Principles of Scientific Management*, Harper & Row, New York.

Toffler, A. (1970) *Future Shock*, Random House, New York.

Trist, E. L. and Bamforth, R. (1951) 'Some Social and Psychological Consequences of the Long Wall Method of Coal Getting', *Human Relations*, 4(1), 3–38.

Urwick, L. (1933) *Management of Tomorrow*, Nisbet & Co., London.

Warman, C. (1980) 'Business School Training Urged for Council Chiefs', *The Times*, 5 September 1980, 3.

Weber, M. (1930) *The Protestant Ethic and the Spirit of Capitalism*, Allen & Unwin, London.

Woodward, J. (1965) *Industrial Organization: Theory and Practice*, Oxford University Press, London.

Section 3: The Organization and Change

11
Creativity

Introduction

About 200 years ago the world's equivalent of today's Silicon Valley was not a valley at all. It was the Pennine Hills to the south-east of Manchester in England. At the far side of these hills Arkwright established the first factory in the world — Masson Mills in the tiny village of Cromford. The mills were powered by the streams cascading from the rainy Peak District plateau between Manchester and Cromford. The dominant mode of transport at the time, the canals, could not cope with the gradients of the Peak District plateau so a railway was built between the canal terminus at Whaley Bridge and Cromford. According to modern standards, it was a strange railway with only stationary engines at the either side of the plateau. Wagons were hauled up the inclines by systems of chains and pulleys. The wagons then travelled the rest of their way under the force of gravity, with a little help from horses. By the standards of that time the railway was completely orthodox. Machinery was nearly always fixed in one place. It required a genius to make the second greatest creative leap in the history of mankind and appreciate that the power source could be placed on wheels. That single creative leap led to the railway systems of the world. It lead to the first station at Liverpool Road in Manchester. It led to the great railways which opened up the midwest of the USA and allowed the granary of the world to get its products to market.

This chapter is concerned with creativity, creative leaps and their impact on industrial and commercial organizations. The mechanics of Manchester who concentrated upon the routine matters of stationary engines and wagons travelling on the incline saw their organizations wither and perish. The mechanics of Manchester who concentrated upon the problems of engines on wheels and who exploited the opportunities saw their organizations flourish for generations.

The term 'creative' has been used in many ways — to describe a product, an idea, a person, a situation, and so on. To provide a way into this diverse topic, we shall follow MacKinnon (1978):

> the starting point, indeed the bedrock of all studies of creativity is an analysis of creative products, a determination of what it is that makes them different from more mundane products. This is the problem of the criterion, and only after we have come to some agreement about the criterion, which . . . is the creative product, are we in a position to study the other facets of creativity.

Consequently this chapter begins by exploring the nature of *creative products* and the ways in which they may be distinguished from 'more mundane products'. Then it examines a series of interrelated concepts, such as: the *creative idea*, which is developed into the creative product; the *creative process*, a mental activity, or series of activities, which results in creative ideas; the *creative person*, as the sort of person who acquires or possesses and uses the abilities required for carrying out the creative process; and *creative situations* as situations which allow creative people to *be* creative.

The creative product

Imagine you are one of a panel of judges appointed to draw up a shortlist of the most creative products in the history of mankind. You are sitting around a table at the first meeting of the panel, and the chairman asks each person to make a personal list of the twenty or so most likely candidates for the shortlist. What would you put on your list? Make a list. Here is ours: the silicon chip, the first use of fire, the first city, the first railway, the Parthenon, Beethoven's symphonies, Picasso's paintings, Shakespeare's plays, Michelangelo's *David*, Einstein's theory of relativity, Newton's laws of motion, the first cultivation of plants and domestication of animals, radar, and so on (not, of course, forgetting the wheel, which has been re-invented possibly more times than any other product).

Which criteria did you use for selecting products for your list? On what grounds did you include one product and reject another? Try now to make a list of the criteria you used. You might find it helpful to compare products on your list with products you decided not to include. In what ways are the listed products different from the non-listed ones?

What others say

Just about all writers on creativity agree that to be regarded as creative a product must be new or original in some way. One sense of the word 'original' is that the original product has not existed before, it is unique, the first of its kind. This degree of originality is characteristic of only a few creative products — the first aeroplane, the first railway and the first hovercraft are examples. Many other products are variations on an original theme, improved versions or developments. The truly original product can produce responses ranging from what Bruner (1962) calls 'effective surprise' to shock and rejection.

A good example of 'effective surprise' is provided by the following problem. Imagine there is a chemical manufacturing company located on the bank of a river. The problem is to get the company to reduce pollution in the river which results from its discharges. List some ideas that might achieve this. Edward de Bono (1972) provides a neat solution to the problem (see Figure 11.1). Usually water is taken in upstream of the factory and pollutant discharged downstream. Reversing

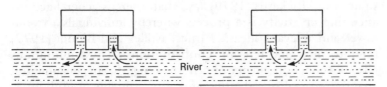

Figure 11.1   *The pollution problem*

the positions of inlet and outlet would encourage the company to treat its effluent before discharge. It is obvious when you see it done, and this is the typical response to this type of creative product. The solution has immediately acceptable features. This aspect of obviousness is shared to some extent by new scientific theories which explain previously puzzling phenomena.

Sometimes a new theory has additional implications which some interested parties find unacceptable, and the initial response is to reject the theory because of its implications rather than for its effectiveness at explaining the phenomenon of central concern to the theorist. Thus, if Darwin's theory of evolution were correct, the long-held belief that God created the world in 4004 BC is incorrect. Rather than change a belief which had been venerated for almost two millennia, the religious establishment rejected the new theory. This consideration of the impact of creative products introduces the second major criterion: the product must be significant in some way to some people.

Chiselin (1963) says that 'creative action . . . alters the universe of meaning itself, by introducing . . . some new element of meaning or some new order of significance or more commonly both'. MacKinnon (1978) uses the phrases 'adaptive to reality', in the sense that the creative product 'serves to solve a problem, fit a situation or accomplish some recognizable goal', and 'adaptive of reality': 'The . . . highest criterion for a creative product . . . requires that the product create new conditions of human existence, transcending and transforming the generally accepted experience of man by introducing new principles that defy tradition and change radically man's view of the world.' Hayes (1978) asserts that 'A creative act must have some valuable consequence, that is, the act should have an effect which is interesting or useful in some way.' Rickards (1979) says that 'there is general acceptance that creativity is a process whereby individuals arrive at novel and relevant ideas'. Parnes, Noller and Biondi (1977) refer to 'new and relevant configurations'. These quotations give us a coherent cluster of criteria — significant, meaningful, adaptive to reality, adaptive of reality, valuable, useful, interesting and relevant.

Clearly there are degrees of significance; putting it rather crudely, the more potential a product has for changing reality and the more people's reality it could change, the more significant it could be. Perhaps the last sentence should have been written in the past tense, since so far we have been considering only creative products of the past. It is much easier to assess the originality and significance of a product in retrospect than it is in prospect. It might be interesting at this point to attempt another imagination exercise.

Imagine you have been asked to produce a script for a television programme entitled *Creative Products of Tomorrow*. Your main task is to choose five recent products which you think will be significant in the future. Which products would you choose and on what grounds? Until now we have made no distinctions between different types of product. Looking back it is difficult to decide which has had more impact on mankind — Darwin's theory of evolution or the motor-car. It is probably true to say that the motor-car has had a more direct impact on more people than has Darwin's theory. Looking ahead to the future is a different matter entirely.

There is currently little attempt to control the product of scientific theories, and little consideration is given to the implications or possible alternative uses of a theory. (However, there are some indications of concern over certain types of research, such as that in the field of genetics.) For the producer of consumer products, however, the significance of a potential new product is of central concern. Before deciding to tool up for the manufacture of a new product the policy-maker in an organization needs to be reasonably sure that the product in its final form will be sufficiently significant for enough people to purchase it. Thus companies are in the business of predicting the future significance of creative products. Similarly, creators of new processes must attempt to take into account the likely responses. For example, there is not much point in producing Acts of Parliament that cannot be implemented or which create more problems than they solve.

The creative product must be differentiated from the creative idea. The main distinction between a creative product of the past and a creative product of the present is that the significance of the latter is more open to doubt, largely because of uncertainty about the future environment.

The creative idea

Imagine you are responsible for the development of new products for a manufacturing company. You have set up a project team with a brief to generate ideas for new products. The project team is about to present its report to you. What criteria would you use to assess the ideas it has produced?

What others say

Few authors distinguish clearly between creative products and creative ideas. The assumption generally held is that a creative idea shares the same characteristics as the creative product — it is new and significant. MacKinnon (1978) draws our attention to a third criterion: 'true creativeness involves a sustaining of the original insight, an evaluation and elaboration of it, a developing of it to the full. Creativity from this point of view is a process extended in time and characterized by originality, adaptiveness and realization.'

For our imaginary manager the issue is whether a creative idea is realizable. Interestingly the criteria 'new' and 'significant' take on additional connotations in the context of new-product development. The test of originality might be whether the idea is patentable or not. Patent office records might show that the idea is not new in the absolute sense, even though it would be new for the company in question but it might still be worth considering production under licence. Significance of an idea pertains not only to the potential market but also to the company. Does the new idea help solve the problem of maintaining utilization of production facilities? Is it the sort of product that is consistent with the company's self image?

MacKinnon's criterion raises the problem of realizability. Past and current creative products have already been realized, but creative ideas have not. We can now summarize the simil-

Table 11.1 *Taxonomy of ideas*

Criteria	Past creative product	Current creative product	Creative idea
New?	At the time	At the time	Perhaps— needs checking
Significant?	Yes, in retrospect	Perhaps— producer thinks so (at least)	Perhaps
Realizable?	Yes	Yes, at least on current form	Perhaps

arities and differences between past and current creative products and creative ideas (see Table 11.1). This summary suggests that there is considerably more uncertainty associated with creative ideas than with creative products. Many creative ideas do not become products because they are deemed not to meet the three criteria, particularly the criterion of realizability.

The creative process

According to MacKinnon (1978), 'the creative process starts only when one sees or senses a problem'. It finishes with the realization of the creative idea — the creative product. Clearly 'not all instances of problem solving are creative' (Hayes, 1978). Hayes also suggests that the underlying psychological processes required for creative problem solving 'appear to be the same as those required for non-creative problem solving'. If these statements are true, then the main difference between creative problem-solving and non-creative problem-solving should stem from the nature of the problems being tackled. As an example try the following problem and make notes of your thought processes as you go along.

Given a plane right-angled triangle ABC with the lengths of AC and BC as shown, use Pythagoras's theorem to find the length of *AB* (see Figure 11.2). Assuming you know the theorem this is a simple problem. So simple, in fact, that there is virtually nothing of your thought processes to record: *AB*, the hypotenuse, is simply the square root of the sum of the squares of the lengths of the other two sides. Many of you will not even have had to go into this amount of detail, because you recognized the basic 3—4—5 triangle. It is doubtful, however, that this puzzle even qualifies as a problem. You are told everything you need to know in order to solve it. The structure of such problems is described by Wickelgren (1974) (among others) as consisting of three components: the *givens*, the *operations* on these givens, and the *goal* to be reached by operating in the permissible way on the givens. If the 'givens' as stated are accepted and the permissible operations understood, the solution is reachable, and it is the same for all solvers — it is not a creative problem.

Now try another problem. Imagine you are responsible for organizing a political campaign. What recommendations would you incorporate for beating inflation? Clearly this is a different sort of problem from the first one. None of the components is clearly defined *for* you. What are the 'givens'? What are the permissible 'operations'? What is the 'goal'? If you were to choose another political party, it is quite likely that the answers to these questions would be different. For this sort of problem there is disagreement concerning the nature of the current and developing situation, uncertainty as to what to do about it, differences in what sorts of actions are acceptable, and difficulty in defining the goal. Such problems are characterized by uncertainty and conflict — nobody

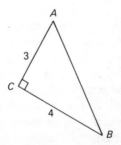

Figure 11.2   *The right-angle triangle problem I*

has come up with a definitive (i.e. universally agreed) formulation of the problem, nobody knows what will happen if one strategy is followed rather than another. Some authors have sought to distinguish between the two sets of problem presented so far. Hayes (1978) writes of *well-defined* problems and *ill-defined* problems. *Well-defined problems*

> are presented in such a way that they leave little to one's imagination. They state the essential conditions of the problem and just what it is one is expected to find out. Their solutions are the same for all solvers. Many school problems such as those in algebra, geometry and chemistry, are well-defined (Hayes, 1978).

'A problem is *ill-defined* because the problem solver takes an active role in specifying what the problem is' (Hayes, 1978). Hayes further suggests that

> There are two sorts of activities which an ill-defined problem may demand of problem-solvers:
>
> (1) They may be required to make decisions which fill gaps in the problem definition.
> (2) They may be required to 'jump into' the problem — that is they need to attempt a solution to the problem before they can fully understand it.

The crucial difference between the two sorts of problems lies in the active contribution of the problem-solver. Different problem solvers will act differently.

Rittel and Webber (1974) distinguish between what they term 'tame' and 'wicked' problems and describe ten characteristics of wicked problems (see Table 11.2).

Rickards (1974) makes a distinction between 'closed-ended' problems and 'open-ended' problems:

> An open-ended problem-solving situation exists if a problem has been recognized and the solver believes that he can usefully challenge one or more of its boundary conditions. The less he is prepared to challenge the boundaries the less open-ended the problem is — as far as he is concerned.

Table 11.2   *Characteristics of wicked problems*

1. There is no definitive formulation of a wicked problem

2. Wicked problems have no stopping rule

3. Solutions to wicked problems are not true or false, but good or bad

4. There is no immediate and no ultimate test of the solution to a wicked problem

5. Every solution to a wicked problem is a 'one-shot operation'; because there is no opportunity to learn by trial-and-error, every attempt counts significantly

6. Wicked problems do not have an enumerable (or an exhaustively describable) set of potential solutions, nor is there a well-described set of permissible operations that may be incorporated in the plan

7. Every wicked problem is essentially unique

8. Every wicked problem can be considered to be a symptom of another problem

9. The existence of a discrepancy representing a wicked problem can be explained in numerous ways; the choice of explanation determines the nature of the problem's resolution

10. The planner has no right to be wrong

Source: H. W. J. Rittel and M. M. Webber (1973) 'Dilemmas in a General Theory of Planning', *Policy Sciences*, 4.

He then lists some ways in which open-ended and closed-ended problems may be distinguished from each other (see Table 11.3).

There are obvious similarities between the three sets of distinctions: Well-defined, tame and closed-ended problems form one cluster, and ill-defined, wicked and open-ended problems form another.

The major implication of this set of distinctions is that problems that are already well-defined, closed-ended or tame do not provide much opportunity for creativeness. The way the problem is formulated largely determines the solution. On the other hand, wicked, open-ended or ill-defined problems can provide opportunities for creativeness. Tackling a

Table 11.3 *Characteristics of open and closed problem situations*

Open	Closed
Boundaries may change during problem-solving	Boundaries are fixed during problem-solving
Process of solving often involves production of novel and unexpected ideas	Process marked by predictability of final solution
Process may involve creative thinking of an uncontrollable kind	Process usually conscious, controllable and logically reconstructable
Solutions often outside the bounds of logic can neither be proved nor disproved	Solutions often provable, logically correct
Direct (conscious) efforts at stimulation of creative process to solve problems are difficult	Procedures are known which directly aid problem-solving (algorithms or heuristics)

Source: T. Rickards (1974) *Problem-Solving through Creative Analysis*, Gower Press, Epping, England.

wicked, ill-defined or open-ended problem involves the problem-solver making decisions as to what the problem is. He has to define it, but there are potentially many ways of defining a problem. The success of the problem-tackling process and the creativeness of the solution depend on the choice of formulation of the problem.

The puzzle shown in Figure 11.3 can be used to illustrate this point. This puzzle has been presented to many people and only a very few have come up with what is currently believed to be the most elegant solution. If you wish to solve it yourself but want to continue reading before you have, turn to line 30 of page 220 and do not read the discussion below. If you do solve it or if you think you have given it the effort it deserves, carry on reading below.

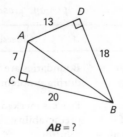

Figure 11.3   *The right-angle triangle problem II*

At first sight this problem looks like a well-defined problem. But as soon as you compare the answers to $AC^2 + CB^2$ (= 449) and $AD^2 + BD^2$ (= 493) it becomes clear that there is something amiss. (It wouldn't be much of a puzzle if the two sums *were* the same.) What solvers tend to do next is to start questioning various aspects of the diagram. For example, they ask if the two triangles are in the same plane or if the triangles are on a curved surface rather than a flat one, or if the numbers are in different units of measurement, or if the angles ACB and/or ADB are really right angles (one architect imagined the right-angle signs to be the tops of two columns supporting a roof-like structure). If you imagine, for example, that the two triangles are not in the same plane, then solutions become possible (see Figure 11.4).

Some people are satisfied if they produce one or both of these solutions; they are, however, interpreting the question '$AB = ?$' slightly loosely in permitting two solutions (21.2 and 22.2). For some solvers there is something not quite satisfactory about this and they continue the search.

What seems to be going on in the problem-solver's mind is that he makes assumptions about the nature of the problem, and seeks a solution on the basis of these assumptions. If he cannot find a solution, he begins to examine these assumptions and imagine what the diagram might represent if they are not true. Some avenues are easier to explore than others. It is generally more difficult to visualize the triangles on a curved surface than as being in different planes. So curved-surface solutions tend not to be produced as often as biplanar solutions.

1. One triangle tilted

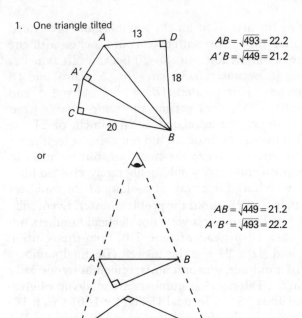

$AB = \sqrt{493} = 22.2$
$A'B = \sqrt{449} = 21.2$

$AB = \sqrt{449} = 21.2$
$A'B' = \sqrt{493} = 22.2$

2. One triangle above the other. *AB* appears to coincide with *A'B'* if the eye is the right distance above, i.e.

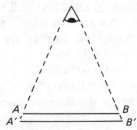

Figure 11.4 *Solutions to right-angle triangle problem II*

Some people, having exhausted their repertoire of possibly false assumptions about the diagram, begin to examine assumptions about the problem setter, either indirectly ('It's impossible'; 'Can *you* draw it to scale?') or directly ('Are you trying to trick me'; 'Are you trying deliberately to make me flounder for some covert purpose of your own').

One person solved the problem as follows: he eventually

started focusing his attention on the numbers and pretended or imagined that they represented feet and inches with the feet and inches symbols left out. So 20 became 2ft 0 inches (or 24 inches), 13 became 1ft 3 inches (or 15 inches) and 18 became 20 inches. This yielded $AB^2 = 7^2 + 24^2 = 25^2$ and $AB^2 = 15^2 + 20^2 = 25^2$, thus getting the same answer from both triangles, which he formulated as 2ft 1 inch, or 21. He was still a bit dubious, because he did not think it legitimate of the problem-setter to leave the signs out, but he also did not think the problem-setter would deliberately mislead him. So he started searching for a way of looking at the numbers consistent with his beliefs about the problem-setter. Eventually he realized that if the numbers were not decimal numbers but duodecimal (base 12 instead of base 10), then the solution was obvious, and $AB = 21$ was the answer. (Decimal numbers are made up of hundreds, tens and units; remember your early school arithmetic. Duodecimal numbers are made up of grosses, dozens and units.) So in decimal 164 is $(1 \times 100) + (6 \times 10) + (4 \times 1)$, whereas in duodecimal it is $(1 \times 144) + (6 \times 12) + (4 \times 1)$, or more succinctly $(1 \times 10^2) + (6 \times 10^1) + (4 \times 10^0)$ and $(1 \times 12^2) + (6 \times 12^1) + (4 \times 12^0)$ respectively.

There are two main reasons why this puzzle is difficult for people to solve. First, most people are not too well-versed in number bases, so explorations in this area are unlikely. If you do not know that other bases exist, you can hardly explore the possibilities. Second, and probably more important, it seems to be difficult to identify and question very commonly held or 'over-learnt' assumptions: '20' means 'twenty' (there is no verbal expression for '20' in the duodecimal system).

Further characteristics of the creative problem-solving process

The main reason for introducing this puzzle was to illustrate the importance of finding a way of looking at the problem which facilitated finding a solution. There are further aspects. Many attempts have been made to describe the mental processes involved in problem-solving. One model, used in creativity courses, is shown in Figure 11.5. Using this model with the hypotenuse problem, you *recognize* that there is a problem when the two triangles give different results. *Definitions* of

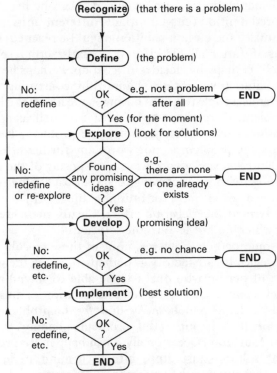

Figure 11.5   *Problem-solving process*

Note: This flow diagram is one of many that have been proposed for describing the general process of problem-solving. It has been developed and used extensively by Ron MacLean, ICI Central Management Services.

the problem are then sought. A redefinition might suggest that the triangles are really in different planes, *Exploration* of possible three-dimensional configurations conforming to this redefinition now take place. Perhaps a number of ideas are produced. These are then *developed*; in essence the problem-tackler tries to visualize or represent the solution ideas. If one looks as though it might work, he then performs the calculations and achieves (or *implements*) the solution. This is then checked. If satisfactory, the *end* is reached. If not, the problem tackler returns to an earlier point in the sequence. Probably he looks at another related solution idea, implements and checks it and so on until no more ideas based on the biplanar definition are produced. Then he may look for further redefinition (curved surface, different units, etc.).

Eventually the elegant solution might be reached; but what happens if (after all his efforts) no satisfactory solution is achieved? Perhaps he decides to give up. Perhaps he rationalizes his failure (explains it to himself) by construing the problem-setter as a trickster, or as having made a mistake in setting the problem. Or perhaps he construes himself as not having the mathematical ability to solve the problem. Perhaps he construes the problem as not worth any further effort on his part. All these strategies are ways of disposing of the problem, of *finishing* with it. According to gestalt psychologists people have a need for closure, for finishing things off. This effect is usually termed the *ziegarnic* effect. Clearly there are ways of closing which do not lead to the solution.

For some people, however, none of these no-solution closure strategies is satisfactory — perhaps they see themselves as the sort of person who ought to be able to solve this puzzle and they cannot accept the disconfirmation of this view of themselves. These people *shelve* or *defer* the problem without closing on it. It is put in the 'problems pending' tray rather than the 'out' tray. Occasionally it can happen that some time later the solution just drops into their mind, perhaps when they are occupied with something completely unrelated. This is the by now famous moment of illumination, the 'aha' or 'eureka' experience, which sometimes follows a period of disengagement of the conscious mind from the problem. This period has come to be known as the 'incubation' period. During this time the mind seems to continue working on the problem below the level of conscious thought. Finally, the new solution is evaluated, elaborated if necessary and applied.

MacKinnon (1978) named the parts of the creative process as follows:

(1) *Preparation*. This is a period of time in which the skills, techniques and experience are acquired which make it possible for the person to pose a problem. This could be the person's whole life to date or just the immediate experiences leading to the posing of the problem.

(2) *Effort* to solve the problem follows. This may be successful, but if not it can involve frustration, tension and dis-

comfort. These may be severe enough to lead to withdrawal from the problem (not a finishing with it), which is often called a period of incubation.

(3) *Incubation*. Little definite is known about what goes on in the mind during incubation. It has been suggested that the unconscious mind continues working on the problem to produce a restructuring of the 'whole mental landscape' (Koestler, 1964), that the mind 'seems to select and arrange and correlate . . . ideas and images into a pattern . . . largely without conscious effort' (Sinnott, 1959). MacKinnon (1978) refers to a time away from direct and conscious attention to the problem as permitting the unfreezing of a fixated and inappropriate way of seeing the problem. Kubie (1958) disputes the role of the unconscious. He believes that both the conscious and the unconscious are rigid and do not allow for fantasy and imaginative thinking. He suggests that the preconscious system (the intermediate region between the conscious and unconscious, whose contents can easily be brought into consciousness (the seat of the memory), is the essential ingredient of creativity. Whatever the explanation of the mental process during incubation, the result can be a moment of insight or illumination.

(4) *Insight or illumination*. The solution suddenly seems clear, and this is accompanied by feelings of pleasure and emotional release – the 'exhilaration, glow and elation of the "aha" experience' (MacKinnon, 1961; cited in Whitfield, 1975). Koestler (1964) describes this moment as the creative act in which there is a 'sudden shaking together of two previously unconnected matrices (or systems of thought) which produces a satisfying synthesis'. Gordon (1961) thinks of the moment of insight as 'The pleasurable excitement itself (the feeling of being on the right track), a purposeful psychological state, recognized unconsciously as an indicator of the direction to take.' The state of illumination can therefore be regarded as that which permits movement on solving the problem. Whereas the problem-solver was previously stuck, he now sees a way of proceeding. Often the new insight is sufficiently well-informed to permit verification.

(5) *Verification* is the final stage of the creative process, during which the solution is checked out, elaborated where

necessary, and applied. Of course, the problem-solving process, may not end here. As Koestler (1964) observes:

> verification comes only *post factum*, when the creative act is completed: the act itself is always a leap into the dark, a dive into the deeps, and the diver is more likely to come up with a handful of mud than with a coral. False inspirations and freak theories are as abundant in the history of science as bad works of art: yet they command in the victim's mind the same forceful conviction, the same euphoria, catharsis and experience of beauty as those happy finds which are *post factum* proven right.

The feeling of elation is of itself no sure indicator of the birth of a creative product. The new idea is a solution to the *problem* as *formulated* (originally or eventually), and if that formulation does not match up with reality, neither will the solution.

The creative person

So far we have looked at the nature of creative products, creative ideas and the creative process. It is now time to turn our attention to the creative person. What sort of person is he? One way of answering this question is to say that he is the sort of person who produces creative products. There are other ways of answering the question. These depend on why you want to know what sort of person a creative person is. For example, if you are an employer wishing to hire creative people, one of the best predictors is past creativeness — the person's track record. However, if you are someone concerned with helping the development of other people's creative potential — a teacher, or management trainer, for example — then you may have different questions which require different sorts of answers.

You may be dealing with people who for one reason or another have not yet realized their creative potential. A person's track record is less useful in this case. Perhaps there is something about the creative person's background or his personality that distinguishes him from the less creative.

Perhaps these characteristics can be used to suggest where to start in order to develop a person's creativeness. And finally, one important reason for wanting to know what creative people are like is that you may want to know how creative *you* are.

In measuring yourself against the creative person described below, you should bear in mind that much of what is known has been discovered by studying eminent people whose achievements have been significant at least on a national and often on a world scale. For example, Vernon's (1970) readings include Galton's (1869) and Terman's (1947) studies of men of genius, along with Anne Roe's (1952) examination of sixty-four eminent scientists. Vernon also contains the writings of Mozart, Tchaikovsky, Stephen Spender and Henri Poincaré.

Obviously very few of us reach this level of eminence. Nevertheless, one can be creative at a lower level, and perhaps the reasons why we are or are not creative are due to the extent to which we share the characteristics and abilities of eminently creative people. Of course, creativity in different fields requires different abilities. For example, Roe (1952) found that experimental physicists 'tend strongly to dependence upon visual imagery in their thinking – images of concrete objects or elaborate diagrams or the like', whereas theoretical physicists 'tend to verbalization in their thinking – a kind of talking to themselves'. Roe's study of sixty-four of the most eminent scientists in the USA – biologists, physicists and social scientists – also revealed personality differences between these groups:

> The characteristic pattern among the biologists and physicists is that of the shy, over-intellectualized boy; among the social scientists the characteristics picture is very different. They [were involved in] social activity and intensive and extensive dating at an early age. They are often presidents in their classes, editors of yearbooks and literary magazines, frequently big shots in college. This contrast between the natural and social scientists was still evident after they grew up (Roe, 1952).

Clearly there is considerable variety among even the highly

creative. In MacKinnon's (1978) words, 'There are many paths along which persons travel toward full development and expression of creative potential, and . . . there is no single mould into which all who are creative will fit.' A brief summary of the 'creative person' cannot reflect this variety. However, a relatively small number of themes occur throughout the findings of investigators of creativity; and this makes it possible to produce a coherent picture of the creative person. A person's level of creative achievement in a particular area is dependent upon three main characteristics: (i) the extent and appropriateness of his knowledge; (ii) the nature and extent of his abilities to make use of that knowledge; and (iii) his disposition to make use of it.

Guilford (1959) describes a set of traits that are believed to be related to creativity. He includes *generalized sensitivity to problems* (people with this sensitivity tend to be dissatisfied with situations — they judge 'that things are not all right; that goals have not been reached; or that not everything to be desired has been achieved') and *ideational fluency* (the ability to produce ideas to fulfil certain requirements in limited time: 'There are certain stages in most problem solving where there must be searching for answers').

Guilford also hypothesizes 'that creative thinkers are *flexible* thinkers. They readily desert old ways of thinking and strike out in new directions.' Two aspects of flexibility are *spontaneous flexibility* — the ability or disposition to produce a great variety of ideas even when it is not necessary for a person to do so — and *adaptive flexibility*. This second type of flexibility appears to be important for problem-solving, particularly when the problem requires an unusual type of solution.

Originality is another trait described by Guilford. A person's level of originality may be assessed by the degree to which he tends to produce unusual responses to problems, to see non-obvious or remote consequences of events and by various other means. Barron (1955), for example, describes altogether eight ways of measuring aspects of a person's originality. Some of these tests measure the quantity, whereas others assess the quality (or goodness or cleverness), of these responses. MacKinnon (1978) points out that some people seem to be brimming over with original but foolish ideas, while others produce only a few original ideas, which, however, tend to be useful. He argues that the ability to produce lots of unusual ideas is not conducive to creativity if the person cannot think through the consequences of his ideas in order to make them realistic:

> To nurture the fullest creativity in those most fertile with new ideas, greater emphasis must be placed upon seeking the implications and deeper meanings and possibilities inherent in every idea. This is a matter of pursuing ideas in depth and in scope, not of criticizing and rejecting — which is so easy to do and which is so crippling to creativity . . . mere fluency in unusual ideas will not alone make for fresh and creative solutions to problems (MacKinnon, 1978).

The last of Guilford's traits, *redefinition*, refers to a person's ability to give up old interpretations of familiar objects in order to use them or their parts in new ways in order to solve problems.

So much for the cognitive or intellectual aspects of creativity — the knowledge and thinking skills related to creativity. What of the temperament of the creative individual? What is it that disposes some people towards originality and others towards conventionality? Certain characteristics recur throughout many of the studies of creativity. MacKinnon (1962) presents a summary description of the creative architect:

> He is dominant; possessed of those qualities and attributes which underlie and lead to achievement of social status: poised, spontaneous, and self-confident in personal and social interaction; though not of an especially sociable or participative temperament; intelligent, outspoken, sharp witted, demanding, aggressive, and self-centred; persuasive and verbally fluent, self-confident and self-assured; and relatively uninhibited in expressing his worries and complaints. He is relatively free from conventional restraints and inhibitions, not preoccupied with the impression he makes on others and thus perhaps capable of great independence and autonomy, and relatively ready to recognize and admit self-views that are unusual and unconventional.

He is strongly motivated to achieve in situations in which independence in thought and action are called for. But unlike his less creative colleagues, he is less inclined to strive for achievement in settings where conforming behavior is expected or required. In efficiency and steadiness of intellectual effort however, he does not differ from his fellow workers. Finally, he is definitely more psychologically minded, more flexible, and possessed of more feminity of interests than architects in general.

Cattell and Butcher (1968), reporting a study of the lives of eminent research scientists, describe their men as typically 'skeptical, withdrawn, unsociable, critical and precise' as well as 'displaying a characteristic resourcefulness, adaptability and adventurousness'. Research scientists also

> appeared to have the socially rather uncongenial and 'undemocratic' attitudes, associated with dominance . . . this dominance, amounting to a belief that most people are rather stupid, seems to be the root of a rugged independence of mind, and a readiness to face endless difficulties and social discouragement, which are needed in any pursuit of a completely novel project (Cattell and Butcher, 1968).

Barron (1955) also refers to 'dominance' as 'a strong need for personal mastery, not merely over other persons, but over all experience. It initially involves self-centredness, which in its socialized form may come to be known as self-realization. One aspect of it is the insistence on self-regulation, and a rejection of regulation by others.'

Roe (1952) emphasizes the contribution of 'the need and ability to develop personal independence to a high degree as possibly the most important single factor in the making of a scientist'. She also cites a 'driving absorption in their work' as being characteristic of the participants in her study.

Whitfield (1975) provides an interesting and cogent summary of the personality behind innovation (see Table 11.4). Whitfield distinguishes between three types of personalities involved in the innovation process: 'the creative person (the ideas man) . . . the innovator (the ideas man who translates

Table 11.4 *The personality behind innovation*

Knowledge	Intellectual abilities	Temperament
General knowledge	Adequate IQ	Tolerant of uncertainty
Specialist knowledge	Sensitive	Energetic
	Perceptive	Dedicated
	Use of all senses	Self-confident
	Openness to new experience	Forceful
	Imaginative	Emotionally expressive
	Flexible	Driven to complete tasks
		Non-conforming
		Challenging

Source: P. R. Whitfield (1975) *Creativity in Industry*, Penguin, Harmondsworth, England.

his ideas into reality) and . . . the entrepreneur, who by his business ability takes an idea and develops it into a money making propostion'. The author's summary of the 'personality behind innovation' is a conglomerate of these three types. Whether one ever finds all these characteristics in one person is an open question. It is more likely that in any organization one finds people who between them share the characteristics of 'the personality behind innovation'. This raises the interesting and important challenge of creating and maintaining the creative organization. What sort or sorts of people do you need for innovation? How can their individual and joint creativeness be facilitated and developed?

The creative situation

To the extent that 'creative action . . . alters the universe of meaning' (Ghiselin, 1963) or is 'adaptive of reality' (MacKinnon, 1978) it is *destructive* of the previous 'universe of meaning' of the current 'reality'.

The person who is creative is thus also destructive; he is an agent of change. In a pluralistic society change in one direction benefits and is supported by some interested parties and penalizes and is resisted by others. Also, change in one direction might conflict with change in another. That is, there are those who resist change because they want to keep things as they are and others who resist a particular direction of change because they wish to promote change in a different direction. The creative person is at the centre of the conflict – it is his ideas that provide the impetus for change. Not surprisingly creative people are often regarded with disquiet. Their assertiveness, independence, distrust of others, energy, etc, can make them difficult employees, hard taskmasters and formidable opponents. Nevertheless, even the highly creative individual does need other people. He needs the time and opportunity to generate his new ideas and very often requires other people to make space for him to operate. For example, Cattell and Butcher (1968) discuss working conditions suitable for creative work, particularly for research scientists. They argue that a university may not always be the best place for a researcher to work, particularly if he has to teach – the necessity to present simplified explanations of phenomena to students could have rigidifying effects on his own thinking – or if he has administrative responsibilities – the need for long periods of preparation time and especially for periods 'off the problem' to allow incubation is difficult to achieve. They suggest that special institutions be set up to support creative work and that attention be paid to 'providing suitable working conditions and incentives in such institutions and elsewhere'.

These writers are saying that working conditions should allow the creative process (preparation, effort, incubation, illumination and verification) to take its natural course. The production of a creative product, especially in the field of technological innovation, is not a one-man job. What organizational characteristics inhibit or facilitate the production of creative products? Whitfield (1975) refers to three levels of influential factors – those relating to interpersonal interactions, those relating to the characteristics of the organization, and cultural or national influences – and describes facilitators and inhibitors of creativeness originating at each level. For a creative idea to be realized, other people and organizations with the will and the resources need to become involved in the development and production of the fruits of the creative person's thinking.

The challenge of setting up special institutions or of changing existing organizations in order to foster creativeness is no simple matter. There are some tentative prescriptions being suggested, however. Steiner (1965) uses the characteristics of the creative individual as a model for the creative organization:

> The creative organization is different from others and it knows it. It is not an organization trying to be like others or one that conceives of itself as being another institution like so-and-so. A creative organization is independent. The creative organization is a hard worker — and largely out of its interest in what it is doing. The creative organization separates source from information; that is, it has an objective, fact-founded approach . . . It is able to draw on facts wherever it can find them and evaluate them in their own right, rather than depending blindly upon the authorities in the field. The creative organization has more irrational impulses within it, and on the other hand, more effective controls for keeping these in the appropriate channels. Here you might conceive of a creative organization as having a wider range of people within it — some of whom are just terribly good idea generators and others who are just terribly good channelers — people who are able to take these ideas, see their implications, and put them into effect. These functions need not exist in the same individual in a specific organization. Finally, the creative organization often appears to be wasteful . . . to the outsider.

(Steiner had earlier referred to the fact that the creative individual may, for sometimes quite long periods, appear to be doing nothing, whereas he is actually musing on a problem, holding back from acting until he has got a total grasp of the situation. Unfortunately, the person who *is not* actually doing anything may appear very similar to an observer — hence the idea of the individual — and the organization — appearing to be wasteful.) Steiner's analogy suggests possible principles for designing the structure of an organization (Whitfield's 'company' level).

MacKinnon (1978) aims his recommendations at interpersonal relationships (Whitfield's 'colleagues' level). His recommendations are based on findings of research into the biographies of creative individuals — for example, 'an extraordinary respect by parents for the child and an early granting to him of unusual freedom in exploring his universe and in making his own decisions' (a recurrent theme in the childhood of highly creative people) is converted into 'respect for and confidence in the ability of the younger person to act autonomously and responsibly' as a necessary condition for encouraging the creativity of young workers and managers. Other suggestions include:

> the granting of considerable freedom for action; a plentiful supply of models of effective resourceful and innovative behavior on the part of managers with whom the younger employee can identify; a variety of challenging assignments; encouraging rather than forcing the development of skills and interests for effective and creative performance in a managerial role (MacKinnon, 1978).

Rickards (1979) has also produced a list of environmental factors influencing managerial creativity:

> Creative behaviour is reinforced by encouragement and reward.
> Job objectives should be challenging yet attainable.
> Jobs should contain interest and variety.
> There should be freedom to try new methods, and sometimes to fail.
> The atmosphere should be supportive.
> Commitment to meet deadlines flows from motivation, but continuous pressure to perform will reduce flexibility and imaginative behaviour.
> Hygiene factors are satisfactory.
> Management is alert to the dangers of over-stressful conditions which make workers prone to habitual and uncreative responses to change.

'Experts' are not allowed to dominate the culture. (An expert domination leads to refusal by others to challenge the views of the experts, and a refusal by the experts to accept that problems may have remedies outside their areas of competence.)

Acceptance that there will be differences of viewpoint between individuals and departments which will influence final decisions.

Resolution of differences in open ways.

Attitudes to risk are realistic: neither fearsome of uncertainty, nor blind to the difficulties of change.

'Overall,' suggests Rickards, 'the factors suggest that a favourable environment is open, risk-taking, supportive and self-regulating.'

Steiner (1965) makes an interesting distinction between getting people to be more creative and getting creative people to be more productive. Facilitating creative people's productivity is largely a matter of achieving an appropriate organizational climate — no easy task, as a reading of Chapter 13 will reveal. But behaving creatively can also be regarded as skilled behaviour that can, with suitable instruction and practice, be learnt. Several centres exist with interests in creativity training. Perhaps the most influential is the Creative Education Foundation at the State University College at Buffalo, New York. A quarter of a century of course development and research into the effectiveness of creativity training programmes has gone into the production of a variety of instructional guides for those interested in enhancing creative potential. This material, together with information on several hundred methods and programmes for stimulating creativity, a listing of 175 films on the subject, on tests of creativity ability and a 2,000-book bibliography can be found in Parnes, Noller and Biondi (1977).

In the United Kingdom the creativity courses at the Manchester Business School deserve mention. For several years now an annual intensive course on 'Creative Problem Solving' (originally called 'Creativity Step-by-Step' and now named 'Ideas Into Action') has been run for participants from industry and the public services. R & D managers, personnel officers, entrepreneurs, new-product developers, marketing managers, management development officers and the like have participated in the past. The year 1980 saw the inauguration of the European Innovation Network. A quotation from the *EIN Bulletin* will serve as an indication of the intentions of the members of the Network:

> It is a shared belief of members of EIN that problems can often be approached more constructively, that social and technological change can be brought about more effectively and with less adverse consequence, and that resources can be deployed to greater advantage. The EIN was formed in order to facilitate implementation of these beliefs through education, training, consultancy, practice, publications and good example. It was felt that there were benefits to be gained from the merging of existing activities in various European countries and that communications between them should be improved and the overall concept expanded. The EIN is therefore a loosely co-ordinated Network with an administrative centre based at Manchester Business School. Through the centre, or through any of the members of EIN, it is possible to make contact with a wide range of professionally competent individuals in academic life, industry and public administration, who will be able to discuss sensibly and imaginatively the problems of a particular situation, and suggest how the network could assist. There are no particular technological, industrial or commercial fields to which the Network and its aims are restricted (Butler, 1980).

A central feature of many creativity courses is the acquisition of skills through the use of creativity techniques – what Rickards (1980) calls 'structured aids to creative behaviour'. The exercises are intended to provide people with experiences of creative thinking and to help them assimilate some of the principles. Rickards (1980) provides a review of the state of the art concerning 'structured aids to creativity' and he includes a neat summary of the four main types of creativity techniques – brainstorming, synectics, morphological methods and lateral thinking (see Table 11.5). For further information on these techniques and a discussion of their usefulness, the reader is referred to Rickards (1980), Parnes, Noller and Biondi (1977), Jones (1970), Rickards (1974), Schlicksupp (1977), McPherson (1969), Gordon (1961) and Osborn (1957).

One of the currently interesting issues concerning participants on creativity courses relates to their reception back at work — to the responses of colleagues, superiors and subordinates to their attempts to practise their creative problem-solving skills. If a course has been successful for a participant, it will to some extent have changed him. He will think about things differently, he may want to do his job differently. It is likely that some at least of his co-workers will wish him to be as he was; there will be attempts to resocialize him into the work setting.

As an exercise imagine you are about to encounter a colleague newly returned from a creativity course. What would you say to him that would save you having to listen to all the boring details and get him back to working as he did before? To set you off, here are a few such comments reported by course participants: 'Back in the real world, I see'; 'I'd like to hear about the course . . . sometime'; 'Hello! Had a nice holiday?'

Another way of discouraging creativity in one's colleagues and subordinates (whether they are newly returned from courses or not) is the skillful use of the 'killer phrase'. This is a device used for making sure that any new idea will be strangled at birth. The crude version is simply to use authority — the expert's 'It can't be done that way' or the old hand's 'When you've been here as long as me.' More subtle is the delaying tactic: 'Let's test it thoroughly before committing the company', 'Let's keep this up our sleeves', or 'OK, leave it with me.' A favourite killer phrase is 'I wonder why our competitors haven't come up with this idea.' There are many more. The really effective killer pharse sounds eminently reasonable but carries with it an ulterior message that casts enough doubt on the idea to prevent its further development.

Perhaps you can think of other phrases that have been used against you or perhaps even that you have found useful yourself. Devising killer phrases can be quite a creative activity — a creative product that is truly destructive!

Table 11.5   *Structured aids to creative problem-solving*

Technique	Operational mechanisms ('what')	Precepts (links with theory—'why')
Brainstorming	1. Generate many ideas 2. Avoid evaluation while generating ideas 3. Seek new combinations ('hitchhike, freewheel')	Fundamental precept—postponement of judgement overcomes habitual responses Wide range of ideas increases efficiency of idea search When used in a group may have positive effect on interpersonal relationships and climate
Synectics (a) Gordon (1960s—1970s)	1. Seek ways of making the familiar strange and the strange familier 2. Use metaphors and analogies to assist the process	Metaphoric state has been identified as important during the creative process A metaphoric excursion may compress the 'incubation' period prior to insight
Synectics (b) Prince/ Gordon (1970s)	1. Identify a range of problem definitions 2. Separate process tasks (group leader) and content decisions (client) 3. Encourage positivity to ideas via 'itemized response' — client notes positive aspects of an idea — client and group try to overcome negative points	Importance of channeling and motivating the client has been recognized
Morphological chart	1. List possible dimensions that together describe a system being studied 2. List alternatives within each dimension 3. Examine as many combinations of sub-sets as possible 4. List any promising and unusual new ideas suggested	To widen the area of search (Jones, 1970) To avoid overlooking obvious possibilities To postpone selection (judgement) until a wide set of alternatives have been listed

Table 11.5   *continued*

Technique	Operational mechanisms ('what')	Precepts (links with theory—'why')
Lateral thinking (a) Random stimulus de Bono (1960s–1970s)	1. Sample any rich set of random stimuli ('walk through Woolworth, a dictionary, science museum') 2. Seek relationships with your problem needs	Restructures perceptions away from preferred patterns Enriches content of solution set
Lateral thinking (b) Concept challenge	1. Consider in depth any important statement usually taken for granted 2. Challenge (signal 'PO' to denote non-evaluation) in as many ways as possible	Assists suspension of judgement
Lateral thinking (c) Intermediate impossible	1. Move from a realistic idea to an imaginative impossible one 2. Treat this as stepping-stone to a new realistic idea	Encourages the imagination Weakens censorship mechanisms of repressed ideas

Source: T. Rickards (1980) 'Designing for Creativity: A State-of-the-Art Review', *Design Studies*, 1 (5), IPC, Guildford, England.

References for Chapter 11

Barron, F. (1955) 'The Disposition towards Originality', *Journal of Abnormal and Social Psychology*, 51, 478–85.

Butler, J. (1980) 'Introduction to EIN', *European Innovation Network Bulletin*, 1, Manchester Business School, Manchester, England.

Bruner, J. S. (1962) 'The Conditions of Creativity', in Gruber, H. *et al.* (eds), *Contemporary Approaches to Creative Thinking*, Atherton, New York.

Cattell, R. B. and Butcher, H. J. (1968) *The Prediction of Achievement and Creativity*, Bobbs-Merrill, New York.

De Bono, E. (1972) *PO: Beyond Yes and No*, Penguin, Harmondsworth, England.

Galton, F. (1869) *Hereditary Genius*, Macmillan, London.

Ghiselin, B. (1963) 'Ultimate Criteria for Two Levels of Creativity', in Taylor, C. W. and Barron, F. (eds), *Scientific Creativity: Its Recognition and Development*, Wiley, New York.

Gordon, W. J. J. (1961) *Synectics: The Development of Creative Capacity*, Harper & Row, New York.

Guilford, J. P. (1959) 'Traits of Creativity', in Anderson, H. H. (ed.), *Creativity and its Cultivation*, Harper & Row, New York.

Hayes, J. R. (1978) *Cognitive Psychology: Thinking and Creating*, Dorsey Press, Homewood, Ill.

Jones, J. C. (1970) *Design Methods: Seeds of Human Futures*, Wiley, New York.

Koestler, A. (1964) *The Act of Creation*, Hutchinson, London.

Kubie, L. (1958) *Neurotic Distortion of the Creative Process*, University of Kansas Press, Kansas.

MacKinnon, D. W. (1961) 'Fostering Creativity in Students of Engineering', *Journal of Engineering Education*, 52, 129–42.

MacKinnon, D. W. (1962) 'The Nature and Nurture of Creativity', *American Psychologist*, 17, 484–95.

MacKinnon, D. W. (1978) *In Search of Human Effectiveness*, Creative Education Foundation, Buffalo, New York.

McPherson, J. H. (1969) *Structured Approaches to Creativity*, Stanford Research Institute, Menlo Park, California.

Osborn, A. (1957) *Applied Imagination*, Scribner, New York.

Parnes, S. J., Noller, R. B. and Biondi, A. M. (1977) *Guide to Creative Action*, Scribner, New York.

Prince, G. (1970) *The Practice of Creativity*, Harper & Row, New York.

Rickards, T. (1974) *Problem-Solving through Creative Analysis*, Gower Press, Epping, Engalnd.

Rickards, T. (1979) *Checklists on Creativity for Managers*, Centre for Business Research, Manchester Business School, Manchester, England.

Rickards, T. (1980) 'Designing for Creativity: a State-of-the-Art Review', *Design Studies*, 1(5), IPC, Guildford, England.

Rittel, H. W. J. and Webber, M. M. (1974) 'Dilemmas in a General Theory of Planning', *DMG–DRS Journal*, 8(1), Department of Architecture, University of California, Berkeley.

Roe, A. (1952) 'A Psychologist Examines Sixty-Four Eminent Scientists', *Scientific American*, 87, 21–5 (in Vernon (1970)).

Schlicksupp, H. (1977) 'Idea Generation for Industrial Firms', *R & D Management*, 1(2).

Sinnott, E. W. (1959) 'The Creativeness of Life', in Vernon, P. E. (ed.) (1970) *Creativity*, Penguin, Harmondsworth, England.

Steiner, G. A. (1965) *The Creative Organization*, University of Chicago Press, Chicago.

Terman, L. M. (1947) 'Psychological Approaches to the Study of Genius', in Vernon, P. E. (ed.) (1970) *Creativity*, Penguin, Harmondsworth, England.

Vernon, P. E. (ed.) (1970) *Creativity*, Penguin, Harmondsworth, England.

Whitfield, P. R. (ed.) (1975) *Creativity in Industry*, Penguin, Harmondsworth, England.

Wickelgren, W. A. (1974) *How to Solve Problems*, Freeman, San Francisco.

12
Participation and Technology

We have heard a great deal recently about the need to democratize or humanize the work-place in industry, to improve the quality of working life by providing the industrial worker with greater participation in the decisions involving work — participation has been a term constantly used throughout this book. Generally participation can be achieved by including employees on Boards of companies and involving them in the long-term policy-making issues of the organizations or by increasing their participation in the decision-making processes of their work-group by allowing them greater freedom in deciding how to organize and conduct their own jobs. These two approaches to industrial democracy, which, it might be added, are not mutually exclusive, have been termed by Strauss and Rosenstein (1970) as *distant* and *immediate* participation respectively.

This chapter considers the work that has been done in the field of *immediate* participation, because, at least in the initial stages of the 'participation revolution' (Preston and Post, 1974), these developments are likely to have the most impact on increasing people's job satisfaction, performance, and improving industrial relations generally. A substantial number of employee or immediate participation programmes have been introduced throughout Europe and other countries under differing labels over the last decade; autonomous work-groups, job-enrichment schemes, work restructuring, etc. (Cooper and Mumford, 1979).

Each of these forms of immediate participation are slightly different, though they share certain characteristics. Autonomous work-groups, for example, are groups of workers who have almost total control over the production or assembly of a particular product or service. Semi-autonomous groups have only partial control, while job enrichment refers to the characteristics of a particular job. When a job is enriched, it is changed in some way to make it more interesting and/or less boring. This may mean that where two different individuals are doing specialized jobs, they may share some aspect of each other's job. In terms of concepts like job enlargement and work reconstructuring, this means a change in a particular or related job in a defined work-place. Job redesign or work restructuring are phrases indicating that the job or work site has been altered in some way to make it more interesting, humanistic or in some way meeting the needs of the workers.

Each of these approaches to employee participation attempts to meet any one of a combination of the objectives put forward by Herrick and Maccoby (1975):

1. *Security* — employees need to be free from fear and anxiety concerning health and safety, income and future employment.
2. *Equity* — employees should be compensated commensurately with their contribution to the value of the service or product.
3. *Individuation* — employees should have maximum autonomy in determining the rhythm of their work and in planning how it should be done.
4. *Democracy* — employees should wherever possible manage themselves, be involved in the decision-making that affects their work, and accept greater responsibility in the work of the organization.

The experiments in the humanization of the immediate work environment vary enormously: some emphasize 'participative decision-making'; others attempt to nurture 'work autonomy'.

Since in most industrialized nations there is likely to be a move towards greater participation in industry, it might be worth while exploring some of the examples and results of the recent work undertaken to humanize the work-place in different countries, so that we may be able to plan and organize more effective programmes. We will explore first the developments in the EEC and then those in Sweden, the USA and Japan.

Developments in the European Economic Community (EEC)

Many companies within the EEC have begun to experiment with employee participation and 'quality of working life' programmes; indeed many of the Community countries have introduced legislation to set up concerned government agencies. We will try to provide a 'thumb-nail' sketch of some of the better-documented examples in each of the Community countries, in order to give the flavour of their approach.

United Kingdom

A report by the Work Research Unit (1975) on work-restructuring projects and experiments in the United Kingdom claims to have traced 111 industrial examples, including schemes of job rotation, job enlargement, job enrichment and autonomous work-groups. These programmes most frequently occur in the chemical, food and drink, manufacturing, engineering, electrical, paper and printing, and electronics industries. Of the 111 experiments, only slightly over a dozen seem to be documented or to show sufficient objective economic and human results to draw any firm conclusions. The United Kingdom has a longer history of work-humanization efforts than is often appreciated. The work of the Tavistock Institute of Human Relations began in the early 1950s (Trist and Bamforth, 1951; Trist, Higgin, Murray and Pollack, 1963) with the application of socio-technical system concepts. But it is only recently that UK approaches to employee participation and humanization have developed systematically. For example, the objective of the Work Research Unit is 'the stimulation of changes in the ways in which work is organized in industry and commerce'.

One of the best-documented (Hill, 1972) and well-designed programmes in a UK company was one carried out by Shell UK Ltd at their Stanlow Refinery. This took place in their micro-wax department, where morale was very low, costs were high, and maintenance poor. A major restructuring of job tasks was then introduced and employees worked as a team to complete *all* of the job tasks and the workers were given more decision-making power. As a consequence the company obtained greater commitment and increased morale. On objective criteria, sickness and absenteeism decreased by 50 per cent, off-plant wax testing was reduced by 75 per cent, and output increased by between 30 and 100 per cent. Another example is Ferranti's avionics plant in Edinburgh. The firm introduced group-cell technology, with teams of four workers controlling six machines to deal with 300–400 different components. Each group cell was left to organize the job tasks and methods of production. It was found (Clutterbuck, 1973) that the time taken to reset tools dropped by 60 per cent, production time for each component was cut by 30 per cent (as was delay in getting parts), and quality improved steadily.

Although the bulk of the UK experiments in this field are production- or assembly-orientated, there are also some notable white-collar ones as well. In 1967 Imperial Chemical Industries introduced greater autonomy and responsibility for their sales representatives in order to increase the sales effort. Sales representatives were given discretion on reports, complaint refunds, some pricing policies, etc. A job-reaction survey showed a significant increase in job satisfaction and also an 18.6 per cent increase in sales (a control group of salesmen whose jobs had not been changed showed a drop in sales of 5 per cent) (Paul and Robertson, 1970). Other white-collar humanization projects in the United Kingdom include design engineers and researchers (Paul and Robertson, 1970), managers (Cooper, 1979; Taylor, 1973) and stock-control office staff (British Oxygen Company, 1971).

Denmark

Denmark, like other Scandinavian countries, has approached both the 'immediate' and the 'distant' participation fronts simultaneously (shop-floor humanization in the late 1960s; company law concerned with Board participation in 1973). A notable Danish example of participation is Foss Electric, a small manufacturer of dairy product testing equipment (Taylor, 1975). In 1969 the firm introduced semi-autonomous work-groups for natural parts of the production process. These groups planned and manufactured their segments of the operation, were paid on a flat rate, had flexible working hours, recruited staff, and had a say in designing the immediate socio-technical system. It was found that labour turnover dropped in one year by 10 per cent and quality errors were reduced by 33 per cent. Not as much information about results is available from another study at Sadoin & Hohmblad (paint manufacturers), which introduced a major change in organizational structure by creating interlocking managerial groups throughout the company. It has been reported that production improved as a result of solving the production problems more quickly and efficiently (Jenkins, 1974). The final example of Danish efforts at work humanization took place in a small corrugated-board plant, Colon Emballage, in southern Jutland in 1970. Autonomous work-groups of between seven and eight workers were formed to decide on work roles, wage system (shifted from piece rates to uniform flat rates), etc. — they were restricted, however, on production scheduling. It was found that production rose 8 per cent and the employees expressed greater satisfaction with their own work.

On the basis of these and many other work-humanization examples, the Danish government introduced a Working Environment Bill in 1974 to promote further improvements in the quality of working life in industry. At roughly the same time 'distant' participation legislation was also passed for limited liability corporations (of over 500 employees), in which the employees were eligible to appoint two members to the Board of Directors to represent their interests. Denmark seems to be one of the few countries to be pursuing a policy of introducing worker-participation programmes at all levels of the organization, dealing with political as well as human issues.

The Netherlands

By far the most extensive and interesting examples of work redesign and participation programmes in the Netherlands comes from Philips, the manufacturers of electrical appliances and other equipment. Most of these experiments took place during the 1960s. For instance, autonomous work-groups were set up in the bulb assembly and finishing departments, where thirty individual jobs were combined into groups of four, with a certain amount of job rotation. It was found that production costs were reduced by 20 per cent, rejects were halved, and output increased; worker satisfaction was not any higher but workers indicated a strong preference for the current job design in contrast to the old (Hertog, 1974).

In the company's black-and-white television factory, Philips achieved similar results when autonomous work-groups were introduced between 1969 and 1972. They formed seven-person work-groups with twenty-minute work cycles and multiple job tasks (e.g. quality control, work distribution, material ordering, etc.). The 1972 evaluation programme in this department revealed that there were significantly lower absenteeism, lower waiting time for materials, better co-ordination and improved training, while component costs were reduced by 10 per cent; unlike the bulb department, greater job satisfaction was expressed as well. Also worthy of note was the white-collar experiment in the order department of Philips. There, the department was reorganized by product; three operational lines became three product lines. Within each product line every employee learnt all the tasks and rotated them; and each unit decided on their work-group leader, who (in conjunction with his team) was responsible for delivery of a complete product. Philips found that productivity doubled and the majority of employees expressed a preference for the new system, though some indicated that the supervision was 'too close'.

France

There are at present only a few well-documented cases of participation in France (Jenkins, 1974) and they are illustrated by two particular cases. Guillist SA, a woodworking machinery manufacturer in Auxerre, introduced semi-autonomous work-groups of between seven and ten persons covering the manu-facturing process of its machinery. Each of these work-groups assembled nearly an entire piece of equipment by themselves. The programme was carried out in 1969 and covered nearly 800 employees. The most positive outcomes for the company were increased sales and substantially enhanced job satisfaction. Another example reported by Taylor (1972) was that of a nylon-spinning plant of 100 workers. The employees introduced a work redesign scheme (with the co-operation of the management) in which each worker used more skills, including maintenance, than normal, (replaced five jobs with two), and in which the work-group took on the decision-making responsibility in the areas of quality control, staffing and work assignments. The experiment was carried out between 1969 and 1972 with the following encouraging positive results: absenteeism was reduced by two-thirds, no grievances or strikes were initiated, and labour turnover was significantly reduced — indeed, workers refused transfers to other plants. This accommodation with management was achieved through worker councils, which met with management on a regular basis.

West Germany

Although West Germany has been the model of Western European countries for worker participation at Board level (i.e. distant participation), or what is termed 'co-determination of employees in the economic enterprise' (*mitbestimmung*), the country has progressed very slowly indeed on immediate or shop-floor participation. It was not until a federal government research programme into job satisfaction indicated that the low paid were the least satisfied with their job and their career prospects that any immediate participation programmes were encouraged. In 1974 the Federal Ministry of Labour and Social Affairs planned a programme for 'Research for the Humanization of Work', which was similar in objectives to the French 'Agence National pour L'Amélioration des Conditions du Travail'. Its 'brief' was to collate information on issues related to stress at work, worker participation, work and job design, etc., and to stimulate further research. There is very little work reported on German experiments of employee participation, mainly because this is not particularly strongly supported by the German Federation of Trade Unions (DGB). As Mire (1975) has emphasized:

> The DGB continues to pay lip service to the demands for direct representation of the workplace, but only as part of its broader demand for worker participation at the top . . . Most efforts of the trade unions are directed at this aspect of their legislative programme rather than at bringing about worker participation at the plant level.

Indeed, there is only one well-reported case of employee participation and that is the work at the Singer Company of Germany (Ruehl, 1974). At Singer autonomous assembly work-groups were introduced to make electric and electronic equipment, precision parts and house appliances – the groups were described by the company as 'assembly islands'. Unfortunately, no information is available on the objective consequences of these innovations, so we are left with very little evaluative data.

The Germans are very much aware of the need to develop their programme for improving the quality of working life and participation. This was particularly highlighted when ex-Chancellor Brandt set up a working party in the early 1970s to consider new approaches to the organization of work life (Butteriss, 1975). Work from this group should help to provide the foundations and framework for work humanization in the future.

Italy

An example from Italy took place at Olivetti's Ivrea plant, where the 'long assembly line' was abolished and 'integrated assembly units' or 'assembly islands' were introduced. These are composed of a group of thirty people whose job is to assemble, inspect and maintain the whole product. Briefly, the following changes were evident from the work system change programme at Olivetti: (i) increase in the speed of the product throughout and decrease in processing time to less than one-third of the time of the line system; (ii) quality of product improved significantly, with lower wastage; and (iii) increased job satisfaction and worker motivation under the new schemes. However, *per capita* costs had increased, as well as training costs, but there was a greater flexibility in the system for allocating human resources in the plant (Butera, 1975).

Belgium

At the level of central government little is happening in the way of quality of working life policies or practices in Belgium. The Office Belge pour L'Accroissement de la Productivité has responsibility for the dissemination of information in this area, but little is known about the work of firms in Belgium to humanize the work-place. The only exception to this is the apparel manufacturer, Inbelco at Poperinge, reported by Jenkins (1974). It has restructured its organization with a series of nine interlocking management groups, each of which was broken down into three or four sub-groups. Within these groups joint decisions are made about job tasks, with opportunities for job rotation and enlargement encouraged. There is very little objective data available about this particular experience, however, except that measured job satisfaction seems to have increased since the introduction of the experiment.

Ireland

Ireland is another country in which work-humanization projects are not very well developed. This is due to some extent to the absence of large-scale industrial organizations in the Republic. Butteriss (1975) suggests that this is partly a function of the prevailing attitudes of management and trade unions, which have been less than enthusiastic about work redesign and quality of working life issues. This is ironic in view of the Council of Europe's decision to create a 'European Foundation for the Improvement of Living and Working Conditions' and to base it in Dublin. The only documented evidence of Irish interest in the quality of work environments comes from a government working paper on *Job Enrichment* in June 1974 and proposals (on the 'distant' participation side) in July 1975 for a Bill on Worker Directors.

Luxembourg

Of the documented work available to us in the quality of working life field, we are unable to find any evidence of government activity or individual industrial projects being pursued in Luxembourg.

Developments in other countries

Other countries have been extensively involved in quality of working life projects over the last decade, particularly Sweden, the USA and Japan.

Sweden

There are literally hundreds of examples of serious, systematic efforts at work redesign and participation in Sweden (Agervold, 1975). Although many of these have not been published in English or fully evaluated by objective criteria, Sweden has certainly been at the forefront of recent ventures in this field. Much of the work was prompted by the country's need to 'overcome an inability to recruit Swedish workers to Swedish factory work (particularly in the 1960s) and to respond to union demands for better quality of working life' (Taylor, 1975). One of the best-documented Swedish examples is, contrary to general expectations about Volvo, the Saab engine-assembly line (at the Sodertalje truck and bus plant). The process of moving towards autonomous work-groups began in 1969 with the expansion of the works council, the formation of development groups, and the formation of small-team production groups of between seven to eight workers — where job tasks were decided collaboratively by foremen and workers. By 1974 the plant had ninety development groups and 200 production groups, and decisions about work organization were jointly reached. In the first year capital costs were higher and absenteeism and turnover were at about the same level, but significantly more labour was attracted into the plant (and a more flexible work system was materializing). By the third year labour turnover was reduced from 70 to 20 per cent, unplanned stoppages were down from 6 to 2 per cent, production had increased, costs were 5 per cent below budget, and absenteeism was markedly improved (Norstedt and Aguren, 1974).

Another interesting Swedish example, involving a comparative analysis of two different forms of work restructuring, was carried out in Granges AB, a die-casting foundry near Stockholm. The company introduced in one unit of the plant a job-enrichment scheme and, in another unit, autonomous work-groups (Jenkins, 1974). Labour turnover rose from 60 to 69 per cent and productivity declined by 7 per cent in the former case, but productivity rose 20 per cent for the self-managed work-group, with turnover falling from 60 to 18 per cent (in addition, absenteeism fell 5 per cent and quality spoilage 2 per cent in the latter case).

The Swedish government enacted legislation in 1971 to set up the Work Environment Fund to sponsor more research and work in this field. In addition to immediate participation programmes, Sweden is also moving rapidly towards Board or distant participation by legislation enacted in 1973.

The USA

There are a large number of industrial cases of work-humanization projects in the USA, some dating back to the late 1940s (Coch and French, 1948) and 1950s (Morse and Reimer, 1956). Most of these examples are found in small plants of up to 250 employees and involve predominantly assembly or production operations. Many of these can be found in O'Toole's (1973) classic book *Work in America*. An example of the kind of programme carried out in the USA is best illustrated by the Corning Glass and Texas Instruments experiments. At the Corning Glass factory in Medfield, Massachusetts, the company introduced autonomous work-groups in their electric hot-plate assembly department. Groups of six workers assembled an entire electric hot plate and had the freedom to schedule work any way they chose. Absenteeism dropped from 8 to 1 per cent, rejects dropped from 23 to 1 per cent and expressed job satisfaction increased. A similar experiment was carried out among 120 maintenance workers in the Dallas plant of Texas Instruments. The maintenance workers were organized into nineteen-member cleaning teams, with each member having a say in planning problem-solving, goal-setting and scheduling. It was found that turnover dropped from 100 to 10 per cent and cost savings were $103,000 in two years between 1967 and 1969.

There are also examples of quality of working life experiments in government departments. The Operations Division of the Ohio Department of Highways established three experimental construction crews with differing degrees of self-determination of work schedules and division of labour, and compared them with three crews who maintained the traditional assignment of duties and work schedules. It was found (Powell and Schacter, 1971) that as participation increased, so did morale and job satisfaction (but not productivity).

Japan

During the post-war period there has been a strong wave of opinion for the democratization of work life in firms. The largest national labour union *Sohyo* has been at the forefront of promoting and encouraging *hatarakigai*, or the quality of working life.

One of the better-known Japanese examples (Kato, 1974) was initiated within the large Mitsubishi Electric company in 1968. At the Fukuyama plant a nine-position conveyor-line system was reorganized into autonomous work-groups of seven workers. Although the work-teams received monthly production goals from top management, they were given the authority to set immediate work targets, to take on quality control and inspection, to organize and supply parts and materials, etc. The scope of the worker's job was immeasurably widened, with only peripheral services provided centrally. It was found that productivity increased by over 50 per cent, while errors dropped by nearly 80 per cent. In addition, perceived job satisfaction had increased and industrial-relations problems minimized. Another well-documented example is Kanto Seiki, an auto-parts manufacturer. The engineers at Seiki decided to carry out a comparative study of two work-restructuring approaches. In one part of the plant they maintained their traditional conveyor-belt system for assembling speedometers and in another they reorganized themselves into autonomous work-groups of differing sizes (seven-, four- and three-worker modules). In contrast to the conveyor system, productivity increased between 70 and 90 per cent for the autonomous work-groups (with the three-man modules producing the largest increase), with absenteeism and labour turnover significantly decreasing as well.

There are an enormous number of quality of work life studies in process at the moment in Japan (Takezawa, 1974) and they are likely to increase in the future. In a recent Japanese government survey of 700 influential national leaders from the unions, industry and the institutions of higher education, it was concluded that wages and salaries would be less important in the 1980s than job satisfaction and working conditions – this was particularly strongly supported by the trade-union officials.

What have we learned from this work

It is important to attempt to answer a number of more general questions raised by these examples of work-humanization schemes. First, why were these programmes undertaken: what did they hope to achieve? Second, how successful were they in achieving their objectives? Third, what are the problems raised by the implementation of such innovations in industry and how might they be improved upon in the future?

Reasons for implementation of quality of working life experiments

There are a wide range of reasons which firms give for doing this kind of work: recruitment difficulties, high labour turnover, automation, introduction of new technology, etc. By far the three most common reasons are low productivity, high absenteeism and high labour turnover; together they represent about 50 per cent of the stated reasons why organizations are undertaking these change programmes. The next category of expressed overt problems is comprised of industrial-relations difficulties (e.g. poor worker–management communication) and lack of worker job satisfaction, which together represent roughly 25 per cent of the problems needing resolution. Of the remaining 25 per cent the following are given as reasons for introducing change (in order of frequency of expression): experimentation of new work designs, poor quality, encourage participation, unnecessarily high costs, inability to recruit, introduction of new equipment, productivity deals.

It can also be seen that most of these experiments apply to manufacturing or assembly-type operations with few white-collar, clerical or middle-management programmes. This supports Taylor's (1975) survey of the 100 best-documented international cases of work restructuring, in which he found that most of them were in assembly operations (33 per cent), semi-skilled machine tending (23 per cent), and process operating (21 per cent), while only 9 per cent were among white-collar workers, and maintenance tasks were a poor fifth, at 3 per cent.

How successful are these quality of working life experiments?

It seems unwise to draw any wide-ranging conclusions about the efficacy of the quality of working life and participation projects which are available to date. First, it may be the case that we are only hearing about the successful interventions, while the ones which are less successful or of marginal benefit are buried under piles of reports or are forgotten altogether. Second, most of the reported work does not have objective criteria by which we can confidently judge it. Third, not enough of the work in this area is comparative: that is, where one approach, for instance to absenteeism reduction, is compared with another or two other possible approaches.

Nevertheless, given these caveats there is still convincing evidence that many of the participative and work-humanization projects have had positive individual and organizational consequences. The empirical work associated with these types of experiments has been summarized by two University of Michigan researchers in diagrammatic form (see Figure 12.1). It can be seen that many of the sources and manifestations of stress for the individual at work are minimized (e.g. job-related threat, alienation, etc.) and many of the organizational objectives are achieved (e.g. lower absenteeism, higher productivity, etc.) when the conditions for improving the quality of working life through involvement and participation at the work site are introduced.

Problems associated with work humanization

Despite the fact that we have reason to believe that quality of work life experiments have many beneficial outcomes, there are a number of problems and difficulties associated with their implementation. The following are only the tip of the proverbial iceberg of potential problem areas:

1. The changing roles of management and workers.
2. Designing and recreating training programmes to meet the specific needs of the different varieties of work-humanization projects.
3. Coping with the fears of first-line supervisors.
4. Dealing with the resistance of the unions, who may feel threatened that some of these approaches may affect the number of jobs and manning levels.
5. Increasing costs during the initial phases of these interventions.
6. Organizations may have to pay more for workers taking increased responsibility.

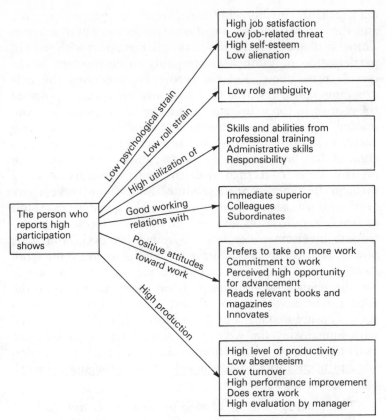

Figure 12.1   *The consequences of high participation*

Source: J. R. P. French and R. D. Caplan (1973) 'Organizational Stress and Individual Strain', in A. J. Marrow (ed.), *The Failure of Success*, American Management Association, New York.

Ottaway (1975) has suggested several ways of mitigating these problems. First, it is vital that there is a *psychological contract* between those changing and those advocating or implementing the change. This will involve all employees concerned with the change, discussing the 'what', 'how' and 'when' of the change programme. One approach at this stage is to encourage the formation of a working party of all interested participants, to oversee the quality of working life intervention to fruition. Second, it is important to diagnose the *quality* of working life problem areas: job design, style of management, quality, industrial-relations difficulties, etc., and then to introduce a small-scale project as a pilot scheme. Third, it is necessary to *design* the change effort with the full participation of those who are going to be involved in the change programme. Fourth, before implementing the new programme, it is essential to 'take back' any possible proposal for change to top management and the unions, who first contracted the change programme and established the working party, to endorse the suggested project. Fifth, once the programme has been accepted, training must be introduced to prepare those concerned with the skills necessary to carry through the experiment successfully. Shop-floor workers may need to learn, for example, how to make decisions in groups or first-line supervisors need to know how to facilitate greater worker involvement or how to relinquish decision-making power. And finally, in addition to helping to create the work structure in which change can take place and preparing people for the change by training, it is necessary to *reinforce* the appropriate new behaviours that emerge. These six steps should ensure that many of the potential difficulties associated with humanizing the work-place are minimized or to some extent contained. In addition to these stages are four underlying principles which must be adhered to throughout (French and Caplan, 1973):

1. The participation or change programme *is not illusory*, that is, it is not used as a manipulation tool (for example, when management asks employees for advice and then ignores it).
2. The decisions on which participation are based are not *trivial* to the people concerned (e.g. management asking workers to decide on the colour of the paper to be used for the company's newsletter).
3. Those aspects of the work environment on which participation are based are *relevant* to the needs of the workers.
4. The decisions which people participate in are perceived as being *legitimately* theirs to make.

These conditions seem critical guidelines in designing programmes which encourage involvement and work-sharing.

The nature of future British developments

We can finally consider some of the implications of the above discussion for the managements of British organizations operating within an EEC framework. Some of the implications of these humanization experiments are:

(1) Work-humanization initiatives may pay off in terms of greater organizational effectiveness and enhanced employee satisfaction with the work to be done. Notwithstanding the reservations mentioned earlier, it is difficult to discount the increasing evidence (Cooper and Mumford, 1979) that work-humanization approaches can have real benefits. One implication for British managers is therefore that there should be continuing and wider attention to this feature of the managerial task.

(2) Britain is one of the few countries in the EEC demonstrating satisfactory experience of a variety of work-humanization experiments that have been successful. Other EEC countries have experimented mainly with autonomous work-groups and similar methods, while Britain has a variety of experiments comparable in scale with those of Sweden and the USA.

(3) Although the use of autonomous work-groups appears to be the most widely used and successful method of improving the quality of working life, it may not necessarily prove to be the most popular among managers because of the questions it raises about control. Autonomous work-groups and what we have termed 'distant' participation both reduce the degree of managerial control of the work-place itself to a greater extent than such methods as job enrichment, redesign of the individual job and altering methods of payment. It may be significant that West Germany has moved further than other EEC countries on distant participation and has neglected, until recently, autonomous work-group methods. One can at least speculate that managers can adapt to one or the other but not to both at the same time, and if we are to see legislative moves via the Bullock Report on Board-level participation, these may inhibit moves towards work-group autonomy.

(4) No contemplation of the future can ignore the views

of trade unions. In Britain the Trades Union Congress can be regarded as late-in-the-day converts to both forms of participation and still showing relatively little enthusiasm for the work-humanization developments of the type we have considered.

(5) We must also consider what is likely to be the main stimulus to participation. Innovations in the Netherlands were attributable directly to problems of graduate unemployment, high-quality employees engaged on low-quality jobs, and so forth. It may be a stimulus of this type that will emerge in Britain, or it may be the need for greater productivity, the need to innovate or a feeling for some sense of greater social responsibility. According to the social imperative that emerges there could be varying directions to the development of work-quality programmes.

(6) We must always remember that the experiments we have studied have been carried out in certain types of work in certain types of industry, and we need very much more data before we can generalize about the type of work-humanization programme that is likely to be appropriate in specific environments.

It might be useful to conclude this chapter by reflecting on the words of the Dutch Jesuit priest, Father A. M. Kuylaars, who wrote about job satisfaction in 1951:

> Man needs labour as an occupation which in more than one sense gives meaning and content to his life. Besides, man needs the guidance and social compulsion which are conditioned by labour. Especially owing to this latter circumstance labour has a unique function which practically cannot be replaced by anything else. As a human activity labour is also *internally* productive, that is to say it is directly a personal enrichment for the worker. Therefore, the economic system has to provide work which is both internally and externally productive. As to the former, certain necessary conditions will be required with regard to the quantity and quality of the work.

References for Chapter 12

Agervold, M. (1975) 'Swedish Experiments in Industrial Democracy', in Davis, L. E. and Cherns, A. B. (eds), *The Quality of Working Life*, Free Press, New York, vol. 2, 46—65.

British Oxygen Company (1971) *Stock Control Office*, Manpower Development Unit Paper, London.

Butera, F. (1975) 'Environmental Factors in Job and Organization Design: The Case of Olivetti', in Davis, L. E. and Cherns, A. B. (eds), *The Quality of Working Life*, Free Press, New York, vol. 1, 166—200.

Butteriss, M. (1975) *The Quality of Working Life: The Expanding International Scene*, Work Research Unit Paper No. 5, London.

Clutterbuck, D. (1973) 'Creating a Factory with a Factory', *International Management*, October.

Coch, L., and French, J. R. P. (1948) 'Overcoming Resistance to Change', *Human Relations*, 1, 512—32.

Cooper, C. L. (1979) *The Executive Gypsy*, Macmillan, London.

Cooper, C. L. and Mumford, E. (1979) *Quality of Working Life in Western and Eastern Europe*, Associated Business Press, London.

Davis, L. E. and Cherns, A. B. (eds) (1975) *The Quality of Working Life*, 2 vols, Free Press, New York.

French, J. R. P. and Caplan, R. D. (1973) 'Organizational Stress and Individual Strain', in Marrow, A. J. (ed.), *The Failure of Success*, American Management Association, New York.

Herrick, N. Q., and Maccoby, M. (1975) 'Humanizing Work: A Priority Goal of the 1970s', in Davis, L. E. and Cherns, A. B. (eds), *The Quality of Working Life*, Free Press, New York, vol. 1, 63—77.

Hertog, F. J. den (1974) *Work Structuring Philips' Gloeilampenfabrieker*, Philips, Eindhoven.

Hill, P. (1972) *Towards a New Philosophy of Management*, Barnes & Noble, New York.

Jenkins, D. (1974) *Industrial Democracy in Europe*, Business International, Geneva.

Kato, H. (1974) 'Job Enlargement as Viewed from Industrial Engineering', paper delivered to the Japan Psychological Association, 38th National Conference, Tokyo.

Mire, J. (1975) 'Trade Unions and Worker Participation in Management', in Davis, L. E. and Cherns, A. B. (eds), *The Quality of Working Life*, Free Press, New York, vol. 1, 166—200.

Morse, N. C. and Reimer, E. (1956) 'The Experimental Change of a Major Organizational Variable', *Journal of Abnormal and Social Psychology*, 52, 120—9.

Norstedt, J. and Aguren, S. (1974) *The Saab—Scania Report*, Swedish Employers Confederation, Stockholm.

O'Toole, J. (1973) *Work in America*, MIT Press, Boston.

Ottaway, R. (1975) 'Working in the Right Direction', *The Guardian*, 15 September.

Paul, W. J. and Robertson, K. B. (1970) *Job Enrichment and Employee Motivation*, Gower Press, Epping, England.

Powell, R. M. and Schacter, J. L. (1971) 'Self Determination at Work', *Academy of Management Journal*, 15, 165—73.

Preston, L. E. and Post, J. E. (1974) 'The Third Managerial Revolution', *Academy of Management Journal*, 17, 476—86.

Ruehl, G. (1974) 'Work Structuring II', *Industrial Engineering*, February, 52—6.

Strauss, G. and Rosenstein, E. (1970) 'Worker Participation: A Critical View', *Industrial Relations*, 9, 197—214.

Takezawa, S. (1974) 'The Quality of Working Life: Trends in Japan', unpublished paper, Rikkyo University, Japan.

Taylor, J. C. (1972) 'Quality of Working Life: Annotated Bibliography', unpublished paper, University of California, Berkeley.

Taylor, J. C. (1975) 'Experiments in Work System Design: Economic Human Results', unpublished paper, University of California, Berkeley.

Taylor, L. K. (1973) *Not for Bread Alone: An Appreciation of Job Enrichment*, Business Books, London.

Trist, E. L. and Bamforth, K. (1951) 'Some Social and Psychological Consequences of the Long Wall Method of Coal Getting', *Human Relations*, 4, 3—38.

Trist, E. L., Higgin, G., Murray, H. and Pollack, H. (1963) *Organizational Choice*, Tavistock, London.

Work Research Unit (1975) *Work Restructuring Projects and Experiments in the United Kingdom*, WRU, London.

This chapter is based on a contribution by C. L. Cooper to *Comparative Industrial Relations in Europe*, edited by D. Torrington, and published by Associated Business Press.

13
Organizational Change

Introduction

This chapter discusses organizational change. We will first discuss the difficulty of bringing about organizational change and then suggest some helpful perspectives for viewing change. These two sections will be followed by a discussion of the change process, where we view organizational change as a discrete, observable process of social behaviour. Since there are a number of change agents involved in a change process, they will be defined and discussed next. Organizational development (OD) is the application of behavioural-science concepts and skills to the change process in an organization. Under the topic of OD we discuss strategies and interesting methods of bringing about change in an organization. Lastly, we will suggest a variety of opinions on the advantages and disadvantages of well-known ideas about organizational change.

What do we mean by organizational change? Kahn (1974) says that 'To change an organization means changing the pattern of recurring behaviour.' A significant aspect of organizational change has to do with behaviour, particularly regular, recurring patterns of behaviour. Shepard (1970) uses the word 'culture', which is more comprehensive and nearer to our concept: 'Cultures are maintained through the operation of self-validating processes. Changing a culture requires interventions that invalidate old processes and conditions that facilitate the creation of new self-validating processes.' Lewin (1952) calls this culture 'customs' or 'social habits'. Such habits are held together in a field of forces (see discussion of Lewin's personality theory in Chapter 4), within the social system (a broad term including organizations). Some forces encourage change and others resist change. Generally, the forces balance and are in a 'quasi-stationary equilibrium'. A balanced field of forces is institutionalized into an organization which is then supported and justified with a value system. It is the difficult task of changing that behaviour which we will discuss in this chapter.

The difficulty of bringing about organizational change

One often gets the impression that change is going on all the time, but we must be careful not to lose our bearings in the swift tides of change. Almost the opposite approach is taken in this chapter. 'Change is our business', often said by dynamic managers, is thought to be a misnomer. Toffler (1970) raised the alarm about the uniqueness of the present situation in regards to change: 'We may define future shock as the distress, both physical and psychological, that arises from an overload of the human organism's physical adaptive systems and its decision-making processes. Put more simply, future shock is the human response to over-stimulation.' He is talking mainly about changes such as changing jobs, residences, personal habits, financial situation, and family relationships due to marriage, birth or death. These changes raise the anxiety level of people, but organizational change is a different matter.

Changing the behaviour of an organization is nearly impossible. Organizations are not meant to change. They are a form of social life that is means to endure. As Weber says, 'Once it is fully established, bureaucracy is among those social structures which are the hardest to destroy' (Gerth and Mills, 1958). Weber saw the development of the bureaucracy as the natural protection against the whims of the nobles of previous periods. The rationalization and depersonalization of behaviours is intended to make them more predictable and efficient. All the bureaucratic sophistication of modern organizations works against organizational change.

Another early twentieth-century conceptualizer of organizational behaviour was F. W. Taylor. He focused his attention on the behaviour of the people in the work organization, rather than the structure, as Weber did. He articulated new duties for the managers and legitimised their duties. The four duties he saw for managers are: (i) develop a science for each element of work to replace the old rule of thumb; (ii) scientifically select and train the workers to follow this scientific method; (iii) ensure that all work is done according to the method; and (iv) see this work as equally as important as the actual doing of the work (Taylor, 1967). Weber and Taylor conceptualized modern work organizations as structured, ordered and stable patterns of behaviour intended to remain predictable. It is fair to say that much of the thought in the area of organizational change has been aimed at reducing the severity of organizations operating strictly according to bureaucratic concepts. However, it is also fair to say that we value the predictability and efficiency of modern, structured organizations.

Organizations would probably be difficult to change even if they were not as bureaucratised as they are in modern Western societies. Cannon (1932) thinks that all social systems are homeostatic. That is, they tend to balance external and internal forces. He thinks this is indicative of nature. There are many examples of this from nature: balance between needs and drives in the personality, balance of energy in physics, balance of general intake and output of biological systems, etc. In other words, we like to keep things as they are. When a group of people work together they tend to develop justifications for behaving in that way, and these are called *norms*: 'Norms: the code of behaviour which, implicitly or explicitly, consciously or unconsciously, the group adopts as just, proper, or ideal' (Homans, 1951). Once the justification for behaviour is internal to a group, it is very difficult to change it. Sherif (1936) and others have shown that members of groups conform to the norms of the group. In work organizations norms for production rates and other behaviours are established and workers conform to them or are rejected by the group (Roethlisberger and Dickson, 1939, 1966; Roy, 1952). So even without the structure and the scientific methods of today's work organizations, there is much evidence that they would be difficult to change.

One of the results of the difficulty of changing the behaviour of an organization is that it is a little-understood process. Many managers fear change: 'Managers within our business institutions are apprehensive about change. Fear of change causes many managers to ignore or fight change instead of attempting to deal with it constructively. Day-to-day work pressures often prevent managers from taking positive steps towards achieving long-term change in their organizations' (Burgher, 1979).

Some helpful perspectives on change

There are several perspectives on change which may be helpful to ensure the maximum opportunity for survival of the change and minimal disturbance to the organization. The first is that *no one likes to change*. If one begins with this view, the approach to change will be more realistic. Of course, we know that people and organizations do change, and that leads to the second perspective: *when people want to change, it is because they see the new behaviour as being in their own self-interest*. When the members of the organization cannot see how the change benefits them, they may *appear* to change in order to test it or show loyalty, but such change is not likely to survive for long. This form of accommodating new behaviours but not internalizing them is one of the problems with imposed change. Another course often taken by members of an organization when they cannot see a benefit in the change is to resist it. This can lead to some distrubances but may be easier to cope with.

Another helpful perspective is that *people change most easily on needs they feel*. This is based on the discussion of Rogers (1951) in Chapter 4. One of his hypotheses of learning is that people only learn what they feel they need. Lewin (1952) discovered early in his work that there are two types of habits, which he called 'need habits' and 'execution habits'. Need habits are based on a source of energy in the person which demands satisfaction. The execution habits are in response to a pattern of restraining forces determining a certain path. Most managers try to change behaviour by restraining undesirable habits. We suggest that the better perspective is to focus on the needs of the members of the organization. A need is a force which a person sees as important and wants to answer or to satisfy. We use the term *felt need* to mean the needs that the individual identifies in himself rather than those that have been identified for him by someone else. People are most motivated to change when it meets a felt need. They will then give their energy to the new behaviour rather than have to be constrained to act in the new way.

People change most easily when they have a say in the change is the fourth perspective. Beginning with the Coch and French (1948) experiments of introducing new work patterns by participation in the pyjama factory in Marion, Virginia, behavioural scientists have been convinced of the merit of involving the persons who are expected to change in the planning of the change process. Beckhard (1969) says that 'People support what they help create.' Argyris (1970) contrasts the mechanistic and organic approaches, concluding that the organic has the more desirable outcomes for the organization:

> The intention is to involve the clients in the introduction, design, execution, feedback, and evaluation of any and all aspects of the program and to provide for them many opportunities for psychological success, feelings of essentiality, development of confidence and trust in others, and effective group relations.

Resistance is often seen as the enemy of change. But at the same time many of the desirable characteristics of an organization, such as predictability and reliability, are due to the resistance of its members to new patterns. From this we suggest the fifth perspective: *resistance is a healthy reaction to change*. Change can be brought about without observable resistance. Two dangers may result from this. The first is that if the resistance is too costly for the members of an organization, they may change, but along the execution needs level that Lewin discusses. The next result is that the manager, or advocate, of the new behaviour has to constrain the changes to the new behaviour. Consequently the manager finds his life filling up with an increasing number of behaviours to keep tabs on. This is a reductionist view in that it reduces the opportunities to be more concerned with directing, co-ordinating and managing the interface of the energy of his group with that of others in the organization.

Another common result of this form of resistance is for members to adopt new behaviours without commitment. They appear to work within the constraints of the new behaviour, but all the time they are complaining (in the canteen and informally). The net result of this is a drag on the system. This drag will become one of the norms and the group itself will enforce this as new behaviour. This subtle resistance is very difficult to overcome. Many organizations will identify this condition as poor morale, lack of motivation, no commitment to the work and other descriptions of a vague malaise in the organization.

A third form of resistance to the introduction of change is overt, open resistance to change. This is the most easily managed form of resistance and the one which we suggest the change process should encourage. It is better to have the resistance out in the open. Resistance is a signal that the change is important and far reaching in the minds of the critic. One might say that until there is resistance the change is not significant. Many managers try to avoid open resistance. This could be because they do not know how to cope with resistance in a productive way. Organizations often go to elaborate lengths to avoid dealing with resistance. This tends to push the resistance into the other two categories.

When discussing resistance we should reiterate that we are referring to helpful perspectives for viewing change. That is, when viewing change it is more helpful to view resistance as a natural, healthy part of change than to take the opposite view. Of course, there is a degree of relativity. Extreme resistance to the point of shutting down the organization or threatening its survival is not healthy. The same can also be said at the other extreme: no resistance at all means a constantly changing organization. A constantly changing organization is impossible to finance, rely on for goods and services, to integrate into, or interact with as a supplier or competitor. Resistance will be discussed in more detail later in this chapter.

The sixth perspective we suggest is to *view the social setting for change as a whole — no just selected aspects of it*. If the organization is viewed as a system, it will be viewed with an assumption that movement in one area of the organization will affect many other areas of the organization. It increases the problems of changing behaviour when a few patterns are selected as the target of change and their interactions with other patterns are ignored. For instance, to increase participation of machine operators in decision-making about their work has direct influence on supervision, maintenance of machines, supply and collection of parts in progress, payment and work methods. All of these departments may resist the change of the behaviour of machine operators. To use Lewin's ideas about quasi-stationary equilibrium, one can see that behaviour between groups in an organization tends to set up a working balance. The change in one group will affect the behaviour of other groups.

Looking at these six sets of lenses which we think are helpful in viewing change, several skills can be identified for those wishing to bring about change in an organization. Generally speaking these are skills which most of us need to develop: helping the changes; identify felt needs; designing change participatively; and handling resistance.

How change takes place

The Dynamics of Planned Change by Lippitt, Watson and Westley (1958) was the first book on organizational change and it treated change as a discrete, observable social behaviour.

Lewin, to whom Lippitt, Watson and Westley dedicated their book, is credited with providing the basic theories and we will use his theories to describe how change takes place. Before the change process begins, life is going on in a dynamic field of forces. This might be called state A. We could describe it, measure it to some degree and most of the members in the organization would know what it was. They would be living their lives in accord with this state. These are the norms of an organization, the unwritten acceptable code of behaviour for that group.

This state A of behaviour is held in place by a field of forces which Lewin calls the quasi-stationary equilibrium. It is a balance with forces encouraging change and forces resisting change. This balance is linked and supported by values, customs, rationale, rituals and other activities which might be called 'culture'. The forces for change are always trying to include new forces to improve the organization.

Yet, the driving-forces for change are not alone. Also present are the restraining forces. These are the efforts for the organization to stay as it is — which has been found workable in the past. The restraining forces are constantly raising questions of stability, predictability and of changing too quickly from the tried and proven ways that have served everyone well in the past. Such criticisms of change are desirable activities. They guard against fatigue and over-extension of the organization which would result if the organization attended to every fad and fancy.

Each type of force is present in each organization as well as in each department and each person. This is a concept which might help one understand change. Figure 13.1 is a summary of these activities. The activities for change are seen by restrainers as destabilizing and radical. Drivers might see themselves as pro-active, imaginative, future-orientated and problem-solving. The activities which are restraining against change are seen by drivers as tradition-orientated, resistant to change, conservative, exclusive, and putting great value on procedures, rules and maintaining tight boundaries.

Within this field of forces there will be much activity—called *dynamics*. Organizations are not equally divided between those for and against change, as Figure 13.1 suggests. It is more a collage of activities that might give the impression of an organization in constant change. Those managers referred to earlier in this chapter are probably seeing the dynamics of an organization as change. Organizational change in its purest sense is moving from state A, such as no women managers, autocratic decision-making, no unions, or highly centralized power structures, to state B, such as having women managers, participative decision-making, unions, or decentralized power structures.

Most of the daily work of organizations is restraining. Most training is aimed at teaching the standard required skills in the organization and is a refreezing activity. Training in organizations is often intended to tell the member what the organization expects of him: how to dress, speak and what values are important. Supervisory practices to maintain these

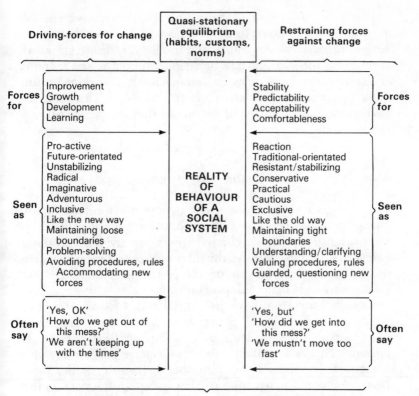

Figure 13.1 *Field of change forces*

company-approved behaviours is also an example of refreezing. Refreezing activities are healthy and required for every organization.

Such a field of forces will function well until a new force intrudes which cannot be accommodated. Lewin says that this unfreezes the quasi-stationary equilibrium. Systems do not like being out of balance and there is a tendency for the system to rebalance itself. *Change takes place when the field is reorganized into a new state which incorporates the new force*. The organization cannot survive if it stays in this phase too long. There will be a natural tendency to refreeze into the new field (phase three).

When the behaviour of an organization is changed special attention must be given to the unfrozen and refreezing phases. If the organization stays unfrozen too long, it disintegrates. If it refreezes too soon, no new behaviour will occur and it could revert to state A. Most behavioural scientists working on the topic concentrate their attention to this phase. This problem is discussed in more detail in the section on organizational development.

Many change agents required for change

For change to take place many people must complete the change process. Ten types of person have been identified by Ottaway (1980). These 'change agents' are divided into three categories corresponding to the three phases of Lewin's change model: change generators (unfreezers), change implementers (changers), and change adopters (refreezers).

Change generators have the initial task of converting the issues into a feeling that change is needed. In most cases they work outside the organization. In essence they say 'You must change.' They are lead by *prototype change generators*, who are gifted individuals selecting the right issue at the right time leading the conversion of that issue to a felt need in the proper target population. They become well-known personalities. Ralph Nader of the consumer movement is a good example of the prototype change generator.

If their action solicits support, demonstrators appear. The first of these are the *barricade demonstrators*, so called because they are the first line of confrontation with the public. Once their effect begins to be felt, *patron demonstrators* emerge to supply money and status. Their confrontation is more polite, formal, and uses channels of power rather than channels of public display. An interesting example was Marlon Brando's gesture of sending an American Indian woman to receive his Oscar award for his role in *The Godfather*, thereby acting as a patron to the cause of the American Indian.

The third group of generators are the largest and least directly involved. They are the *defenders* who defend the action of the other generators. They write letters to the editor, act as discussants in debates or be the village liberal who keeps the topic on the agenda. The beneficiaries of the change are important defenders. The defenders determine the presence of the felt need. When this group gets large and represents the typical person who feels the need for change, the existing field of forces admits new forces and the system unfreezes. Unfreezing may happen very quickly, or it may take a long time. The first three groups may develop and exist for a long time but lack the key member, the defender, in sufficient numbers to bring about the felt need for change.

Once the organization realizes that it needs to change the unfreezing has completed its task and a new type of change agents are required for the second phase: the change implementers. The first of the implementers are the *external change implementers*. They are invited into the organization from outside to assist it to implement the change. They have special knowledge and pioneering tendences which make them highly experimental; they value working in unknown situations. They are usually freelance consultants in development work. Their task is to set up implementers within the client organization who are the next group of change agents. The *external/internal change implementers* usually work at the headquarters and assist the organization implement change. Sometimes the members of the organization go to headquarters, or to a staff college, to learn the new behaviours. Whereas they are internal culturally, their clients are external to their immediate work environment.

The largest group of implementers work at the grass roots of the organization. The *internal change implementers* work with a particular part of the organization on a long-term basis. They include personnel in organization development, operations research, training specialists, planners, managers and shop stewards. They have a specific job of implementing change within their group. Sometimes they experience stress (see Chapter 5) due to role conflict because they are expected to socialize new personnel into acceptable company habits, whereas they prefer to inculcate change.

By this stage the change process is becoming difficult to observe and may remain in this state for a long time. Trainers may be training people into a new behaviour which should be refrozen but the training does not transfer to the work situation where old habits prevail. For change to occur the new behaviour has to be adopted and normalized into the day-to-day behaviour of the organization. This is the task of the third category, the adopters. The first type in the adopters is the *prototypic change adopter* who are the first to say 'I'll try it in my group.' They are not professionally engaged in work that puts them in the implementer category but they will often call themselves 'change agents'. They liaise closely with the implementers and they may be managers, supervisors, shop stewards, or significant informal leaders. It is important that they be prototypic since they must exhibit the new behaviour in a way that contributes to the change process. Sometimes, however, the first adopter is not highly regarded in the system and might deter the implementation.

Often change will get this far and fail to refreeze. The final two groups are very large and unconscious of their role as change agents, but they are the key to the adoption of a new behaviour. The *maintainers* are those who run the organization on a day-to-day basis. It is *they* who will have to adopt the new behaviour for it to be a change. Often there is low commitment to change and a high commitment to the old behaviours. If the change is aimed directly at this group it often fails. If the old habits are engrained in this to this group, the change agents have to be particularly careful to ensure that felt needs are present, that implementers have done their task and that a prototypic adopter is present. Maintainers are the most important group in the organization if the change is to have a good chance of surviving in the long term.

Once the organization has changed its behaviour, it is up to the tenth group to support that new behaviour by using the goods or services of the changed organization. These are the *users*, and in many cases they can determine the failure or success of a change process. For example, if the public did not use the reorganized health service in the United Kingdom, it would not be a changed health service. The same thing could be said about Ralph Nader and safer products. If the public did not buy a safer car, he would not be so well known. If the organization's output is consumed, it will be changed.

Organizational development (OD)

Organizational development (OD) is one of the best-known applications of Lewin's change concepts. It is mostly aimed at the implementer phase, but instead often occurs at the refreezing phase. French and Bell (1978), in one of the most widely used textbooks on OD, provide an exhaustive definition:

> organization development is a long-range effort to improve an organization's problem-solving and renewal processes, particularly through a more effective and collaborative management of organization culture — with emphasis on the culture of formal workteams — with the assistance of a change agent, or catalyst, and the use of the theory and technology of applied behavioral science, including action research.

As a direct outgrowth of the work of Lewin, Lippitt and others, OD had an early predisposition towards laboratory research: the use of unstructured small-group settings for training members of an organization in group skills and intergroup behaviours. Often the strategy was to have most of the members of the organization attend such a training event in work-teams. About the same time Likert (1967) began work with surveys and feedback of the results to the participants in the organization. The University of Michigan group, which Likert headed for many years, had a strong interest in changing the structure of an organization rather than the individual behaviour of a series of individuals (Katz and Kahn, 1966).

In the United Kingdom OD was developed by the Tavistock Institute for Human Relations. It, too, had two foci (De Board, 1979), one of which followed the work of Bion (1963) and the psychoanalytical Freudian approach. Another emphasis was the socio-technic approach based on the work of Trist and Bamforth (1951) — see Chapter 12. This approach may be seen as working for the best fit between the technical demands of the work-place and the social needs of its members.

Action research is a term widely used to describe OD. French and Bell (1978) say:

> A basic model underlying most organization development activities is the action research model — a data-based, problem-solving model that replicates the steps involved in the scientific method of inquiry. Three processes are involved in action research: data collection, feedback of the data to the clients, and action planning based on the data.

But as Foster (1972) remarks this is difficult to accomplish and 'Among the approaches to planned organizational change the term action research has not been popular lately. This may be in recognition of the fact that those involved are either doing research with little action, or action with little research.'

Change strategies and interventions

Change strategies are particular sequences of activities in which change agents engage in order to bring about change. Chin and Benne (1969) divide concious change strategies into three categories: rational—empirical, normative—re-educative, and power—coercive. The rational—empirical is the strategy based on the views of englightenment and classical liberalism — which means that people will change when knowledge is used as a reason for it. The normative—re-educative is the view held by therapists, trainers, and organization development practitioners. The power—coercive is the view held by non-violent leaders such as Martin Luther King and political institutions. Chin and Benne's list of strategies might be seen as fitting Lewin's three phases: power—coercive being the unfreezers, normative—re-educative being the changers, and the rational—empirical being the refreezers.

Schein (1969) suggests a strategy of OD which has seven stages:

(1) initial contact with the client organization; (2) defining the relationship, formal contract, and psychological con-

tract; (3) selecting a setting and a method of work; (4) data gathering and diagnosis; (5) intervention; (6) reducing involvement; (7) termination.

This change strategy, called *process consultation*, emphasizes the change agent contracting the right place in the organization, obtaining the right 'contract' of expectations and relationships, and terminating the relationship in accord with the psychological dynamics of the consultation.

Ottaway (1976) describes a strategy designed to change the norms of an organization. It too has seven stages: (i) contracting, (ii) diagnosis, (iii) design of intervention, (iv) implementation of intervention, (v) skill training, (vi) reinforcement of new norms, and (vii) replication at other sites or levels of the organization. This strategy commences by changing the bottom of the organization using a pilot site where the organization learns how to change. The strategy suggests that training follows change rather than brings change about and has a strong emphasis on contracting throughout the process.

Describing a strategy does not state what the change agent does during the change process. French and Bell (1978) describe a wide variety of interventions in detail. They list the major 'families' of OD interventions and activities such as: diagnostic team-building, survey feedback, education and training, structural modification, process consultation, grid organization development, third-party peacemaking, coaching and counselling, life and career planning, and planning and goal-setting.

Katz and Kahn (1966) suggest that changing the organizations system is particularly effective:

The study and the accomplishment of organizational change has been handicapped by the tendency to disregard systemic properties of organizations and to confuse individual change with change in organizational variables. More specifically, scientists and practitioners have assumed too often that an individual change will produce a corresponding organizational change. This assumption seems to us indefensible.

The second edition of Katz and Kahn (1978) includes more

approaches to organizational development and groups than into individual approaches (adding selection and placement, termination, and behaviour modification), group approaches, and changing organizational variables (including authority, participation and the distribution of power, rewards and reward allocation, and division of labour such as job enlargement and job enrichment).

An empirical study of the effectiveness of different OD approaches is given by Bowers (1973) who reports research in twenty-three organizations using five OD approaches (laboratory training, interpersonal process consultation, task process consultation, survey feedback, data feedback), plus a control group which received no treatment. He found that the most effective intervention was survey feedback.

Unfortunately Bowers's work is exceptional. Research in OD is often lacking. Kahn (1974) lists only three experimental treatments of organizational change, and these are regarded widely as the classics: 'Coch and French's (1948) work on the effects of participation, Morse and Reimer's (1956) on hierarchical locus of decision-making power, and Trist and Bamforth's work (1951) on changes in sociotechnical structure.'

Conclusion

In conclusion we emphasize that changing the habits of an organization is very difficult. Organizations are not meant to change: we organize when we find a way of behaviour that we want to *continue*. But change must take place. Often it is a tense moment in the life of the organization because many of the skills which would facilitate change are new to most managers. Change is a process beginning with an interruption of existing habits (state A behaviours) and concluding with a new set of behaviours (state B) and this process requires many change agents. The process can be managed and influenced by the use of change strategies. Organizational development and its strategies are a possible resource to the manager when managing a change process, and we have included a discussion of such strategies in this chapter.

References for Chapter 13

Argyris, C. (1970) *Intervention Theory and Method*, Addison-Wesley, Reading, Mass.

Beckhard, R. (1969) *Organization Development: Strategies and Models*, Addison-Wesley, Reading, Mass.

Bion, W. R. (1968) *Experience in Groups*, Tavistock, London.

Bowers, D. G. (1973) 'OD Techniques and their Results in 23 Organizations: The Michigan ICL Study', *Journal of Applied Behavioral Science*, 9(1), 21–43.

Burgher, P. H. (1979) *Changement*, D. C. Heath & Co., Lexington, Mass.

Cannon, W. B. (1932) *Wisdom of the Body*, W. W. Norton & Co., New York.

Chin, R. and Benne, K. D. (1969) 'General Strategies for Effecting Changes in Human Systems', in *The Planning of Change*, ed. Bennis, G. W. *et al.*, 2nd edn, Holt, Rinehart & Winston, New York.

Coch, L. and French, J. R. P. (1948) 'Overcoming Resistance to Change', *Human Relations*, 1(4), 513–33.

De Board, R. (1978) *The Psychoanalysis of Organizations*, Tavistock, London.

Foster, M. (1972) 'An Introduction to the Theory and Practice of Action Research in Work Organizations', *Human Relations*, 25(6), 529–56.

French, W. L. and Bell, C. H. (1978) *Organization Development*, 2nd edn, Prentice-Hall, Englewood Cliffs, N.J.

Gerth, H. H. and Mills, C. Wright (1958) *From Max Weber: Essays in Sociology*, Oxford University Press, New York.

Homans, G. C. (1951) *Human Groups*, Routledge & Kegan Paul, London.

Kahn, R. L. (1974) 'Organizational Development: Some Problems and Proposals', *Journal of Applied Behavioral Science*, 10(4), 484–502.

Katz, D. and Kahn, R. L. (1966) *The Social Psychology of Organizations*, Wiley, New York (2nd edn 1978).

Lewin, K. (1952) *Field Theory in Social Science* (ed. D. Cartwright), Tavistock, London.

Likert, R. (1967) *The Human Organization*, McGraw-Hill, New York.

Lippitt, R., Watson, J. and Westley, B. (1958) *The Dynamics of Planned Change*, Harcourt Brace, New York.

Morse, N. and Reimer, E. (1956) 'The Experimental Change of a Major Organizational Variable', *Journal of Abnormal and Social Psychology*, 52, 120–9.

Ottaway, R. N. (1976) 'A Change Strategy to Implement New Norms, New Styles and New Environment in the Work Organization', *Personnel Review*, 5(1), 13–18.

Ottaway, R. N. (1980) *A Taxonomy of Change Agents*, 3rd edn, Department of Management Sciences, University of Manchester Institute of Science and Technology, Manchester, England.

Roethlisberger, F. D. and Dickson, W. J. (1939) *Management and the Worker*, Harvard University Press, Cambridge, Mass.

Rogers, C. R. (1951) *Client-Centred Therapy*, Constable, London.

Roy, D. (1952) 'Quota Restriction and Goldbricking in a Machine Shop', *American Journal of Sociology*, 57.

Schein, E. H. (1969) *Process Consultation*, Addison-Wesley, Reading, Mass.

Shepard, H. A. (1970) 'Personal Growth Laboratories: Toward an Alternative Culture', *Journal of Applied Behavioral Science*, 6(3), 259–66.

Sherif, M. (1936) *The Psychology of Social Norms*, Harper, New York.

Taylor, F. W. (1967) *The Principle of Scientific Management*, W. W. Norton & Co., New York.

Toffler, A. (1970) *Future Shock*, Random House, New York.

Trist, E. L. and Bamforth, R. (1951) 'Some Social and Psychological Consequences of the Long Wall Method of Coal Getting', *Human Relations*, 4(1), 3–38.

Section 4: Other Matters

14
Additional Areas in Organizational Behaviour

The material covered in this book clearly shows the variety involved in studying organizations. At one level we are talking about an individual manager, the job he has to do, his motives, the way he learns and his personality. At another level, we are talking about the way individuals function in work-groups, how they judge each other, how they communicate and how they work together. At a third level we are talking about the organization and how it changes. Yet even this array does not reveal the full range of topics that lie within the domain of organizational behaviour. The normal constraints inherent in any book that seeks to introduce a subject have meant that only a selection of topics could be covered while equally fascinating material has to be omitted.

For example, Section 2 deals with groups and how they function. But an organization rarely consists of a single group; once several groups exist there is the possibility of them either *conflicting* or *co-operating*. New issues appear. Is conflict to be welcomed or discouraged? Conflict could be either an impediment to effective performance or it could be a healthy characteristic which plays a vital role in the organization's processes for dealing with changes in its environment. Under what circumstances does conflict arise between groups? How can conflict be reduced? In a situation where it is in everyone's interests to co-operate will groups learn to trust each other or will dog-in-the-manger tactics prevail?

Another topic of clear importance to organizational behaviour concerns *socialization* — the way that the organization 'teaches' individuals to behave in the way that is required. The discussion of the managerial job in Chapter 2, the specific mention of learning and socialization in Chapter 4 and the discussion of groups and their norms in Chapter 8 are all relevant and integral parts of the socialization process. However, the socialization process is a topic in its own right. The continuous process of socialization and its reciprocal nature whereby the individuals also influence the organization are important additional features which are exhibited in the interesting descriptions of the socialization of new recruits into organizations such as the military services.

A third topic which might have been included in this book is the *cross-cultural* dimension in organizational psychology. The vast majority of the studies quoted in the previous chapters are set in the USA, the United Kingdom or Europe. It is true that many of the findings are consistent irrespective of their setting. For example, Rosemary Stewart's findings on the jobs of British managers and Henry Mintzberg's findings on the jobs of American managers (see Chapter 2) are quite consistent. Similarly, Milgram's experiment on obedience, which was briefly described in Chapter 4, has been replicated in many countries. However, it is always dangerous to generalize blindly across cultures. It is often dangerous to generalize even within cultures. It has been shown, for example, that there are significant rural–urban differences in the way that potential for growth in a job affects employees' performances. There are also cultural differences in the goals which managers pursue for their organizations. Bass (1967) simulated a hypothetical company and observed the decisions of managers from different countries. All managers, except the Italians, thought that 'making a profit' was the most important objective (the Italians gave pride of place to smoothness of operations), but there were noticable differences in subsequent choices. The British saw 'beating the competition' as an important objective, while the French-speaking Belgian managers placed this at the bottom of their list. Another relatively wide national difference concerned 'pollution': 65 per cent of US managers were prepared to spend money cleaning up a polluted stream, while only 25 per cent of French-speaking Belgian managers were prepared to spend money on this problem. They preferred to spend money on management development (Schaninger *et al.*, 1973).

One particular aspect of the cross-cultural dimension of organizational behaviour deserves specific consideration: the match between organizational and cultural values. Multinational organizations may hold one set of values while they operate in a country where a different set of values are maintained. For example, Kagitcibasi (1970) noted that many values in the USA are self-centred in the sense that an individual feels that his main obligations are to himself, while in Turkey a great deal of obligation is vested both in the nation and in the family. Williams *et al.* (1966) also produced an interesting contrast in preferences in supervisor—subordinate relationships. In contrast to American workers, who preferred considerate supervisors, Peruvian workers preferred supervisors who emphasized meeting production targets. Barrett and Bass (1976) provide an excellent summary of cross-cultural issues in organizational psychology and point to the cross-cultural dimension in areas such as selection, training, the prediction of success in working in foreign environments and preparation for work in another culture.

A final perspective on organizational behaviour concerns methodology. As an academic discipline, it is concerned with building up a body of scientific facts by an iterative, bootstrapping cycle. On the basis of previous experience hypotheses constructed. The hypotheses are then used to make specific predictions. Data are carefully gathered in order to check whether the predictions are true. If the predictions are false, the hypothesis is rejected or modified. The prestige of the scholar making the prediction is irrelevant since the findings must be objective and based on empirical observations. Thus, in principle, the science of organizational behaviour is no different from the sciences of chemistry or physics. In practice, however, there is a world of difference. Both physics and chemistry are older and more advanced – as sciences, many of their techniques and theories are well established. The science of organizational behaviour is, in contrast, only a few decades old, and we are at the stage where we are unsure whether our thermometers – our attitude scales, etc. – really are more accurate than individual, subjective estimates. Furthermore, we have no agreed structure equivalent to the chemist's periodic table for our subject, we have not identified the basic particle of our subject-matter and indeed we are not sure whether we ought to be looking for one!

In addition, there is the difficulty of the subject-matter. Organizations and the individuals within organizations are very complex and varied. They do not always react in accordance with pre-established laws. An organization can be structured in a way to induce creativity, yet the effective productivity of the R & D department can be neglibible. Except in unusual circumstances the physicist and chemist can rely on pure water boiling at 100°C, plus or minus one or two degrees. In other words, the science of organizational behaviour has a higher level of error variance, and this prevents it becoming an exact science. There are practical difficulties, too. Research into organizational behaviour is a painstaking process. Every organization and every individual studied needs to be convinced that the investigation is worth while. This is no easy task since other activities are often competing for their attention and they may sense that the research may prove them to be wrong in some way. Furthermore, the investigator is under a heavy ethical responsibility to preserve both the dignity of his subjects and the confidentiality of the information he obtains. In many ways the physicist, chemist and biologist are in a fortunate position: there is no need to ask a bar of metal's permission; drosophila fruit flies wait until the experimenter is ready; and a prism does not object to a scientist revealing its refractive index.

The practical difficulties of research on organizational behaviour produce two consequences. First, theorizing becomes very attractive. The confines of a comfortable armchair are much more attractive than the inconvenience and disappointments of field experimentation, and furthermore theorizing does not always require the stringent requirements to define and apply the concepts in practice. As the previous chapters have shown, organizational behaviour is very well endowed with theories, but unfortunately not all of them have been subjected to searching empirical scrutiny.

A second consequence of the practical difficulties of research into organizational behaviour is that the investigations that are conducted tend to use very small samples. For example, probably the best and most comprehensive set of measures of organizations was developed by Pugh and Hickson (1976), yet their scales were based on data from just fifty-two firms in the Birmingham area. Although there are statistical safeguards which can be employed when small samples are used, it is clearly preferable to obtain a data base which is sufficiently comprehensive to produce results that are generally valid.

The final section of an introductory book on organizational behaviour ought to say something about methodologies used in the study of organizations. Probably the greatest methodological distinction lies between surveys and experiments. From the scientific viewpoint the experiment has many advantages compared with the survey. In an ideal experiment a situation is carefully established in which everything is carefully standardized so that all influences are controlled except the one or two aspects under study. In this way causes can be established and precise estimates can be obtained (e.g. leadership style causes 10 per cent of the variance in productivity.) An example of the experimental approach is given by Litwin and Stringer (1968). They set up three simulated organizations and used them to investigate the effects of organizational climate and motives on management performance.

But, in the context of organizational behavour, experiments and simulations of the Litwin and Stringer kind have two disadvantages. First, it is not always possible to set up experiments because it is impossible to isolate the effects or because the experiments would involve unethical practices. Second, because experiments are so carefully controlled and contrived they may be so artificial that their results do not carry over into the real world.

Often the only realistic way of investigating organizations is by use of a survey, and the majority of the findings in this book have been obtained using survey methods. However, one particular disadvantage of such methods concerns surveys where people are asked questions about their actions and opinions. Even though they have no intention to deceive, what people say they will do is often different from what they do in practice, and this difference may make research findings inaccurate. Another disadvantage of most surveys is the fact that they do not usually give sufficient information to establish which factor is the cause and which the effect. For example, a number of studies (see Chapter 8) have shown that high-producing units tend to have supervisors who are considerate, and it is tempting to believe that by training supervisors to be more considerate production could be increased. However, because surveys do not usually establish causality, such a conclusion could be wrong. Highly productive units could have a tendency to have considerate supervisors because their supervisors appreciate the efforts of employees and do not therefore feel the need to emphasize production.

The objectives of these few paragraphs on methodology are limited solely to providing some context in which to evaluate the work described in the book. Inevitably such a summary must be inadequate. However, provided the central issues have been identified and the reader's interest stimulated, the reader can turn to more detailed texts (e.g. Bonchard, 1976; Cook and Campbell, 1976). Indeed, this has been one of the major objectives of every chapter. This book will have served its purpose if the reader goes on to read other texts on organizational behaviour.

References for Chapter 14

Barrett, G. V. and Bass, B. M. (1976) 'Comparative Surveys of Managerial Attitudes and Behavior', in Boddewyn, J. (ed.), *Comparative Management and Teaching, Training and Research*, Graduate School of Business Administration, New York University, New York.

Bass, B. M. (1967) 'Use of Exercises for Management and Organizational Psychology', *Training and Development Journal*, 21(4), 2—7.

Bonchard, T. J. (1976) 'Field Research Methods', In Dunnette, M. D. (ed.), *Handbook of Industrial and Organizational Psychology*, Rand McNally, Chicago.

Cook, T. D. and Campbell, D. T. (1976) 'The Design and Conduct of Quasi-experiments and the Experiments in Field Settings', in Dunnette, M. D. (ed.), *Handbook of Industrial and Organizational Psychology*, Rand McNally, Chicago.

Kagitcibasi, C. (1970) 'Social Norms and Authoritarianism: A Turkish—American Comparison', *Journal of Personality and Social Psychology*, 16, 444—51.

Litwin, G. H. and Stringer, R. A. (1968) *Motivation and Organizational Climate*, Graduate School of Business, Harvard University, Cambridge, Mass.

Pugh, D. S. and Hickson, D. J. (1976) *Organizational Structure in its Context*, Saxon House, Farnborough, England.

Schaninger, M., Barrett, G. V. and Alexander, R. A. (1973) *National Organizational and Individual Correlates of Simulated Decision Making*, Technical Report 65, ONR Contract N00014—167, University of Rochester Management Centre, Rochester.

Williams, L. K. *et al.* (1966) 'Do Cultural Differences Affect Workers' Attitudes', *Industrial Relations*, 5, 110—17.

Author Index

Subject Index